In this beautifully written book, Eric Motley shares his personal odyssey of grace and gratitude. This is a memoir about love—love of family, community, literature, language, and ideas.

FORMER FIRST LADY LAURA BUSH

The roots Eric L. Motley traces in his hometown of Madison Park, Alabama, a place founded by former slaves not long after the Emancipation, serve as a powerful reminder of the shaping influences that family, faith, and community have in African American lives—so, too, the love of mentors, neighbors, and teachers who nurture those lives in the crucial years of their development. In the personal odyssey of this remarkable black Renaissance man, in whom a passion for learning was cultivated at a young age and through whom others have been touched from the Deep South to the White House, we find inspiration in the history that binds the citizens of a place across generations and hope for every child, whatever their birth, blessed to be raised among those who see education not only as a value but as a vital spark to be shared.

HENRY LOUIS GATES JR., Alphonse Fletcher University Professor, Harvard University

In writing as clear as water, *Madison Park* tells a moving story of hope: how members of a small African American community in Alabama joined together to enable a young man with no "worldly advantages" to realize his potential, even beyond their—or his—imagination.

ELAINE H. PAGELS, Harrington Spear Paine Professor of Religion, Princeton University; author of *Gnostic Gospels*

As a 1970s first-grader, Eric Motley was dubbed a "turtle" because of his poor reading skills. Two decades later, he became the youngest appointee in George W. Bush's White House. In this compelling memoir, Eric shows how his life trajectory was shaped by the self-reliance instilled by his grandparents—but also the timely support of a close-knit community of mentors and supporters. Whatever attributes we ourselves bring to the table, our networks propel us further.

REID HOFFMAN, cofounder of LinkedIn and co-author of the
#1 *NYT* bestsellers *The Startup of You* and *The Alliance*

Eric Motley has crafted a beautiful volume, an inspiring tale of family, community, determination, and hope. His is a deeply moving and deeply American story. The lovely prose brings to life those who raised him and taught him and opened doors for him, as well as those who tried to keep those same doors firmly shut. The book is sharply observed and utterly engrossing. Once I started, I could not put it down.

STEPHEN L. CARTER, William Nelson Cromwell Professor of
Law, Yale University; author of *Civility: Manners, Morals,*
and the Etiquette of Democracy

MADISON PARK

MADISON PARK

A PLACE OF HOPE

ERIC L. MOTLEY

ZONDERVAN
BOOKS

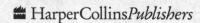
HarperCollins*Publishers*

ZONDERVAN BOOKS

Madison Park
Copyright © 2017 by Eric L. Motley

Requests for information should be addressed to:
Zondervan, *3900 Sparks Dr. SE, Grand Rapids, Michigan 49546*

Zondervan titles may be purchased in bulk for educational, business, fundraising, or sales promotional use. For information, please email SpecialMarkets@Zondervan.com.

ISBN 978-0-310-35696-7 (softcover)
ISBN 978-0-310-34966-2 (audio)
ISBN 978-0-310-34964-8 (ebook)

Art direction: Curt Diepenhorst
Cover design: Darren Welch
Cover photos: BJ Ray/My Portfolio/Shutterstock
Interior design: Kait Lamphere

Printed in the United States of America

21 22 23 24 25 26 27 28 29 30 31 /LSC/ 15 14 13 12 11 10 9 8 7 6 5 4 3 2 1

I'm tired of sailing my little boat,
    Far inside of the harbor bar;
I want to be out where the big ships float—
    Out on the deep where the Great Ones are! . . .

And should my frail craft prove too slight
    For storms that sweep those wide seas o'er,
Better go down in the stirring fight
    Than drowse to death by the sheltered shore!

Daisy Rinehart, 1905

CONTENTS

FOREWORD BY WALTER ISAACSON

When I first met Eric Motley, I knew there must be a wonderful backstory.

He was the youngest appointee in the George W. Bush White House, but he had the demeanor of a courtly collector of antiquarian books, which he happened to be. Despite his youth, his face went blank when the name of any contemporary pop star came up, but he had a passion for comparing renditions of Bach's *Goldberg Variations*. He was an African American from a tiny tight-knit black community in Montgomery, Alabama, but he had the worldly outlook of someone who got his doctorate from the University of St. Andrews in Scotland. He had the deferential deportment that comes from having been taught by his elders to consistently err on the side of formality rather than familiarity. But after a while, I realized that there was something much deeper behind that respectful demeanor: a true inner strength based on spiritual humility.

After four years in the White House, Eric became the director of the State Department's Office of International Visitors. When his term was up, I was able to recruit him to the Aspen Institute, where he had been part of a small cadre of young leaders in our Henry Crown Fellowship program, and he now serves as one of our executive vice presidents.

Along the way, Eric nurtured a diverse array of consuming intellectual passions that would seem quirky were he not so serious about them. His office, piled with books and journals, is graced by a large color portrait of Samuel Johnson. Eric is an avid collector of rare and first-edition books, with Dr. Johnson being his foremost passion. His faith was shaped by the sermons of the Reverend Lee Chester Washington of Montgomery's Union Chapel African Methodist Episcopal Zion (AMEZ) Church, which his great-great-grandfather had built and his grandfather rebuilt, and his doctoral dissertation was on the application of German theologian Reinhold Niebuhr's philosophy to contemporary geopolitics. He has written about the Scottish-born American founder James Wilson, and he has collected the books and personal papers of the classical scholar Sir Kenneth Dover, who once tutored him in Greek. An avid poet, he published a volume of his own verse in 2006.

Of course Eric does have a few blind spots. We once ran into Peyton Manning walking down the street, and Eric afterward confessed he had no clue who that was. When our colleague Peter Reiling was heading off to a concert, Eric asked him whether Led Zeppelin was a good singer. The only celebrity he feels a kinship with is Tiger Woods. He tells a funny story—once you get to know Eric you discover that he has a wry sense of humor—about walking on a beach below the Royal and Ancient Golf Club of St. Andrews, not far from his university, and being mistaken by a group of excited Japanese tourists for the golfer.

The more I got to know Eric over the years, the more it reinforced my initial impression. What a story he must have, I thought. He does, and this inspiring and exquisitely written book tells it.

First and foremost, it is a story about the importance of community, in this case the one known as Madison Park. A self-reliant enclave in Montgomery, Alabama, it was founded in 1880 by a small band of freed slaves, including Eric's great-great-grandfather. It has a cohesiveness and communitarian spirit that survived Reconstruction, Jim Crow, and the turmoil of Civil Rights era-Alabama.

There Eric was raised by his grandparents and by the embracing community. When he was put into a slow-learner's track in first grade, an aunt announced it at church the next Sunday and asked the congregants to bring him books. Soon he had a library that included Gwendolyn Brooks, Keats, Tennyson, Wordsworth, copies of *Life* and *Jet* magazines, and volume L of the *Encyclopedia Britannica*. More importantly, the trove came with six women neighbors who volunteered to tutor him in the afternoons. "And in that little place," Eric writes, "as evidence of God's grace, I became what one of my childhood tutors, Mrs. Sarah Pearl Coleman, called the D.U.K, the 'designated university kid.'" Not only was he nurtured intellectually, he was offered afternoon jobs so he could save money in his college fund.

Among the lessons his community taught him, he says, is "we are all responsible for one another." Those of us lucky to be in his orbit know that it also taught him the value of creating community. "For him, Madison Park is not just a place, it's an idea that he recreates everywhere he goes," his friend Jim Spiegelman points out. "He himself becomes a magnet drawing people together through ideas, interests, and shared values."

This book is also about mentorship. Each step of the way, Eric sought out and was able to attract someone who would mentor him.

Each tale of generosity is inspiring. But also inspiring is Eric's own talent of bringing out the generosity of others. When he finished his White House service, he had the opportunity to have his picture taken in the Oval Office with the president. Instead of doing it alone, he asked that three people who had mentored him as a student be allowed to join in the picture.

Above all, this book is about gratitude. Eric has an uncanny ability to remember everything, in part because he possesses an enormous sense of gratitude. At times, he recounts, his memory of all those who helped him has been so intense it felt like a burden. "Blessings come at us so relentlessly, we are forever in a deficit position," he writes. "We never get all of the thank-yous or goodbyes properly said, which leaves us, each one, living with a burden of gratitude." For all of us who have the joy of knowing Eric, there is a counterpart to that sentiment. In his life, and now in this book, he teaches us about the grace that is bestowed by gratitude.

PROLOGUE

On my grandmother's dressing table in her farmhouse near Montgomery, Alabama, there was a snow globe containing a tiny fairy-like replica of the White House. It was given to her by the daughter of a family whose house she used to clean. As a child, it inspired my wildest imaginings. "One day," my grandmother would always tell me, "you can be in this snow globe."

That seemed unlikely. I was an African American child born in 1972 to a teenage mom and raised by her adoptive parents—my grandparents. I called them Mama and Daddy. We lived in Madison Park, a rural, always struggling Southern community founded after the Civil War by freed slaves. A safety net of neighbors, church friends, tradespeople, and most of all, Mama and Daddy, held me up. The whole town had a vested interest in me. They determined to educate me and give me bone-deep confidence in my values, my abilities, and who I was. The first in my family to go to college, I went on to receive a Ph.D. After graduation I moved to Washington, D.C. A favorite college professor warned me, "D.C. ain't Alabama! You gotta have thick skin to survive!" A Samford trustee was optimistic. "Boy, the world is yours," he said. "Your name is the best thing you got, so don't hold back."

I didn't. I was twenty-seven, and I was inside the globe, working for President George W. Bush in the office of presidential personnel. My first day of work, I set my alarm for 6:00 a.m. The phone rang at five. It was Mama.

"Bugs, I didn't want you to oversleep, so I'm giving you a wake-up call."

"Thank you, Mama."

"I heard the locust sing all night long," she said. "It's a clue."

"A clue to what, Mama?"

"I don't know, but everything means something. One day you'll be able to piece all of these things together."

As I walked through the front gates of the White House later that morning, the snow globe crossed my mind. This was one of the few times when childhood fantasy was meeting adult reality. Perseverance, hard work, and good luck had brought me here. But I knew Madison Park was the thread that stitched my life together.

CHAPTER 1

THE MOTLEY BOY

Amos and Bernice Perry lived with their fourteen children in Madison Park, a close-knit cocoon of several hundred self-reliant descendants of former slaves, on the outskirts of Montgomery, Alabama. Short on money and long on faith, the Perrys went to church and aspired to little more than survival and a lightened burden. Six Perry children lived on their own or were parceled out with relatives, while eight still lived at home. Amos, a slender man with a dark complexion, was a warehouse laborer who farmed his own land. Bernice, a bright-eyed and fair-skinned beautiful woman, was a round-the-clock homemaker and had to put aside her soft-spoken ways to command her boisterous brood. She occasionally had to take on housekeeping jobs for white families in Montgomery to help make ends meet.

Amos and Bernice's best neighbor-friends were George Washington Motley and Mamie Ruth "Mossy" Motley, a childless couple in their forties. For more than twenty years the Perrys and the Motleys had swapped stories and apple pies, wandered unannounced in and out of the other's home, and cried and laughed together. Each family was in the other's innermost circle.

In the spring of 1964, Bernice received devastating news. She had terminal cancer. As she lay dying, she asked George and Mossy for an almost unimaginable favor: to adopt her fourth youngest child, Barbara Ann, age ten, and bring her up as their own.

I've often wondered why Barbara Ann was chosen to go live with George and Mossy. Did Bernice fear that Barbara Ann was the most vulnerable? Did Bernice hope that George and Mossy, relatively better off and with more time to put into a child, might

My adopted grandfather George Washington Motley (left) and my biological grandfather Amos Perry (right) were longtime friends (c. 1945).
The collection of Eric L. Motley

be able to nurture her in a way Amos couldn't? Or was Bernice offering them the opportunity to become parents?

George and Mossy likely never told Bernice and Amos about their failed attempts to have children. But Bernice had to have picked up on Mossy's disappointment over the years. Whatever lay behind it, Bernice's request came as a surprise to the Motleys.

Most people would want to fulfill the dying wishes of a cherished friend. But adopting a child was a major decision. Taking in a youngster was a financial liability and needed to be considered carefully. For the Motleys it wasn't a difficult calculation. They made a lifetime promise without considering how disruptive a child would be to their marriage. Invariably the will of God mysteriously unfolds just as it should.

As Bernice lay stretched out in an ambulance for her final ride, with

Mrs. Reeves holding her hand, she asked about the adoption proceedings. Mrs. Reeves, a white woman for whom Bernice cleaned house, had paid for Bernice's cancer treatments and arranged for Barbara Ann's adoption. Mrs. Reeves reminded her that the papers had been signed two days earlier. "The Motleys are officially Barbara Ann's parents."

"I know. I just needed to hear it one more time."

She passed away forty-eight hours later.

Barbara Ann lost her mother and went from being one of fourteen to an only child in just a few days. A sunny girl, she burst into George and Mossy's quiet home. The new name, Barbara Ann Motley, brought privileges and opportunities unlike anything she might have imagined. She had spent most of her early life wearing one of three dresses, recycled from older sisters. Now the Motleys fitted her for new dresses and matching ribbons for every day of the week. For the first time in her life she had her own pair of new shoes. Other firsts followed. Barbara Ann got her own bed—even her own room. She was used to competing for yesterday's leftovers. Now she was one of only three to share the feast of a chicken dinner.

Barbara Ann left a free-spirited household, where discipline and orderliness were relaxed. She suddenly shared a home with two people who set rules and abided by them precisely. Curfews, dressing for dinner, and the manners of the Motley household unnerved her. Barbara Ann's tendency was to push back. The older Barbara Ann grew, the more prone she was to argue and assert her independence. Still, the Motleys experienced unanticipated joy because finally they had a child to love.

The years 1964 to 1972 were turbulent for Barbara Ann. As fate would have it, her struggles coincided with the political and social upheaval rippling across the country. Barbara Ann rode the wave of black students integrating Robert E. Lee High School and, in 1973, was among the first to earn a diploma from the formerly all-white school.

She eagerly looked toward her future. But in 1972, when Barbara Ann was eighteen, she found out she was pregnant. She gave birth in a Tuskegee hospital a week before Christmas, bringing her newborn home to 34 Motley Drive in Madison Park. They called me Eric.

Answering an infant's middle-of-the-night cry was a new experience for everyone in the family. Just as George and Mossy were about to be comfortably alone, their house revolved around diapers, baby food, and pediatricians visits. Despite Barbara Ann's confidence that she could raise me on her own, George and Mossy sensed that she wouldn't cope well with the emotional, financial, and spiritual demands of single motherhood, added to her own early adulthood pressures. Just after my first birthday, they insisted on becoming my legal guardians.

Though they had made a similar life-changing decision when they adopted Barbara Ann, this time they were under no pressure to honor a dying friend's last request. And at fifty-five and fifty-two George and Mossy faced an obligation that wouldn't end until they were in their seventies. They gave up the tranquility they had earned to parent a rambunctious and unformed thirteen-month-old toddler, with all the capacity to be a nuisance.

After my adoption, Barbara Ann married and moved to Atlanta. For the first decade of my life, she maintained regular contact, calling every day and visiting once a month. Unaware of our biological connection, I understood that she was special to my grandparents and had a particular interest in me. I assumed she was my sister.

When I was ten I began to recognize that Barbara Ann was my biological mother. To George and Mossy's credit, they never attempted to deceive me. I became aware of the facts in the gradual way that any child sorts out his aunts, uncles, cousins, and more distant family. I never received an explanation about how or why I'd come to be George and Mossy Motley's son. The revelation changed nothing. Their sacrifice and love were all that mattered. It is because of their unceasing devotion that I came to believe that oftentimes water can be thicker than blood. That idea and those feelings increased over time. Perhaps unfairly so, I grew to resist not only the temptation to think otherwise, but to allow anyone to make that suggestion. I was in my world, and I was satisfied with it. They were Mama and Daddy before I figured out my connection to Barbara Ann, and they were Mama and Daddy afterward.

Over time, Barbara Ann became a less frequent visitor, a less diligent caller, and less interested in me. Months could go by without any communication. This distance must have pained Mama and Daddy, but they never said so in front of me. The anxious collect phone calls we sometimes received around Christmas and Easter became the only indications that she was alive. Despite these obvious signs of trouble, my grandparents ended each conversation and letter saying, "The door will always be open, and you don't need a key."

No one understood why Barbara Ann lost contact. When I asked, Daddy said, "Sometimes you feel like you need to take a break—from friends, from family, and sometimes from life."

I'm sure I was hurt, and in time, I began to distance myself emotionally from her in the same way that I saw her pulling away from me. Eventually, I almost stopped thinking about her.

I don't remember meeting my biological father. Even his name eludes me. No one seemed to know him well or to care much about him. His relationship to Barbara Ann was temporary, and he speedily drifted from the family's attention. When I was in junior high school my grandparents received a call, and as I overheard them discussing it, I became aware that they were speaking of my biological father who had apparently died. Out of respect for a conversation that didn't involve me, I didn't ask about it or feel the need to know more. Having reconciled myself to the fact that my biological father didn't try to see me when I was a child, I decided that someone who showed me no love deserved none of my curiosity. I've read of adopted children who feel compelled to identify their biological parents, rich or poor, heroes or renegades, living or dead. While I understand their need, that wouldn't have undone my scars.

Looking back, I didn't simply "grow up." I was *raised*. Mama and Daddy had little money but enormous influence. They possessed in abundance all the things that count—optimism, integrity, patriotism, common sense, faith in God, respect for others, and a strong work ethic—and passed those on to me. My grandparents were smart enough not to spoil me, wise enough to indulge my love of books, kind enough to chauffeur me to debates and speech contests, devout enough to get me to Sunday school, and inspirational enough not to allow me to become an angry young man.

Sociologists debate the relative importance of nature versus nurture in childrearing. I would cast my lot with nurture. Whatever my birth parents bequeathed to me biologically has paled beside the years of intense yet patient rearing that my grandparents invested in me. They imparted an inheritance beyond all estimation and far beyond all deserving. And such careful devotion is even more extraordinary when I consider that they had already done it once before.

Over the years I've often pondered the way that silent, unnoticed decisions, made without fanfare in the ebb and flow of routine, can have such enormous consequences. I rush from issue to issue, payday

22

to payday, and year upon year—and suddenly I have a moment of revelation: how a decision made years ago shaped my life and the lives of others.

"Why me?" is a question I've asked myself endlessly, in a way similar to why Bernice chose Barbara Ann to go with George and Mossy. But I can answer no better than anyone else.

It seems that in becoming my grandparents, the Motleys were following the unspoken, ruling passion of their lives: do the right thing. I once asked Daddy for an explanation, and after a long reflective pause, he responded simply, "Why not? What else were we to do? After all, you were our grandson." In one quiet, unheralded act, because of unexpected circumstances and their good hearts, my destiny changed.

It was *the* blessing of my life.

CHAPTER 2

MADISON PARK

Madison Park is a small hamlet lying west of U.S. Highway 231. The town's perimeter is roughly marked out by a line running from Union Chapel Church to the north, Old Elam Baptist Church to the east, Mrs. Martha Moore's old house to the south, and Ezell's Catfish Cabin, a restaurant owned by a white businessman, to the west. The entrance lays at the end of a rickety two-lane bridge that spans a ravine where a low-lying creek runs alongside the train tracks. The creek divides Madison Park in two parts: "This Side" and "Over the Bridge." This Side was more conservative and was home to many of the old, established families, including mine, as well as the Methodist church. Over the Bridge was considered a bit more liberal and is where Big Ben opened the only nightclub for miles around. Henrietta, a.k.a. "Big Hen," the cursing-est lady in all of Madison Park, lived Over the Bridge.

Although I would sometimes accompany Mama and Daddy to visit friends who lived Over the Bridge, I spent little time there. When I was young, almost everything that interested me happened on This Side. Two exceptions were the funerals we attended at the Baptist church and occasional visits to Mama's good friend, Mrs. Evelyn Holmes, who owned one of Madison Park's two general stores. While her competition offered a wider variety of merchandise, we felt an obligation to shop at Mrs. Evelyn's sparsely stocked store because of the family connection. Mrs. Evelyn always invited me to choose the largest dill pickle I could spy through the big glass jar that sat on the front counter next to the pigs' feet and pickled hard-boiled eggs.

No matter which side of the creek they were on, Madison Park residents lived modestly. Most homes were small wood-frame houses, lifted off the earth and resting on cinder blocks. They called them shotgun houses because someone standing at the front door could fire a shotgun straight through the house out the back door. A few were larger white-frame houses and red-brick homes built by the federal government in the 1960s for military veterans.

Most families owned a couple acres of land, with their house close to the road and what lay behind designated as farmland. Stretching back to the settlement's founding in the nineteenth century, Madison Park was predisposed for the rural lifestyle—the sense of community and self-reliance naturally lent itself to farming. Even in the 1970s a lot of families raised their own chickens, and a few kept livestock.

The rainy, humid climate supported many types of trees, such as pecan, maple, oak, pine, magnolia, and crepe myrtle, and a house was thought to be naked without flowers, shrubs, lawn furniture, and lawn decorations. Mrs. Minnie, a long-time friend of Mama's, had her own abstract-impressionist style of horticulture. She painted three car tires white, set them on her lawn, and planted them with Queen Anne's lace, black-eyed Susies, and petunias. Mrs. Clementine, whom Mama never failed to describe without saying, "Mrs. Clementine, bless her heart," had large lemon-yellow painted rocks leading down her driveway to keep cars off the grass. With few fences separating the houses, dogs took long naps on neighbors' front porches, and chickens pecked freely from yard to yard.

With the exception of Old Wetumpka Highway, which ran the length of Madison Park, all of the streets were red clay. They were dusty when it was dry and muddy when it rained. Most people walked. If they did drive, the vehicles of choice tended to be dented pickup trucks and Chevy sedans that had spent their prime as fleet cars or taxicabs and long ago had lost their luster. Many had crudely filled holes where blue lights, sirens, or rooftop taxi lights formerly beamed. I grew up thinking nothing of the roar of an unmufflered V-eight, wheels spinning without hubcaps, trunk lids and hoods missing, wearing the mixed hues of primer and paint. In our neighborhood they were not remarkable.

Most people who called Madison Park home had grown up in the area or had relatives there who took them in. Transition in and out, except by birth, death, and the outward migration of the young—too many going to jail or into the army—was limited. Few, if any, outsiders chose Madison Park after cruising multiple neighborhood open houses on Sunday afternoons. In the eighteen years that I lived there, I don't recall seeing a single moving van.

Dating back to its earliest days, Madison Park's most prominent feature was the absence of white faces. It was built by the hands of people seeking not just a sense of community but a safe haven—free from the perils of their recent enslavement.

When President Abraham Lincoln signed the Emancipation Proclamation on January 1, 1863, approximately three million men and women were set free, at least in theory—the Proclamation immediately affected only twenty thousand to fifty thousand slaves where the Union Army had taken control. It wasn't until two years later, when the Civil War ended, that the Proclamation systematically freed thousands of men and women, with nearly all liberated by July 1865. With almost nothing more than the clothes on their backs, a little farming knowledge, and an extraordinary capacity for resilience, they moved their families to find land they could work—land that for the first time would yield profit and prosperity for them and not a master.

But freedom didn't come without fear. Former slaves were ignorant of legal constraints and general business practices—ironic given that they had been legally constrained all their lives. Most couldn't write their names—and some had only one name until they chose a second. Their perspective and understanding of how the world worked was based on what they'd overheard and seen from their masters' conversations and transactions. Could they succeed on their own? Would they become victims of carpetbaggers and scalawags who migrated south to take advantage of the social turmoil caused by the onset of Reconstruction? Would their freedom be short-lived? What if resentful plantation owners, angry over the loss of their "property," chose to retaliate?

As unequal as their lot in life had been to that point, they cherished a conviction that they were the equals of any other person, blessed by their Creator with inalienable rights. To paraphrase Civil Rights leader Reverend Fred Shuttlesworth, who spoke about our enslaved ancestors' appetite to be free, a "fire got started deep in their souls, and it could not be put out."

What little is known about Madison Park's origins is due to the efforts of African American historian Dr. Gwen Patton and her research among the "Madison Family Papers," housed at Trenholm State Technical College, in Montgomery, Alabama. Eli Madison, the patriarch of the community bearing his name, was born in Alabama in 1839. According to the stories passed down, he was both physically and intellectually a strong man, with an indestructible sense of self-respect. Dr. Patton notes that his "slave-master trusted him, yet feared him." In 1865, after the conclusion of the Civil War, Madison set out with his half-brother Killis Marshall and close friend Gadson Draw, along with their wives, to establish what would become one of the state's first free African American communities. Soon other families from Autauga County, about twenty miles north of Montgomery, joined the pioneers in Hunter Station, five miles down the road. Next Madison moved the families to King Hill, thirteen miles away. They were closer to the city but still deep enough in the country to secure the amount of arable land they needed for the settlement they envisioned.

Within a few years the families had accumulated enough capital to buy a substantial plot. Only modest-sized properties were available in King Hill, but Flatbush, which is near Wetumpka to the northeast, had a number of plantations for sale, land that belonged to financially ruined white Southerners. So, the families pooled their resources in 1880 and made a down payment on the May Plantation. Within two years, Madison paid James and Molly May $2,380 in exchange for the deed to 560 acres, becoming the only recorded group of freed slaves in Alabama to purchase an entire estate.

Madison and his group trusted the Lord's promise to supply their needs. Settling their families on the plantation, they cleared brush, tilled the sandy fields, and planted trees, including oaks, whose height and grandeur now reign as testaments to their industriousness, even while shading what would become their graves. Later they established a sawmill and gristmill and bought a cotton gin.

Unincorporated, without a mayor or town council, the community was organized around the common good. Within the framework of national and state laws, residents made the rules, governed and cared for one another, and meted out whatever discipline and correction a situation required. It was a community where, when a black person spoke, black people listened. The one thing the town fathers hadn't done was to give their community a name.

One night the train that regularly passed along the edge of the hamlet derailed. The booming noise as the railroad cars exploded could be heard for miles, rousing the men from their beds. Madison and the others struggled to put out the spreading fire, or at least to contain it, tend to the injured train crew, and keep watch over the debris scattered in the surrounding field along the tracks. They didn't care that it was white people's property. They prized their community's integrity too much to tarnish it by looting. At daybreak, when officials arrived from Montgomery to investigate and secure the cargo, the all-white posse was surprised to find order, an outcome they'd deemed impossible among African Americans. When the story reached the rest of Montgomery's citizenry, Madison's community was held up as a model for black people. From that day on it was called Madison's Park, and, gradually, Madison Park. The name was not merely an honor bestowed on the founder, it spoke to the unifying sentiment that we were Madison's children.

Eli Madison (1839–1915)—Madison Park's founding father and namesake
Courtesy of William Winston family archive

Despite their lack of formal education, these pioneers took concrete steps to care for their souls, minds, and bodies. They desired freedom not only from slavery but from poverty. Realizing their need to remain spiritually liberated, sometime in 1881 they established a church in the Methodist tradition, an unsurprising choice given Methodist founder John Wesley's outspoken opposition to slavery. The church met first under bush trees before moving into a log cabin that protected them from the wintry winds. Two years later Kate and Killis Marshall donated the land on Old Wetumpka Highway on which today's church, which Eli Madison named the Union Chapel African Methodist Episcopal Zion (AMEZ) Church, still sits.

A few years later the founding families cleared twenty-five more acres to create a park. Shaded by oak trees that lined its perimeter, the land was a vast green lawn broken up with gravel sidewalks, play areas for children, and a central pavilion. The park doubled as a meeting place and vacation spot, since most residents couldn't afford to travel.

CHAPTER 3

A PROUD BLACK COMMUNITY

Eli and Frances Madison had ten boys and two girls. The oral history passed down through his grandchildren and great-grandchildren affirms that the couple imparted to their children a sense that they were part of W. E. B. Du Bois's "talented tenth." Du Bois, the first African American graduate from Harvard, asserted that the spearhead of African American social advancement would be an elite cadre of classically educated blacks (one in ten). Eli told his children, "We need doctors, lawyers, scientists, teachers, bishops and every other profession that will uplift the race."

He saw no contradictions in the philosophies of Du Bois and Booker T. Washington, the founder of Tuskegee Institute. Whereas Du Bois advocated an elite approach to black advancement, Washington emphasized black economic independence through the pursuit of technical and vocational educations. Eli joined Du Bois's notion that some African Americans were more talented than others with Washington's firm faith in the capability of all to lift themselves "by their own bootstraps."

Madison Park's first organized school was convened in Eli and Frances's home and moved a few years later to Union Chapel Church to accommodate the community's growing demand for education. The teachers had learned how to read and write while still slaves, during sessions known as "midnight schools," secret schools where the few men and women who had been taught literacy skills by their owners would pass their knowledge on to other slaves.

In 1914, Chicago-based philanthropist Julius Rosenwald, chief executive officer of Sears and Roebuck, contributed money for the construction of a two-room schoolhouse, on land that Eli Madison deeded to the community, the first of six Rosenwald schools in Alabama. Rosenwald was inspired to help fund schools after meeting Booker T. Washington. Eventually five thousand Rosenwald Schools were established in fifteen Southern states.

Many still believe that Rosenwald donated all of the money for the schools, but the Madison Park community raised $500, twice as much as the $250 grant from the Rosenwald fund. The remaining $200 needed for construction came from taxes, which at the time were segregated by race, meaning that African Americans footed the bill. A single teacher for all grades taught a basic curriculum of reading, writing, and arithmetic, along with shop and vocational skills, including farming, gardening, dress making, and personal hygiene.

Eli and Frances Madison's philosophy of education and uplift was borne out in their family. After Eli's death in 1915, their eldest child, Mr. General Madison (1872–1952), the superintendent of Union Chapel Church's Sunday school for more than fifty years, assumed the role of community leader.

Of all Eli and Frances Madison's offspring, their fifth child, Arthur, was the most diligent. Eli managed to obtain a scholarship for Arthur to attend Bowdoin College in Maine, but each summer he returned to Madison Park to teach "citizenship classes," for both adults and children, encouraging all to register to vote—part of his father's vision for civically educating the community. After receiving his law degree from Columbia University in New York City in June 1918, Arthur set up practice in Harlem, eventually becoming legal counsel for the National Association for the Advancement of Colored People (NAACP). He later became Montgomery's first black attorney, and, in 1944, filed a petition in Montgomery probate court that restricted ownership and residency in Madison Park to "the negro race in perpetuity" to prevent outside speculators from buying up land and increasing its value to the point that it was inaccessible to all but the wealthy. But Arthur's distinguished career was cut short, largely as a result of racial oppression, and he was ultimately blackballed from the legal profession for bringing suit against Montgomery County for voter registration irregularities among black communities. Some years after his disbarment in Alabama, he became a national celebrity because of his tireless work in gaining citizenship rights for southern blacks. Even until the late years of his life, he continued to press for equal rights and opportunities for African Americans generally, and Madison Park residents in particular. When he died in Harlem in 1957, his body was shipped home for burial in the Madison Park Cemetery. Rosa Parks and other Civil Rights pioneers cited Arthur Madison as one of their chief inspirations, having followed the accounts of his legal battles on behalf of the Montgomery Civil Rights movement.

Except for a scattering of whites on the outskirts, Madison Park remains a black community today, justifiably proud of its history. Generations later the descendants of the original settlers still see it as a "shining city on a hill."

CHAPTER 4

MY MOTLEY HERITAGE

I don't know the story of my great-great grandfather John Motley Sr.'s enslavement—whether he worked in the plantation house or the cotton fields and how his owners treated him. But I do know that he was one of the freedmen who left Autauga County to join Eli Madison just before sunrise one summer morning in 1880. Upon arriving, he and his group of former slaves gathered in an open-air temple of arched trees to make a promise under God's heaven and on the altar of God's green earth to start their own community, take responsibility for one another, and make a success of their lives. Later, he was among the pioneers who moved the stones to build the foundation of Union Chapel Church.

John Motley Sr. was in his late sixties when his grandson, my grandfather, George Washington Motley, was born—the third of John and Minnie Motley's six children. Daddy was proud of his beginnings. Like his namesake, he knew from childhood that much was expected of him, and he took pleasure in signing his full name.

Daddy enjoyed retelling childhood stories of visiting his grandfather's simple frame house on the large tract of land that was eventually passed down to his grandchildren. He remembered the large rough-hewn wooden cross shaped by my great-great grandfather's hands;

it hung over the front door, an intensely personal symbol of salvation for a man who never expected to get out of slavery. Over the back door hung a picture of "the Great Emancipator," President Abraham Lincoln, a testament of gratitude and a reminder of the difference that one principled man can make. You might say that in my great-great grandfather's thinking, whether you went out the front door or the back, you were reminded of redemption. Had he lived long enough to see it built, John Motley Sr. would have approved of the brief citation engraved in stone at the Lincoln Monument in Washington, D.C.: "IN THIS TEMPLE / AS IN THE HEARTS OF THE PEOPLE / FOR WHOM HE SAVED THE UNION / THE MEMORY OF ABRAHAM LINCOLN / IS ENSHRINED FOREVER."

John Motley Sr. instilled in his grandson an optimistic spirit that emphasized the importance of building the future for generations to come. He inspired Daddy to dream without letting dreams become his master, to keep the faith in himself and in mankind, to refuse self-pity and never create excuses, to accept responsibility, and to be true to himself. His grandfather emphasized the importance of sure foundations—building on solid ground with firm values and moral rectitude. Perhaps it was from his grandfather that Daddy learned to be economical in all things, especially with words.

Shy and self-contained, Daddy nonetheless understood how to get along with people of different backgrounds. He had learned to swim as a teenager from a lifeguard at the whites-only Montgomery Country Club, where he and his younger brother Chiney, or "Dot," waited tables and worked as valets. Daddy became a favorite of some of the old members, who bent the club's rule against African Americans in the pool on his behalf, allowing a lifeguard to teach him to swim.

One of the earliest pictures I have of my grandfather,
George Washington Motley (c. 1953). Seated behind
him is his brother James Fawcett Motley, and they
are surrounded by their nieces and nephews.
The collection of Eric L. Motley

In the late 1930s, Madison Park residents combined their resources and built a swimming pool in the park, the only one in Montgomery County where blacks were allowed to swim. For twenty-five years, Daddy was Madison Park's sole lifeguard. People traveled from as far away as Birmingham, ninety-five miles north of Montgomery, to take swimming lessons from George Motley. When he went to war in the 1940s, the pool was closed for more than a year.

One story demonstrates Daddy's enormous capacity to live out his beliefs in his own quiet actions. He and Uncle Dot used to catch a city bus to get to and from the country club. One afternoon when they boarded the bus to head home, the driver was shouting at an elderly black woman too frail to climb the steps without pausing to catch her breath as passengers laughed and grumbled that she was taking too long. The woman slowly worked her way down the aisle, ignoring the stares and sighs until she reached her seat in the back. The two Motley brothers had paid their fares, but Daddy grabbed Dot's hand and dashed off the bus before the doors closed, too angry to remain onboard. Daddy didn't say a word to Dot the whole way and never let go of his hand as they walked home, some five miles away, in the hot evening sun. Walking to and from the club, the brothers kept up their silent protest against the unfair forces of society for the rest of the summer—and for the rest of their lives. Neither Motley ever rode a Montgomery public bus again.

Mamie Ruth Cain was born on September 3, 1920, in Wetumpka, Alabama. She was the only child of Annie Ruth "Toot" Cain and Homer Graham. Those present said Mamie didn't come into the world screaming but talking like the radio, which made its debut around the same time, and she never stopped. In the late 1920s Toot went away for a year to work as a domestic housekeeper in Mossy Head, Florida. Grandmother Cain took care of her lively, pig-tailed, eight-year-old granddaughter Mamie but had difficulty remembering the city where her daughter Toot was working. To aid her memory, folks began to call my grandmother "Mossy." The name stuck.

Mama's grandmother was proudly half-Cherokee, and Mama's

distinctive high cheekbones evidenced her Native American birthright. One day in the 1950s my grandparents were filling out papers to transfer land deeds when the county clerk casually told Mama that because she was black she'd have to take a number and wait in the back room. "Well, you know a very good percentage of me is Cherokee," she said. "I'm not just black, I'm part Indian."

Daddy took her hand and joked, "Now, thanks to your heritage, we're damned twice! We'll never get out of here."

But that came twenty years after they met.

Mamie Motley, still dressed in her party attire, having just returned from a friend's wedding (c. 1947). The collection of Eric L. Motley

In 1936, Ernest Wilson's Madison Park Night Club was the social center of Madison Park and nearby black communities, including Wetumpka. It had a full bar, a jukebox, and enough fun-seeking patrons to fill it every Friday and Saturday night. One weekend Dot begged Daddy, then nineteen, to go as his wingman.

Dot worked the room as Daddy stood in a corner, far enough away from the action to prevent anyone from asking him to dance. But at almost six feet tall, with light caramel skin, brownish green eyes that brightened a room like a lantern, a regal bearing, and a strong resemblance to the actor Cary Grant, his effort to go unnoticed didn't work for long. At the instigation of her closest childhood friend, Mama came over and asked Daddy to dance. She'd already caught his attention, fanning her dress in the air as she'd danced with his best friend. "She smiled at me," Daddy said, recalling that night decades later. Just sixteen, Mama was already a take-charge kind of girl. According to Mama, Daddy accepted her offer hesitantly. Then, to the great amusement of onlookers, he stood talking to her as she jitterbugged in circles around him.

Mama was four-foot-six and weighed 140 pounds. She had a light brown-sugar complexion, a round face, small eyes, and thin lips. Though the two made an odd couple, that night was the start of a sixty-one-year relationship.

CHAPTER 5

EVERYTHING ROUNDED OUT

By the nature of growing up on the land, Daddy was a farmer. He liked to think he didn't just "garden," he *farmed* the two acres behind our house, tilling each row with his wood-handled hoe to the same precision as if he were laying ceramic tiles. He grew corn, okra, sweet potatoes, squash, tomatoes, peas, turnips, collards, cantaloupes, and watermelons. He was what many would call "a jack of all trades." But on his official army transcript he listed his occupation as "carpenter."

Even as a boy Daddy had a fascination with building things. His teachers recognized an acute mathematical ability, especially in geometry, and when he was ten, they encouraged him to pursue a career as an architect or carpenter. After he finished high school, he apprenticed himself to an architect in Montgomery, following him to job sites until he settled on home construction as his chosen profession. Daddy, who was mechanically inclined, became a skilled carpenter, brick mason, and an uncertified architect, learning by that time-honored method of imitating those who already knew how and letting them point out his mistakes.

But it's difficult to believe that he made many errors. He always carried a tape measure in his back pocket, ready to verify whatever met the eye, and a little notebook to jot things down, whether it was the imagined dimensions of a future project or the price of a gallon of milk. He believed in taking the time to do things right. To him, shortcuts were inexcusable. Symmetry, precision, and order meant everything.

The many houses he built in Madison Park bore certain trademarks. He would never build a house in the country without a front porch. To him, a porch was as necessary as a roof. He had a signature trim he used to encase windows that made them stand out in importance. And unlike most woodworkers who disdain simple repetition, he loved to build his own window shutters. People in our neighborhood would look at houses and say, "George Motley built that. I can tell by the windows."

Daddy's strict standards extended to outhouses. His refusal to build one within fifteen yards of a home—he preferred at least twenty yards—irritated some of his clients, whose chief concern was convenience. Who wanted to walk five extra yards in winter? But for Daddy, aesthetics were as important as sanitation and health. He had a natural ease and eye for how things should look. When one homeowner complained that his outhouse looked more like a gazebo, Daddy replied, "*You* know what it is! Must everyone else?"

Daddy was especially proud that he had helped build about half the black churches in Montgomery, including Union Chapel Church—a simple, beautiful structure whose foundation and cornerstone were laid by the founders of Madison Park, including his grandfather John Motley Sr. A generous member offered to pay for the altar, to be purchased ready-made from a dealer in Pittsburgh. But in his quiet way, Daddy had a better idea. With lovely wood from trees under which his forefathers had sat and talked—that had been felled on the church grounds to build an earlier extension—he fashioned an altar with far more significance than ever could have been purchased. He didn't talk much about it—he rarely thought it worthwhile to voice what he felt—but he enjoyed the fact that he had lovingly cut, shaped, and stained the wood with his own hands. Every time I kneel at that altar, I am reminded of his many contributions to our community.

The call to enlist during World War II posed a great dilemma. He'd promised to finish a church in Montgomery and two houses in Madison Park. The families were good but poor people, and their homes had fallen into an unlivable state. They knew if they could save money to buy the lumber and supplies, Daddy—perhaps the only man on earth who would work that way—would build them a house and allow them to pay him in installments for as long as they needed.

On April 10, 1945, the jubilant headline in the *Montgomery Advertiser* announced, "Allied Forces Liberate Nazi Concentration Camp in Buchenwald." Two days later the nation's grief was evoked in another headline: "United States President Franklin Delano Roosevelt Dies Suddenly at Warm Springs, Georgia; Vice President Harry S Truman Becomes 33rd President." But on April 11, between those two momentous events, George Washington Motley nailed the last board in place, headed to the recruitment office downtown, and joined a segregated platoon in the U.S. Army. What prompted him to enlist just four weeks before V-E Day, I'm not sure, other than a profound sense of obligation that characterized him all his life.

Eight months later—only days before Daddy's warship sailed for Germany—he was granted a furlough from the base at Fort McClellan, Alabama. By careful plan, he hurried his fiancée and his sister-in-law, Evelyn, to the courthouse where probate judge William W. Hill, affixed his seal and signature to the certificate that read "Rite of Matrimony—Wednesday, January 9, 1946."

The newlyweds attended church the Sunday after their wedding.

Mama walked to the altar holding Daddy's hand and offered her life anew to the Lord, joining his church. The preacher prayed for the casualties of the war and at the end of the service asked Daddy, a long-time member of the choir, to sing a hymn. Without accompaniment, he sang "There Will Be Peace in the Valley":

> *Well, I'm tired and so weary, but I must travel on,*
> *'Til the Lord comes and calls me away,*
> *Where the morning's so bright and the Lamb is the light*
> *And the night is as bright as the day!*
>
> *There will be peace in the valley for me some day*
> *There will be peace in the valley for me, oh Lord, I pray*
> *There'll be no sadness, no sorrow, no trouble I see*
> *Only peace in the valley for me.*

Mama often said if I thought Elvis could sing that song, it was a shame I never heard Daddy. Not an eye in the church was dry when he finished. Tens of thousands had died in the war, with atrocities beyond human telling. Madison Park had sent a good number of boys overseas, so there was great hope in the thought that perhaps there would finally be "peace in the valley."

After the war, despite peace abroad and an economic boom at home, the next decades tested African Americans. Daddy went to war for his country when his country didn't fight for him. A son of the South, he swore allegiance to a commander-in-chief whom he could not elect. He drank from shared battlefield canteens but wasn't permitted to drink at a "whites only" fountain in his home state. He read Army training manuals but wasn't welcome in his hometown "public" library. Blacks, though accounting for 60 percent of bus ridership, were compelled to pay their fares at the front door before walking around to the backdoor to board. But the Army had no qualms about hauling African Americans to the front lines.

Daddy didn't march in the streets, but neither did he silently acquiesce to these inequities. In 1955 when Montgomery's black citizens dared to boycott buses and public transportation in Montgomery, he drove Madison Park neighbors and friends to and from their jobs in the city in his car. The boycott was a pivotal moment in the Civil Rights movement.

He'd learned from his grandfather that we all drink from wells we didn't dig, are warmed by fires we didn't kindle, are nourished by harvests we didn't cultivate, and rest under shade trees we didn't plant. Part of his great legacy to me was that he never became embittered. Unlike many people, who seek only the outward appearance of religious conformity while remaining unchanged by their faith, Daddy was shaped by biblical teachings that prevented him from feeling resentful. Despite disrespect and verbal abuse from Southern segregated society, he maintained a quiet decency and never lost hope that someday this country would rise to a level of God-inspired fairness for all. He displayed a level of stoicism that today would be unimaginable. His childhood remembrance of the cross above his grandfather's door impressed him with the example of the One who was despised and forsaken but who could still pray, "Father, forgive them, for they know not what they do."

In 1947, after his military discharge, Daddy came home and tore down the weakened old house John Motley Sr. had built. To preserve his grandfather's legacy, he incorporated the timbers into the new, stately, white-framed, plantation-style, one-story house that he built for his bride and future generations. Raised on brick pillars and accented with forest-green wooden shutters, it was made up of three bedrooms, two formal rooms—a living room where guests were received and a formal dining room used on special occasions—a family den, kitchen, and a large foyer at the back of the house. Of the eight rooms, five rooms had fireplaces. It was in that house that Daddy stood over his mother as she lay dying and there, early one morning years later, that he found his brother, James Fawcett Motley, had died in his sleep from a heart attack.

But joy far outweighed sorrow under that roof. George and Mossy lived contentedly together for fifty-two years. Although they treated each other with a formality that belonged to another century, devoid of public displays of affection, they were devoted to one another in a way that allowed each to flourish. Until the end of their lives, they never asked what the other could do for them but what they could do for the other.

My grandparents both appreciated precision and design. Mama believed that God's presence could be felt most acutely in beautiful things and worked hard within their budget to make an attractive home. The rooms were handsomely decorated with drapes, framed drawings and paintings, antique furnishings, and lovely rugs.

She had a keen eye for finding treasures in other people's trash. When my grandparents drove by furniture left at the side of the street for the garbage collector, Mama would get out and inspect the haul to decide if it was worth strapping to the roof or stuffing into the trunk. Practicality was rarely a consideration. They'd scavenged a table lamp with a three-foot-high base rounded like an apple and trimmed with gold and elaborate floral designs etched in silver. The lampshade was made of cream-colored vellum that looked like a large bowl of butterscotch candy. It took pride of place in the living room even though it didn't turn on and they couldn't afford to have it repaired. "It's *too pretty* to work," Mama explained.

Mama was not one to overspend, but occasionally beauty trumped thrift. Once when she spotted a mahogany dining table with brass claw feet and six lyre-back chairs made by Duncan Phyfe, one of America's leading nineteenth-century cabinetmakers, in the window of a Montgomery antique shop, she had to have it. She patiently paid a little each month on layaway for two years before she brought it home.

People could ask Mama and Daddy for anything. When bills needed to be paid and someone ran a little short, they came to George and Mossy Motley. A ride to the store for groceries? Daddy said yes. He made concrete headstones for the dead whose families couldn't afford polished granite, using a fine pointed stick to carve their name and dates, removing the excess cement with a clean paintbrush before it dried. They never kept account of deeds done for others; to them, everything "rounded itself out."

CHAPTER 6

YEARS IN TRAINING

With a toddler in the house, after Barbara Ann's departure, the Motley household suddenly was a new troika: George, Mossy, and Eric. When I was about three years old, Mama began calling me Bugs, after Bugs Bunny, because of my love of raw carrots, which I used to gnaw on constantly, as if they were my pacifier.

I never thought we might be considered poor. The critical distinction for me, as explained by my grandparents, was between those who had and those who had not. I had a roof over my head, warm cooked meals three times a day, and clothes for every day of the week. We knew good people in our community who had far less. My grandparents never shielded my eyes from the poorest and most neglected of our neighbors. Daddy always ended his mealtime prayers with the plea, "And Lord make us ever mindful of those who have not."

Word was that Mrs. Sarah Pearl Coleman, her son, Sylvester Jacob Coleman, known as "Silva Jo," and her mother, Mrs. Galloway (people called her "Mrs. Ola"), who lived with them, were the richest people in Madison Park, and Mama believed it, so it must have been so. Both Mrs. Sarah Pearl and Silva Jo had college educations. Silva Jo worked in Birmingham as a government consultant but drove home every weekend to be with his mother. He turned heads as he pulled into Madison Park in his polished silver Toyota convertible sports car, further evidence that they were among the world's rich. After high school in the sixties, he had been privileged to go abroad for a couple of weeks to experience "high-culture." Upon his return, the people of Madison Park remarked that he was a "changed man."

Whether you were rich or poor, sharing came as naturally as sunrise to the people of Madison Park. You'd see tractors, plows, and other implements that belonged to one family parked in someone else's back-yard for weeks. Daddy's close friend Ray never felt compelled to buy a lawnmower, and Daddy implored him not to, because his yard was so small and our mower was available. If someone's roof leaked, half a dozen men would descend on the house one Saturday and reroof it, with no money changing hands and no one keeping score. You always planted a bit more in your vegetable garden than you needed.

But my arrival had a price tag that neighborly generosity couldn't close. Anticipating the extra expense of raising a child, Mama and Daddy sold the bit of extra land they owned. During Barbara Ann's last years in high school, they'd scaled back the number of days and hours they worked. But when I came along Daddy took extra carpentry jobs, and Mama, a maid who kept house for white families in the Old Cloverdale neighborhood in Montgomery—a section of beautiful homes with carpet-pressed lawns and sculpted hedges where Zelda and F. Scott Fitzgerald once lived—stepped up her schedule.

Mondays through Saturdays were ordinary working days, and unless there was a funeral we seldom had a reason to dress up. When Monday morning came, you knew exactly what to do, because our house was superintended by order and routine, with few surprises. Mama was disciplined and extended this to those around her. She governed the affairs of the house with a strong hand, and we obediently obliged her sixty-five rules. I was expected to make my bed as soon as I got out of it, to dress for the day before interacting with others, to be fully dressed at all meals, to habitually reserve a half-hour of quiet for prayer and reflection, and to consistently err on the side of formality rather than familiarity.

Mama saw to it that any tendency on my part to be lazy, slothful, grungy, or rebellious was never given oxygen. I didn't resist, partly because it would have been futile, but more important, because my grandparents imprinted on me a love of order and routine. From them I learned that the way one starts the day largely dictates how it will unfold. A core tenet of the Motley household was that to rise early was to embrace the newness and freshness of the morning, with all of its promise and opportunities, before others started to create noise. All these years later some of these habits continue to dictate my daily life.

Mama was like a clock that never needed winding. She woke up every morning at 4:30, before sunrise, without an alarm; jumped out of bed; and headed to the kitchen as if a gun for the day's marathon had just sounded—a pace she maintained all day. The Good Lord knew if He were to make a woman this determined to do things right, He had to give her a cheerful disposition, a boundless supply of energy, and a sense of humor, lest she take herself too seriously.

In the winter she would turn on all four burners on the stovetop to warm the kitchen and then light a fire in the fireplaces in the den and in Daddy's room. After warming the house Mama would take her bath. This was a process! She'd bring in the buckets of water that the two of us had pumped the evening before, heat it in a large steel basin on the stove, ladle it into a pan, and transfer that to a large galvanized tub that she set down in the hallway, taking it from the back porch, where it hung neatly on two large hooks when not in use.

The closed kitchen door was the signal that Daddy and I were not to enter. When she finished, she put on a print dress and apron, emptied the bath water, and repeated the process for me. She'd wake me at five o'clock by turning on the bright lamp on my dressing table and calling out, "Morning has broken. Rise and shine and give God the glory!"

With that trumpeting call, I'd push back the covers and stumble to the sudsy, warm bath, fresh towels smelling of lye soap piled high to the side. Mama believed everything should be spic 'n' span, including me. You could count on that. Her demand for cleanliness stayed with me, making me the punchline of countless university jokes and comments later in my life.

As I bathed, Mama multitasked, serenading me with church hymns and old Negro spirituals while she cooked breakfast, the bacon hissing on the stove. This routine continued, in slightly altered form, even after Daddy used an unexpected lump-sum payment from the Veterans Administration to "put in a bathroom for my boy," as he said. He could have spent that money on many more urgent necessities, but he hired a plumber, Mr. Dwight, to install a bathtub, toilet, and sink in an old storage room off the back porch, finishing off the space with yellow floral wallpaper and green trim to experience my joy.

Mama and I always ate a full morning meal. Daddy was permitted to sleep until six, so the two of us sat at the table, enjoying the bacon alongside scrambled eggs and homemade biscuits, with small bowls of white rice and a large pot of hot black tea.

Although we chatted easily while we ate, as far back as I can remember, our habit at the end of the meal was to sit for a while in silence. She would close her eyes and move her lips in prayer, and then we would pray together, she, asking God's grace and mercy upon us all, thanking Him for a new day of possibilities, and teaching me to do the same. She would end with, "And, Lord, thank You for the land that feeds us and the hands that plant the seed."

Mrs. Hattie Mae Sherman, known as "Mama Sherman," reigned as the chief operator of the Washerteria, a do-it-yourself laundromat owned by her eldest son, Jessie. Every morning, for three years, Daddy dropped me at the Washerteria where Mama Sherman offered to babysit me. Besides watching me, she welcomed people, helped them pass the time, and measured soap and bleach.

When she became my babysitter, Mama Sherman was seventy-one and had been retired for twenty-plus years, after a long career cleaning the houses and rearing the children of white families in Montgomery. A large-framed woman, she weighed more than three hundred pounds and carried herself as if she had toted a heavy load all her life—which she had. She had lost her husband, "Big Peter," when she was young and was left to raise their eleven children on her own.

Every morning she took me in her powerful arms and squeezed me into her well-cushioned bosom. No one's embrace, not even Mama's, could compare. Her hugs left nothing out. She could make the most alienated soul on the planet feel loved. It was her gift.

The Washerteria was a laboratory of human experience. Mama Sherman's superintendent role allowed her to know almost everything going on in Madison Park. She used to say, "There are three places where Madison Park's people go to get clean: the church, the tub, and here at the Washerteria." Ours was the rare family who did our washing at home. Mama had a Maytag with spinning rollers that extracted the last drop of moisture before she hung our clothes on a long wire line in the backyard to air-dry. Amid the whining and spinning of twenty washers and dryers, Mama Sherman was as much a counselor as a laundry expert. She portioned out advice on marriage, children, the stresses and demands of life, and how to make a crisp potato piecrust.

I appointed myself the official greeter, making conversation with our clientele the same way Mama Sherman did. And like her I found the patrons' habits fascinating. Had I been old enough, I could have edited a gossip column on the housewives of Madison Park.

After the first rush at eight o'clock, there was usually a lull around ten. Mama Sherman would give me the long square broom, so I could sweep up the wooden floor. Next I'd twist a clothes hanger into a hook and fish aggressively for change that people dropped. Easing it out from under the low-hung motor of the machine, I'd shout, "Whew, got it!"

"How much did you get little man?" Mama Sherman would ask.

"Enough to buy us a Fanta!"

"Sho-nuff, little man? Well, you get us a Coke from the machine, and I'll take out this sweet potato I made for us. We'll have a good snack time, just the two us."

I remember the way Mama Sherman emptied the coins

Little Bugs: A three-year-old, energetic, precocious Eric Motley—a wonderful handful for Mrs. Hattie Sherman to watch over at the Washerteria (c. 1975).
The collection of Eric L. Motley

from the machines, the silver quarters spinning themselves flat on the long wooden folding table. It was there that I learned to count—"25 cents, 50 cents, 75 cents, one dollar."

We'd roll the coins in paper wrappers as Mama Sherman told me stories of her papa on their farm when she was a child. During the hours we spent together, she often sang old spirituals that reaffirmed what my grandparents had taught: "You betta' mind. You betta' mind the way you talk; you betta' mind what you talkin' about. You gotta' give an account to Jesus, you betta' mind."

Every day she told me she loved me as much as she loved her own children—a claim I never doubted. Loving me as her own, she felt obliged to tell me how good boys and gentlemen behaved. She would say, "Take off your hat when you come through the door, little man."

I would take it off and lay it in a chair, only for her to grab it and say, "Never lay your hat down low. Always hang your hat up high, 'cause you always want to reach up."

Then she'd hoist me up so I could reach the high-hung hook.

I still hang my hat high.

CHAPTER 7

NOT MY ONLY PARENTS

Daddy had a daily routine that allowed him to live life somewhat on his own terms. He worked every weekday from 8:00 a.m. to 1:00 p.m. Then he'd leave the city, heading home to work in the field until dinner.

Mama's families arranged for her to be dropped off at the entrance to This Side, or at home, at noon. Like Superman stepping into a phone booth to make a last minute change of wardrobe before a mission, she retired to her bedroom and quickly changed from her good work clothes—crisp, neatly starched cotton dresses in an assortment of floral patterns worn with an apron and white, flat, rubber soled shoes—into softly worn plaid or striped housedresses. She never wore lipstick, rouge, or face powder to work; such luxury was reserved for Sundays and special occasions. Then she'd begin cleaning, cooking, and washing for us, as she'd done for other families.

Her tireless spirit kept her in perpetual motion, and she attributed that same energy to God. Once on a Sunday afternoon, I heard her say she was positive God didn't have time to rest on that first Sunday after creating the world, because surely there was a lot of cleaning up afterward. "You just can't form mountains and swirl stars into their silvery sockets and carve rivers out of the hollow earth and expect no

59

dust and nothing needing polishing up." She had a way of squeezing out of every hour what mattered most in life.

Tending her flowers was her favorite thing to do. She loved the rambling pink roses and elegant irises that she planted alongside the front porch and the dozens of potted amaryllises she placed around the pecan trees in our backyard. We had what seemed like hundreds of flowerpots on our porches containing geraniums, pansies, and chrysanthemums. She rearranged them seasonally, numbering each pot so that she could keep track of her flowers when she moved them into the barn for the winter. I secretly worried that, like Mrs. Clementine, Mama might warm to the idea of recycling old car parts or appliances as flower containers and front-yard sculpture. But as with inside, her tastes outdoors leaned to the formal and symmetrical, shaped by her admiration for the English Palladian style. She planted small shrubs to create borders around her flowerbeds and tall boxwoods on either side of our gravel driveway to fashion a grand entrance. She trimmed all the shrubbery herself and tried to sculpt them like the professional gardeners did at the city houses she cleaned.

In addition to Mama and Daddy, all sorts of folks in Madison Park participated in my upbringing. As a result, a community shaped and molded me. People invested their talents and resources in me. While I know my grandparents' love and nurturing set me on a certain path toward adulthood, I'm not certain that path would have opened up the whole world to me if it weren't for these friends, neighbors, and family members who took an extra interest in me.

Chief among them was our next-door neighbor, Mamie Motley Arms, Daddy's youngest sibling, whom I remember as the epitome of love. She was bold in faith, gentle in touch, and strong in charity. Despite her fragile constitution, whisper of a voice, and disinterest in getting out, "Ant Mamie," radiated warmth. With no picket fence separating our two houses, I saw her nearly every time I came and went. On hot, humid summer days we exchanged cups of lemonade and iced tea from each other's back porches.

As much as I enjoyed my aunt's fellowship, I needed a wider world. I was a precocious youngster. Dr. John H. Winston, our family doctor, said that when I began talking at nineteen months, I spoke in full sentences—full paragraphs, even—and never again was I quiet. Mama and Daddy could have easily felt too busy or ill-prepared for my questions, but they never tried to dampen my curiosity.

Dr. Winston helped me make sense of my surroundings. Unbelievably, in this age of drive-through medicine, he drove out to Madison Park from Montgomery every day to see his mother and make house calls, often without charge. He would arrive, listen to our ills, pull strange things out of his black bag, and chat with his patient, all the while addressing my rapid-fire questions. Occasionally, even when no one at 34 Motley Drive was ill, Dr. Winston came to see me, to bring me a book or talk about a sermon he heard. An avid photographer—he was one of the few among us who could afford photography—he'd conclude each visit saying, "Eric, let me get my camera and take a picture of you."

Mama and Daddy did set limits. They taught me early on that sassing was a cardinal sin. I understood the rule about "back talk," but I also held a high opinion of truth and justice. I didn't understand why the truth was the exclusive possession of adults and couldn't be arrived at through the give-and-take of lively discussion. My quest for truth, and the joy I got from correcting other people, often got me into trouble. Our other next-door neighbor, on the opposite side from Ant Mamie, Mrs. Cheney Jackson—"Miz Cheney"—then in her late eighties, often spoke a slightly corrupted version of the truth. Yet no one ever questioned her to her face.

One day I accompanied Mama to Miz Cheney's to take her some fruit. She surprised me by telling Mama a story that I knew to be outrageously false. Overeager to set the record straight, I flashed a look of incredulity—a look that said, "That's not so, and I know it." Though I'd said nothing, my astonishment was enough to propel Miz Cheney right up out of her rickety chair. She glared at me with an almost insane look that the wicked witch of Oz couldn't rival and cursed—yes, cursed (lying *and* cursing were doubly impressive to me). "What you lookin' at boy and wha's that look on your face? You 'sputin' my word? You sayin' I'm tellin' a story?"

As we made our way home through the open cornfield, Mama gave me a tongue-lashing I never forgot. "As long as you live, you never again look in Miz Cheney's eyes when she's speaking with me or any other adult," she scolded. "Do not even visually suggest that you have reason to doubt her."

Lesson learned.

When I was older, I learned that both Mrs. Cheney's father and mother had died as newly freed slaves and that because she was black, destitute, and orphaned, her entire life had been commanded and dictated by others. She'd been told what to do and when to do it. She'd been talked down to and bossed most of her nearly ninety years. But she deserved, and in Madison Park had been granted, the privilege to always be "right;" the community recognized that too much of her life had been spent being "wronged."

Every aspect of the common life was imbued with a sense of "we, not me." Alienation is difficult in a place where we all believed that we were all responsible for one another. I realized this when I started Head Start at age three. Head Start was created in 1965, as a part of President Lyndon Johnson's Great Society initiative and focused on providing early childhood education to children from low-income backgrounds. Johnson believed it would reduce poverty and increase social mobility. In 1967, Madison Park got the program and appointed Mrs. Shirley Peavey as principal. Mrs. Peavey, a large, fleshy woman, cast a frightening figure and, as the head disciplinarian, took delight in being feared. More inclined to scowl than smile, she had a prominent jaw, a few missing teeth, and an intense gaze that could shrivel children into silence. Worse, for me, she was Mama's friend. During my three years there I was sent to her office just twice, for talking during quiet time. But it might have been two hundred times for the impact it had on me. I'll never forget what it felt like when Principal Peavey grabbed up my little hand in her plush palm and stared at me with eyes fit for a horror film. "Boy," she hissed, "If you don't get your bottom in there and behave, I am going to *crucify* you!" The image I conjured of my pudgy body nailed to a cross with all my classmates watching made my knees weak. And I knew if I didn't shape up, I'd have to contend with more than Principal Peavey.

Mama would be next in line.

There were two occasions that I recollect getting spankings at home; one was in response to a tantrum I threw one Sunday, and I no longer remember the reason for the other. But what remains fresh are the many Peavey warnings I received. Had I gotten in trouble with her again, Mama told me I'd get two spankings: the first from Mrs. Peavey and the second from her.

Even though I grew up an only child, I never felt lonely or wished for a sibling. Looking back, I'm sure that spending so much time entertaining myself encouraged my creativity. From the time I learned my ABCs and a few sight-words in Head Start, I loved the lyricism of language and the way words looked printed on a page in different styles, fonts, sizes, and the color of the ink. I remember cutting words out of newspapers and magazines, looking them up in the old dictionary on Daddy's bedside table, and trying to make out their meanings. Then I'd copy the definitions on a clean page in my notebook and sound the words aloud. I'd repeat them over and again to anyone who would listen. Sometimes I'd wander into the woods behind our house, almost singing my new words, lifting them from the page into the air, like a melodious sonnet.

Like language, the natural world was another component of my imagination. Thanks to Mama's influence and her love of flowers and plants, I found the same companionship in nature as I did among people. More than six acres of wooded land stretched across the end of our vegetable garden. The woods weren't deep, but they were wide and thickly sown with brush, broken timbers, and the residue of decay. It was there that I started learning to identify birds, by sight and sound. Although I was close enough to see our house, I was far enough to imagine worlds unknown. In the woods and open fields alongside the creek, I found solace and solitude. The fireflies and red-breasted robins captivated me, as did the sun's daily arc across the sky.

I found nature to be vast but not always benign. I was fascinated by our frequent Southern summer storms. We could expect them in the hot, late afternoons of July and August. Daddy called them "Alabama Thunderstorms." But my religious grandmother took them as a sign that "God was at work," and as the Scripture beckons, "Let all the earth keep silent." The three of us would pass afternoons sitting wordlessly in the den, Mama in her rocking chair and Daddy and I on the sofa, listening to the thunder and watching the lightning flash.

As a little boy I often joined the church ladies on early Saturday morning walks across the bridge and over the hill, through the overgrown brush, to the cemetery, a collection of modest graves, some marked with crosses, others with hand-drawn etchings, shaded by tall pine trees. My companions were the elderly granddaughters of Eli Madison, each in their late sixties and early seventies—Mrs. Emma Madison Bell, a tall, muscular lady whom we called "Aunt Shine" because she possessed both an intellectual light and a physical strength that not even a man wanted to challenge; her sister, Mrs. Frankie Lee Winston, a large-framed stocky woman, who, like her son Dr. John Winston, had a loving touch; and their sister-in-law, Aunt Prince Ella Madison, who, with her unfailing elegance and gentle manner, reminded me of a benevolent queen. The three ladies would trim the wisteria, gather broken branches, replant shrubs, and refill the built-in vases on top of the graves with fresh flowers and vines, adding water that we brought in old milk containers.

I was the official sweeper. Brushing the faded pine straw into piles, I'd go from one grave to the next, listening to Aunt Shine. Without looking up, she'd say, "You're standing on the grave of my father, Mr. General Madison, the son of the founder of Madison Park, Eli Madison." Inspired, I'd sweep harder and more reverently, moving to another grave and then another. "Now you're sweeping Mrs. Emma Drain's grave," she'd tell me. "She believed in prayer and treated everyone as best she could. She was ready to go when the trumpet called."

Graveyard duty might not sound like a child-friendly activity. But as Aunt Shine told me, "Each of these people here, unknown to you, has a story that makes up the larger story of this place we call home. This is your history, Little Motley, and you too will come to rest here one day."

But of course I didn't spend all of my time in the quiet, more-or-less placid environs of Madison Park. Proximity to the city never seemed an important topic of conversation at home. Montgomery attracted my attention and shaped my upbringing from a young age. I couldn't resist a trip to the soda fountain at Kress department store, the scene of lunch-counter sit-ins by African Americans in the Jim Crow days of the early 1960s—and, coincidentally, where I glimpsed my first example of racism. I don't remember the details, but I vividly recall the haunting anxiety of the moment. It was a spring Saturday morning in 1976, when I was four. The department store windows were colorfully decorated with Easter ornaments. As we headed toward the building and turned the corner from the main street, we suddenly heard in front of us the thunderous sound of a marching drum in a parade.

What child doesn't like a parade? Eager to see, and pulling Mama back, I paused long enough to notice two flags hoisted high—one, American, and the other I learned years later, was Confederate—followed by rows of people dressed in full-length white robes and pointed hooded masks. I remember thinking, "They have no faces." It was a chilling sight—one that I will never forget. Neither will I forget the tight squeeze of Mama's hand pulling me fast to her side into the folds of safety.

CHAPTER 8

RABBITS V. TURTLES

The November afternoon that I brought home a letter from my first grade teacher, Mrs. Heikamp, Mama was so alarmed she immediately called Aunt Shine.

"We've got a problem," Aunt Shine agreed.

She hung up the phone, came to our house, and delivered a stern lecture to me about my "unacceptable" performance. The idea was woven into our everyday conversation: "Is that going to help you prepare for college . . ."; "you need to do that if you want to go to college . . ."; "you need to start saving for college . . ." With so much reinforcement, I couldn't help but make this my overriding goal. Everyone in Madison Park knew of the Motleys' dream for their little boy—and my plan to fulfill it.

In church the next Sunday, Aunt Shine suddenly stood, asked the pastor for permission to speak, looked out over the congregation, and announced: "Brothers and Sisters, we have a serious problem. Little Eric Motley has been moved from the Rabbits to the Turtles. Any books you've finished reading, please bring by George and Mossy's house. Little Eric doesn't have a library; and he needs to practice."

Everyone turned to look at me. I was mortified by the unwanted attention. But within a few hours, community folks started dropping by until soon our porch looked as if we were having a paper drive. There were 1945 *Life* magazines and a few way-back issues of *Jet* bundled together. I had *Encyclopedia Britannica*, Volume "L," 1932 edition, and a *Farmer's Almanac* predicting the weather for each day of 1948. Someone brought a dilapidated volume of Gwendolyn Brooks's poetry, powerful and impressive even absent a cover and half its pages. There was a volume of English verse—the poems of Keats, Tennyson, and Wordsworth. Talk about *eclectic*.

Learning was taken seriously in Madison Park. Too many older citizens had been denied the advantages of a formal education and exposure to the arts and ideas. Perfect attendance in school was expected. Only fever-induced delirium warranted an absence. When the Madison Park School was functioning, the teachers, who were neighbors and fellow parishioners, were a part of the community and enjoyed a relationship socially and civically with parents, and the sentiment continued in my day: parent-teacher conferences, PTA potlucks, plays, and pageants were must-attend events. And Mama and Daddy exhibited a far greater level of engagement and oversight of my academic performance than most.

With my low marks in reading identified and books and periodicals at hand, Aunt Shine mobilized a volunteer corps of six ladies, all of whom had been retired from teaching for fifteen to twenty years. All descendants of Eli Madison, the group included the same women who'd taught me Madison Park's history at the cemetery. A rotating team of two came by our house every afternoon to coach, drill, and encourage me. They didn't stop at reading. They must have figured while they were at it, why not tutor me in math too?

A couple of months in, Mrs. Frankie Lee Winston recognized that if I were falling behind in *my* studies, there had to be other kids in the community as bad off—or worse—than me. With a few small donations from townspeople to buy workbooks, flash cards, and other materials, they started a community-wide tutorial program in the back hall of our church to lift up Madison Park's children. Every weekday from four to five o'clock in the afternoon for more than two years about sixty boys and girls—Methodists, Baptists, Church of Christ, and Seventh-day Adventists—came to sit at the elbows of the all-volunteer staff.

The Tutors: The women who had the most formative impact on me as a child. Left to right: Carrie Madison Seay, Prince Ella Madison, Emma Madison Bell (aka Aunt Shine), and Frankie Lee Madison Winston (c. 1980). Courtesy of William Winston family archive

Aunt Shine began every afternoon with the Lord's Prayer, the Apostles' Creed, the Twenty-Third Psalm, the Pledge of Allegiance, the Preamble to the Declaration of Independence, and James Weldon Johnson's famous negro national anthem "Lift Every Voice and Sing." These were words to live by. They informed our lives and reminded us of our heritage and sense of belonging. Too important to be read, they had to be memorized, an underpinning of classical rhetoric and practice used among American slaves who weren't allowed to read. The women didn't have the benefit of research on the importance of oral reading and recitation, but their instincts were perfect. Memorization became an important part of my life. To this day I rely on passages I committed to memory then.

Helping their young charges imagine possibilities was also one of the keystones of their tutoring. One day, Aunt Shine asked us, "What did George Washington do?"

A dozen hands went up. She called on one boy, who stood and replied, "George Washington cut down the cherry tree!"

"No, no, no!" she answered, her voice rising in frustration. "George Washington did not cut down the cherry tree! He led this country through the American Revolution. He refused a crown and became our first president. That is important to remember! Maybe one day one of you will become the president of this country."

Pausing for emphasis, she added, "But only if you are *educated*."

The next day she asked, "Who is Harriet Tubman?"

Every day she asked about a different person to be celebrated for his or her contribution to America or to the world. Those ladies, showing us heroes and heroines and bending over us patiently to check our work as we sat around long Sunday school tables, were lifting us to higher places. They knew the benefits: a generation of children elevated out of their circumstances.

Aunt Shine and her female relatives had seen their educational mission upended by the U.S. Supreme Court's unanimous 1954 decision in *Brown v. Board of Education*, which ruled that separate educational facilities for blacks and whites were "inherently unequal" and demanded that schools be racially integrated. But the road to integration was rough. In 1963, Alabama's then-Governor, George Wallace, barred the door to two African American students at the University of Alabama in Tuscaloosa, just seventy-eight miles from Madison Park, standing down only after President John F. Kennedy called out the Alabama National Guard.

Madison Park Head Start Program—photo day (March 21, 1979)
The collection of Eric L. Motley

Wallace wasn't the only one against mixing white and black children in school. Aunt Shine and other Madison Park elders feared that forced integration would *destroy* their model of community-based education, which assured that every student was taught by someone who knew his or her background, parents, and family situation. Given that blacks and whites in the South lived separately, integration required transporting students to schools outside their neighborhoods. While elsewhere busing might have helped achieve greater diversity, Madison Park's citizens had felt insulated from the abuse of segregation common beyond their boundaries. Thus, they feared that the stability they'd achieved, while not perfect, might be better than the unknown. Aunt Shine once told me, "No one cared for our poor students like we did."

Third-grade photograph at Dozier Elementary—taken when public school integration was in full swing in Montgomery (April 1982)
The collection of Eric L. Motley

In the pre-*Brown* days, and long before schools offered free breakfast and lunch, the teachers often fed their hungry students. When boys and girls came without winter coats, they bought them clothes.

When kids didn't come to school, the teachers went out looking for them. They were in and out of students' homes and ran into them at church, ball games, and at Mr. June Jackson's grocery store. Fearing this spirit of community would be lost, they also feared the children would be failed by a system based on statistics instead of relationships.

But the law was the law. By the time I entered first grade in 1978 all of Madison Park's students were being bused to mostly white public schools to achieve racial balance in Montgomery. The old Madison Park School was converted into a county-run school for physically and mentally ill children, and instead of a ten-minute walk from 34 Motley Drive, the fifteen-mile trip to Dozier Elementary took forty-five minutes each way.

I loved riding the bus. I thought it was an adventure. It opened up new vistas of Madison Park to me, yet unknown, due to the limited bike route that was prescribed to me by Mama and Daddy. I got to know the community better, at least by sight, and daily chronicled in my mind and journaled all the changes that were taking place—house repairs, newly planted trees, or freshly paved roads.

But the bus also came with tribulations. Among the student passengers was Madison Park's number-one bully, a boy named Michael. Michael was an equal opportunist when it came to his intimidation tactics but singled out the most vulnerable, us first-graders, and took a particular interest in me. Or so it seemed. I was quiet yet precocious, and as he once put it, "Eric Motley is a know-it-all, and what I hate most is that he's always right."

The bus driver, Mrs. Ella Miller, a Madison Park local and good friend of Mama's, knew not just the name of every road but the name of every passenger. She seated the first-graders in the first three rows behind her and yelled Michael's name with such fury when she caught him misbehaving that I'm surprised the bus didn't shake. I stayed in the third row for my entire time at Dozier Elementary and, on the advice of Mrs. Ella, decided that the best remedy for Michael was to pretend that he didn't exist. She was a wise woman.

I thought of my demotion to the Turtles as my fall from grace. But unlike Adam and Eve, I left paradise only temporarily. Along with Aunt Shine's volunteer squad, two first-grade teachers staged an intervention. Mrs. Dorothy Thomas and Mrs. Mary Smith spent extra time with me on reading and suggested to Mama and Daddy that I repeat the year to lay a firm educational foundation. I was embarrassed and took this to mean that I wasn't as smart as everyone believed. Worse, I was sure that my intellectual shortcomings would sidetrack my aspirations for college. In retrospect, it's hard to imagine a six-year-old child consumed with worry about the future, but the circumstances of my childhood quickened my maturity.

Mrs. Dorothy Thomas, in particular, was instrumental to my turnaround. Tall and naturally pretty, she took a Southern woman's pride in her appearance, heightening her good looks with lipstick, pink blush, and gardenia perfume. Mama would say, paradoxically, "She was born that way and self-made that way." She was the first black woman I met with freckles, accentuated by her rouged cheeks. When she talked, she got right into your face and left you no personal space. During these frequent, uncomfortable encounters, I would count her freckles. When the good Lord publishes "The Best Teachers of Eternity," Mrs. Thomas's name is sure to top the list. She was strict but fair and resolute. She wanted me to succeed in school—and in life.

Mrs. Thomas represented the ideal that many Madison Park educators believed was in peril after integration in the South. She was among the African American teachers to integrate the Montgomery Public School system, and Madison Park seemed to have had the highest concentration of blacks transferred to Dozier Elementary. I knew she empathized with children who were bused into the city, but I never saw her show preferential treatment to black students. Just the opposite—she demanded even more from us.

When I was in third grade, Mrs. Thomas made a bold stand against what she perceived to be racial discrimination against me. Every day, my white teacher, whom I will call "Mrs. Joy," asked for volunteers to help her clean the classroom after school. I eagerly raised my hand to sweep the floor and erase the chalkboard. I never thought anything of it, but if I had, I would have noticed that all of the volunteers were African American kids from Madison Park.

One day, having heard that I was one of Mrs. Joy's cleaners, Mrs. Thomas bolted into the classroom, grabbed the broom from my hands, and sent it sailing into the closet before pulling Mrs. Joy aside for a private conversation.

Next, she led me by the hand to her room and sat me down. Still holding my hand, she said, "Your grandmother didn't send you to school to clean anybody's floors. Do you hear me? You're here to get an education, and every single *second* of your day you had better be learning what you don't know. If I ever see you cleaning someone's room again, I'll tear you in two. Do you understand?"

"Yes, Ma'am," I said.

"I'm not mad at you," she said, squeezing my hand. "I just love you."

CHAPTER 9

THE D.U.K.

I was restored to Rabbit status by spring. If I'd never been downgraded to the Turtles, it's possible that friends, neighbors, and fellow parishioners at Union Chapel Church would never have rallied around me. The effort, spearheaded by Aunt Shine when I was a first-grader, didn't stop there. Not only did the townspeople see to it that I could read, by God, they would make sure I went to college. And in that little place, as evidence of God's grace, I became what one of my childhood tutors, Mrs. Sarah Pearl Coleman, called the D.U.K., the "designated university kid."

When I was just seven, neighbors began to hire me for odd jobs so I could save up to pay for my education. I mowed lawns, trimmed shrubs, picked blackberries, and stacked fireplace logs. Over time, my monthly calendar expanded to include picking up litter, picking pecans, peeling pears and peaches, weeding vegetable gardens, watering flower beds, cleaning barns, organizing storage sheds, piling bricks, and painting garages. I realized even then that my employers could easily have done the work, but they hired me to put cash in my college fund.

I would just as soon have been given the money outright, but Mama insisted that I earn my way. She believed I would feel better about myself if the rewards were a product of my sweat. Looking back, those folks knew exactly what they were doing—the back-breaking jobs I endured built in me a powerful desire to find a better way to make a living and ratcheted even tighter my resolve to get a university education.

I would climb off the school bus every afternoon around four o'clock and walk home, past Miz Cheney's yard, to 34 Motley Drive, where Mama greeted me with a cup of hot tea and cookies and asked me about my day. Then I'd hastily change into working clothes—worn khaki pants and a hand-me-down denim shirt—to do my chores.

From 4:25 p.m. to 6:30 p.m. I'd mow Mr. Yelder's two lawns, rake and bag the debris, and get home in time for dinner and homework with twenty dollars in my pocket. This was substantial college savings.

But along with the overflow of support, there was a strain of jealousy among a few folks. From the time I was six, there was one woman who was so bitter about the attention I received from others, she couldn't even be kind to me. I'll call her Mrs. Margaret Fillerseed. She was a discontented woman, and she was rancorous with everyone, even her siblings.

Mrs. Fillerseed was wealthier than we were, but as country-music star Gary Allan sings, "You can be the moon and still be jealous of the stars." Like Mama and Daddy, she also was rearing her grandson, Rick, who went to a private school in the city. Apart from that, we were the same age, lived five blocks apart, attended the same Sunday school class, and looked so much alike we were often mistaken for one another. Despite our frequent contact, Mrs. Fillerseed forbade Rick to talk to me, and he avoided me when she was around. Pretending to like me, she would occasionally talk to me, but her expressions were never inviting. While I was mowing every lawn in Madison Park, she spitefully said to one of my employers, "Rick doesn't have to do menial labor to go to college."

I kept quiet, but I remember the anger I felt deep within—a stoicism I'd built inside watching Daddy. Why did this lady who had so much resent me? I never shared the experience with Mama but took comfort from her admonitions that "money doesn't buy happiness" and "the burden of jealousy is a heavy load to carry." Rick never went to college. After high school, he got a job as a deliveryman on a grocery truck. Giving her grandson money, an education, and other advantages wasn't enough; evidently Rick needed something more from his grandmother.

Whatever that intangible was, I received it. Upon reflection, my after-school jobs enriched my life well beyond the money they provided. Some were challenging and had a tremendous impact on my character formation at an early age. Picking blackberries for Mrs. Beulah Byrd was one. I always admired Mrs. Byrd. She had her own style. She always wore a pastel-patterned dress, black shoes with silver buckles, and a brightly colored tam on her head, like men wear in France. Although she was soft-spoken, you could recognize her voice over ninety-nine others in a crowded room. She sounded as if she were speaking through her nose. She swallowed, or seemed to want to swallow, after each word, always suppressing a grainy cough.

She called Madison Park home even though she wasn't a *bona fide* life-timer. She made her way down from the city to Madison Park every Sunday, arriving at Union Chapel Church in a black Cadillac limousine, a complimentary service provided by a Montgomery funeral home. To me there was nothing more impressive than this diminutive lady stepping out from the back seat of that big shiny car.

Mrs. Byrd was physically disabled and used a walker. She lived alone, without any surviving family. Yet she had enormous energy. Given her disadvantages, she was often held up as a model in Sunday school of how we can draw on resources from within. At the close of each Sunday service there were always two lines—one at the main door of the sanctuary where parishioners stood to be greeted by the minister and the other, a mass of children swarmed around Mrs. Byrd. Along with her purse, she came to church carrying a large bag of Tootsie Rolls and Jolly Ranchers. One by one, she'd hand us a piece of candy, using the moment to look us in the eye and exhort us to be good, as if it were a sacrament.

She was a proud, particular woman, bordering on eccentric. But Madison Park tolerated eccentrics well. One Sunday, before the children gathered around her, Mrs. Byrd called my name. "Motley," she said, "Stay afterward. I need to talk to you."

I got my candy and stood waiting nervously as the organist pulled her stops. I'd never spoken to Mrs. Byrd about anything but my preferred Jolly Rancher flavor (sour apple).

Gradually, the church cleared, and she motioned for me to sit next to her, immediately launching into an explanation of her love for blackberries and the many virtues of blackberry pie. Attendees at the annual church picnic had debated for years whether Beulah Byrd's blackberry pie or Rosebud Hall's red-velvet cake was better. She looked at me as if she wanted me to offer a judgment on the spot. Even at that young age, I knew not to comment.

She eventually got around to explaining that she'd always preferred her blackberries handpicked over those sold in the supermarket. "I'm looking for someone new to pick for me," she said in a tone indicating that whoever picked her blackberries last year had not performed up to standard. "Motley, will you pick them for me?"

Blushing at the honor, I accepted on the spot. I was so flattered I failed to ask about the pay.

Mrs. Byrd quickly got down to the particulars: how many containers she needed and when. Then, reaching for her walker and lifting herself up from the pew, she said, "I'm going to pay you *ten dollars*. Plus, I'm going to make you a pie—a big blackberry *pie*."

She got as much satisfaction telling me as I did imagining that pie with a cold glass of milk. "One more thing," she remembered aloud. "You have to be patient picking blackberries. Don't forget or you'll crush them between your fingers."

The choicest blackberries in Madison Park lay hidden in a maze of contorted briers in a field between Fuller's Road and Old Wetumpka Highway, across the street from the Washerteria. A foot-worn path connected the two roads that split the field into two parts.

Berry picking isn't brain surgery, but it does require a proper state of mind, small hands, a good pair of knee-high rubber boots, and a tubful of patience. I was an experienced hand at strawberry picking, a job I did for a neighbor, but blackberries were something new. I quickly learned that they required much more time—they're tinier and much more fragile. To press them too hard is to bruise the berry, possibly crushing it. Picking went so slowly, I had to postpone two other jobs. I moved deliberately to uncover berries tucked under the leafy brush and hidden from the eye while at the same time, trying not to get pricked or scratched among the thorns and snares.

When I finished, my hands were sore and stained red with berry juice, but the tub I delivered to Mrs. Byrd was overflowing. Standing before her, I silently awaited judgment. I felt as if she were inspecting each berry microscopically. Finally, with a nod of approval she said, "Motley, bend down here and let me give you a hug! These are some of the best berries anyone has picked for me." It was a hard-earned ten dollars, and I ran home thinking that I'd never pick another blackberry again.

If Mrs. Byrd taught me patience, Mrs. Nellie, an old friend of Mama's, taught me grace. Mrs. Nellie, whose last name I never knew, had lived in Madison Park all her life. When her health started to decline, Mrs. Nellie's daughter moved her to live with family in Detroit. Mama felt it was a bad move. "You can't take an eighty-year-old woman from the country to the city and expect her to be happy," she said.

Mama was right. After a year Mrs. Nellie longed for home. Like most people in Madison Park, she was a strong, independent woman. She wanted to live out her days in her own house, taking care of herself. She phoned Mama from Detroit every day in tears. With about six months to live and without her daughter's knowledge, Mrs. Nellie bought a one-way Greyhound Bus ticket to Montgomery. On a bright September day, she pulled up in our driveway in a yellow taxi with a small suitcase and a couple of plastic shopping bags.

Mama telephoned the daughter, explained the situation, and promised to do all she could to take care of Mrs. Nellie. Her house had sold, so my grandparents found a small one not far from ours. Daddy installed a wood-burning stove, and Mama supplied three hot, home-cooked meals a day. But since they were working full-time, they couldn't devote themselves to Mrs. Nellie around the clock. Someone needed to remove the ashes from the stove, replenish the wood supply, and make sure Mrs. Nellie had fresh water from the pump. Hardest of all, she needed her porcelain chamber pot emptied in the outhouse.

I've never had a strong constitution, and even now I get queasy around other people's illness and at the sight of blood. Mama felt I needed to get over it. Mama insisted, "Never allow Mrs. Nellie to feel that you're too good to take out her chamber pot."

CHAPTER 10

SHAVE AND A HAIRCUT

It's hard to say which cornerstone was bigger in our community: school or church. Both were sacred spaces in Madison Park. When you rode by one of the community's three churches, you slowed down as a sign of respect. Inside, you didn't run, you walked. On Sundays, you offered your best in song and speech. Church was one of the few weekly rituals we dressed up for. We all wanted to look as good as we could. You might be sitting next to Mrs. Beulah Byrd, but you were standing before God.

For Madison Park's men—which included me, starting at age seven—that meant an eight o'clock Sunday morning haircut. Traditionally, black men have found sanctuary in barbershops, but our trims and shaves took place three doors down from us on the back porch of Joe Simon Jr.'s house. Mr. Simon was known by all as "Little Joe," even though he was neither little nor, at thirty, with a wife, Jean, and four kids, particularly young. Born into barbering, Little Joe had succeeded his father, Big Joe. Even his clippers had been handed down.

Daddy and I would make an early start, leaving right after breakfast. We'd cut through Miz Cheney's back garden next door, passing through her stand of ancient pear trees, and take a seat with the other customers under the Simon's magnolias to wait our turn. Men who didn't need their hair or beards neatened up would come just for coffee and conversation, both offered free of charge. In fact, Joe seemed almost too embarrassed to take money for anything. You'd hear someone say, "How much I owe you for my haircut, Joe?"

"Well," he'd hesitate, "you could give me $2, and we'll call it even."

After a while there could be five or ten conversations going simultaneously. "Any more coffee? Who made this coffee, Joe? Mighty strong today. Did Jean make it? Jean, you got any more coffee in there?"

"Man, did y'all hear about that bad accident over the bridge last night?"

"Melvin needs to stop singing. His voice din started to crackin' so bad the organ can't cover up the sound."

"You don't tell me he died?"

"Did ya hear that Albert Lee and Buster ended up in front of a Montgomery circuit judge after a fight? The judge said, 'Albert Lee, I'm not surprised to see you here, because you get in fights all the time. But Buster, I'm shocked to see you. You've never been in trouble. You've always been an upright citizen. I don't want to see you here again.' Ole Buster was just about speechless. 'Your honor,' he said, 'It wasn't my idea to be here in the first place.'"

No Madison Park "hen" party could ever compete. The men must have brought a backlog of pent-up conversation from home, as if they assembled to accomplish collectively what they couldn't do individually—or with their wives around. At our house, Mama would ask Daddy questions, and before he could form an answer in his laconic style, she would have answered them herself. But even at Little Joe's, Daddy listened more than he talked.

More than the banter, my favorite part of the morning was when

Little Joe winked at me and, motioning, would say, "Bugs, you next. Come on up and get in this chair."

I'd climb into the kitchen chair, and then, in one billowing gesture, Little Joe would spread a white bed sheet over me. "What'cha want me to do?" he'd ask.

"The same," Daddy would say.

In those days, I wore my hair in a mini Afro style. Joe would comb and cut, his clippers zooming around my head as if on autopilot. "You done yet, Mr. Joe?" I'd ask, as the stubble that had grown since the previous Sunday fell invisibly onto the porch floor. He'd finish by splashing a nickel-size amount of green rubbing alcohol into his palm, a backyard antiseptic-refresher, rub his hands together, massage my neck, and remove my backward Batman cape. I'd hopped down from the chair to make room for Daddy. "That sure is a fine haircut you gave him, Joe," Daddy would say, smiling at me, as some older man would stage whisper, "Who is that little boy, anyway?"

"That's George Motley's boy," he'd be told.

And the conversations buzzed on.

As we headed home, I'd look back through the pear trees and see the crowd dispersing. "Look, Daddy, they're all leaving."

"Well, boy, it's nine o'clock. They all got to get home to get ready for Sunday school and church like us."

In the simple act of having my haircut on Little Joe's back porch, I witnessed a coming together, a sharing of common purpose and a bearing of burdens in the small talk of the morning nearly every Sunday for thirteen years, up until I left for college.

By the time we arrived home, Mama would be dressed up, her face powdered, her cranberry-colored lipstick on, and wearing her sweet gardenia signature fragrance sprayed in a cloud from a bottle curved to look like a woman's torso.

All that was left for her to choose was a hat. She had more than a hundred: wool and felt hats for winter, lacy straw for summer, Easter bonnets with colorful flowers attached, and others festooned with feathers, bows, and pins.

Every Sunday she'd come to my room. "Now I have three hats here," she'd say. "Which one do you think matches this dress?"

I knew she didn't consider me a fashion expert, but she liked having someone else's opinion. She had style and grace and, with hat and gloves, she was the essence of an elegant Southern lady. The other kids I knew had younger, hipper parents, but I loved the way Mama carried herself—old-fashioned, yes, but always proper and self-respectful. Then out the door we'd go, Mama, with pocketbook on her forearm that matched her shoes, and Daddy and me both in dark suits, white shirts, and skinny black neckties—our shoes shined.

The same scene was unfolding at the Church of Christ and Old Elam Missionary Baptist Church, where Little Joe Simon and Michael Slaughter, the school-bus bully, prayed. But the Baptists began their worship with an "old-time prayer service," in which the elders and deacons would invoke God's presence by singing spirituals and ecstatic praying in song. The incantations called to mind scenes I'd seen in movies like *Roots*, of plantation slaves keeping time to old spirituals. To me and other young folks, the unbowed devotion seemed like a relic out of sync with the times.

But in other ways the church's influence was decidedly forward-looking. Dr. Martin Luther King Jr. honed his considerable preaching skills at Dexter Avenue Baptist Church, ten miles from Madison Park, before leading the Montgomery bus boycott of the mid-1950s. He and countless others in less famous pulpits espoused full civil rights for all Americans.

And of course the pulpit served as my formal Christian education. Not all sermons were memorable, especially for an imaginative and precocious young child. I did my share of nodding off in the pew when Mama wasn't looking. I often found the dramatic rhetorical style of preaching captivating. It not only fanned the desire to know God better but to love the spoken word.

In Madison Park, some of Daddy's friends were illiterate. Words on a page meant nothing to them. But as Daddy often reminded me, "They can hear." They had the capacity to be tremendously moved by the spoken word and, in turn, to use words in moving fashion. They recognized, and preferred, good English when they heard it. I've often wondered if it's somehow in African Americans' bloodlines to be good storytellers and good talkers because, by law, slaves weren't allowed to learn to read. I marvel, all these years later, how so many of the elderly people of Madison Park, with no formal education, used pitch, volume, pauses, pace, crescendo, even a whisper to make a joke or tell a story such as they did in Little Joe's backyard.

They expected the same from the pulpit and the political rostrum—high-toned, elevated language. The Bible centered their lives—lifting their minds and hearts upward. The Word was always delivered beautifully from the King James Bible. To my mind it is the greatest work of English prose ever written; it became my model for language—elegant, subtle, majestic—music to the ear.

My Sunday school teacher, Mrs. Bertha Winston, believed that even then I had a special gift of speech. Beginning when I was in third grade she'd pull up in front of my house after school in her gleaming black Cougar and drive me down to the Union Chapel Church parking lot, so I wouldn't be distracted from the comings and goings at home. We'd sit in the car under the large oak tree—in the winter, she'd keep the motor running and the heater blowing—and we'd practice the art of elocution. She'd give me a list of words to repeat over and again. There was no such thing as good enough. Mrs. Winston demanded perfection. She paid attention to my grammar, diction, pace, and inflexion, scribbling quotes and passages she deemed appropriate for my recitation on the backs of envelopes, church bulletins, receipts, and scraps of paper.

She taught me that if you "hide verses and lines in your heart" you can "own" them, and they can be retrieved whenever needed. When you can't afford books, memorizing parts of the ones you borrow is a useful strategy, that I used later in speech competitions and my study of rhetoric. She etched in my mind famous quotations from Shakespeare, Milton, and Robert Frost and theological writings of St. Augustine and African American theologian Howard Thurman.

Not everyone was as gracious about helping me find my place in the world as Mrs. Winston. When I was eight, the Creation narrative, colorfully illustrated in our Sunday school books, satisfied my classmates, while the idea baffled me. I wondered if God made the universe, then who made God? I posed the question to a visiting Sunday school teacher, a pinched-faced woman who was the ecclesiastical version of Mrs. Fillerseed. Unprepared and ill-equipped to answer, this poor woman chose to ignore me, no doubt hoping I would turn my attention elsewhere. After I persistently, and I mean *persistently*, pressed the issue, she told me that I was being disruptive and reported the incident to Mama.

Hidden Verses: Mrs. Bertha Winston, my Sunday school teacher
who inspired my love for language, along with Reverend
Robert Lassiter, Minister of Union Chapel Church
Courtesy of Dr. John H. Winston Jr.

When Mama insisted on an explanation, I described what had happened. She immediately suggested that I ask our minister, Reverend Lee Chester Washington. I don't think Mama could acknowledge she'd be unable to answer my questions any better than the substitute teacher could. But she did point me toward a source of greater knowledge, an example of her wisdom.

The community's deep roots in religious faith extended beyond its church sanctuaries, forming a social contract that bound people together and carried as much force as if it were law. Right ruled. If you did a good deed, it wasn't for bragging rights. If a kindness favored one individual, you didn't keep score. You "did" for love, not reputation.

You seldom heard profanity, and if you cursed, it was done softly. You didn't steal. It didn't make sense. We were so closely linked, it would be like taking something from yourself.

The July morning that my grandparents and I discovered five ripe watermelons had gone missing from our back porch stands out as a vivid exception to the norm. News spread quickly, along with the certainty that it had to be an "outside" job. "They must not have known the kind of man they were stealing from" went the common refrain. People were sure that knowledge of Mr. George Motley's upright character would stay the hand of any would-be thief.

Sure enough, the next day, we discovered a guilt offering at the crime site. On the back porch, next to the swing, lay four melons—not the stolen loot—but four juicy cantaloupes offered in the watermelons' place.

When I was in first grade, we went on a daylong road trip to Wetumpka to visit Mama's childhood friends. Before we left, I told Mama we needed a burglar alarm for such occasions. "What for, Bugs?" she asked. "We've got Nee-bo across the street and Aunt Mamie next door. They watch our house night and day."

The idea of looking out for one another was more than superficial, and I was constantly reminded that Christian charity did not just belong in church. A little after eleven o'clock one starless November night, a catastrophic fire broke out and quickly consumed a small, wooden-frame house down Motley Drive from us. As we stood watching the house engulfed in flames, there was a feeling of great loss in the air. All you could hear was the crackling timbers. Worse, a well-liked young man named Ronnie, who was separated from his wife and children and had become almost a recluse, lost his life in the blaze. Madison Park was distraught, especially by the thought that in our little close-knit community, Ronnie had died alone.

Mama and I had hardly finished breakfast the next morning when our phone rang. If we got a call after ten at night or before six in the morning one could be assured that something had *happened* in Madison Park and the news was making its way from house-to-house. Now, a neighbor was on the line. When Mama hung up, she went into Daddy's bedroom and yanked the pull-string that lit the ceiling bulb. Daddy was silent as she delivered more bad news: there was no insurance to cover Ronnie's burial. "We'll have to do something," she said.

"Lord have mercy," was all that Daddy answered.

Mama pulled on her gray and black winter coat and matching tam, took an empty Crisco can from the kitchen cupboard, and headed out the door, motioning for me to follow. I braced myself for the cold air, buttoning my coat as I jockeyed to keep pace with her short, deliberate steps. She didn't explain what we were doing—maybe she thought I already knew—and I didn't ask.

For the next four hours we went house-to-house, neighbor-to-neighbor, collecting money to pay for a proper burial. As we knocked on doors, we found some sitting at the kitchen table with their coffee, some standing at the stove cooking their noonday meal, others gathered around the warmth of their fireplaces, having already prepared a place for two more, expecting us as word had spread. Locating us by phone, Mrs. Lola Mae called one house to say that she'd collected forty dollars. What surprised me most was that no one looked into Mama's Crisco can to see how much had been given. Over and again I heard Mama use the word "community" as she petitioned people: "This is community," "We live in community," "We're all a part of this community."

Billy Joe, working under the hood of his car, covered in grease, stood up when he saw Mama coming around through the field. He so proudly and gently pressed in Mama's hand a wrinkled dollar bill. "Boy, your Momma was a good lady. We were friends for a long time," was all that Mama could say as she was so inexpressibly moved. He looked up with tears rolling down his cheek and said, "And the community buried her too. Y'all sure did. We did not have money to bury her, but y'all did." As we walked away you could hear her faintly declare, "She deserved a decent burial. None of us are that poor."

We didn't go to Good Hope Church Cemetery in Elmore County, some thirty miles away, where Ronnie had been born and where he was to be buried. But we knew he'd be buried in a coffin and have a headstone engraved with his name and the dates of his life. Mama didn't teach me to ask for money that day. It was a lesson about inter-dependence, respect, and collective responsibility. And she taught me to have compassion for those who were truly poor; there was no place for pride when caring for those who had less than we did. God gave his grace to us, and out of gratitude we extended it abundantly to those around us, regardless of circumstances.

But the social contract didn't mean that Madison Park was idyllic. Alcoholism, domestic abuse, and other pathologies went mostly untreated. The township lacked the means to finance social services such as mental health clinics and the educational background to fully appreciate their worth. And these transgressions became fodder for gossip. Even so individuals seemed instinctively to show care and concern for the people who were hurting, and someone typically stepped forward to intervene.

Once the neighborhood garbage collector, Mr. Killis Hendricks, a.k.a. "Mr. Bunk," a World War II veteran and a great grandson of one of the founders, stopped by the home of a man known for hard drinking, fast living, and domestic altercations, and asked him to go for a ride. The conversation was blunt. Mr. Bunk told the man that most of

Madison Park knew of the damage that he was inflicting on himself and his family. Many people were praying for the man and his family, but Mr. Bunk made it clear that fellow Madison Park men had decided to take action. He would be held to account if such behavior persisted. The violence ceased.

CHAPTER 11

THAT OLD-TIME RELIGION

Good ol' time baptisms used to take place in the creek. The preacher and choir would lead the congregation out of the church's front doors and down the ivy slopes to the banks, singing "Take Me to the Water to Be Baptized." Then, shouting prayers to the Hammond-like humming of the parishioners, the minister would lower some soul dressed in white robes into the cool, muddy water.

But one Sunday as the congregation sang its way down to the creek, there were "over a hundred water moccasins" lying out sunning, according to Mrs. Shirley Mae, an old family friend and parishioner. "Black people sho' don't like snakes!"

That was the end of that. Going forward, baptisms took place in the backyard swimming pool of Attorney Solomon Seay Jr., the only Madison Park resident with his own pool. The church elders always described it as "Olympic-size," but since none of them had ever seen one we can excuse their mathematical mistake. I was always tempted to linger behind after a baptism to find out what it was like to swim in that pool, and my friend Ralph, who lived Over the Bridge, had a similar idea. He said that when it came time for his baptism he was going to surprise the preacher by jumping into the pool from the diving board—"And he came to Jesus with a splash!" But when we were baptized at age eight, we didn't dare deviate from the script and walked into the shallow end to be dunked like everyone else, with the Holy Ghost looking on.

A bigger event, and one we looked forward to every year, was the Methodist Church picnic. Always held in Madison Park on the third Saturday in August, it was on par with the Montgomery State Fair and the circus. Everyone in the community was invited to the picnic.

Preparations took two weeks. First, churchmen gathered in Daggerhole, by the creek, for "the clearing." They'd open the great gates and bring in their equipment to mow, clear brush, trim trees and shrubs, and burn the debris and broken limbs. Then Mr. Bunk, who owned a truck—a rarity in Madison Park—would haul a load of sand to fill sand boxes for the children. Cousin David would grease the swings and wash down the sliding boards, and someone would hang a new tire from a tree, making sure the branch was strong enough to support the weight of a man. They spread potent yellow lime over the grounds to deter snakes and lizards. Daddy would connect and prime the pump with the old red handle from our barn.

The day before the picnic, more than a half-dozen men would spend the night in the park, cooking and barbecuing ribs on the big open pit and making the camp stew—a deep-South variation of Brunswick stew—containing beef, sausage, chicken, stewed tomatoes, black beans, buttered beans, greens beans, and just about every other bean imaginable, some corn, peppers, and okra, and copious amounts of hot sauce. It cooked for fifteen hours. Mrs. Rosebud Hall's husband, Harvey, was the camp stew master.

On Saturday morning, we'd rush to get through our chores before the picnic started at one o'clock. By 12:15 the park was so full you could hardly find a place to lay your blanket. People dressed up for the occasion. Most of us got new clothes twice a year—for Easter and the church picnic. You'd hear women poking at the little children: "Little Lady Girl, is that a new sundress you're wearing? I love those bright sunflowers on it. Go tell your mama we're over here under the big oak tree next to the old swimming pool; right across from where the Vincents sit every year. Y'all come over and have some Coca Cola with us."

From a microphone stand under the main pavilion, our minister, Reverend Washington, welcomed everyone and offered a short prayer before the banjos started playing gospel and any other tune they could pick. The games, which included hide-and-seek, ring-around-the-roses, and hopscotch, would last until about six in the evening. The aroma of baked ham, fried chicken, and grilled mullet filled the air, and people shared dishes along with news and gossip. I always felt a little let down when the festivities ended, and we made our way back up the hill and over the bridge to our side of Madison Park. When you're young, next year might as well be eternity.

Besides the picnic, the Baptist and Methodist churches chose one Sunday a year to worship together, rotating between the two. One year, at Old Elam Church, the music was so good that I started to tap my foot and bounce my knees up and down to keep time with the clapping and swaying of the red-robed choir. The spirit was *moving* through that place! Sitting beside Aunt Prince Ella, I could sense that the tempo was a bit much for her. When she saw my toes tapping and my legs moving, she placed her hands on my knee, squeezed it softly, and whispered, in case I had forgotten, "We are *Methodist*. We do not *dance* in Church."

We were born with restraint. At Union Chapel Church, our choir's robes were a somber blue, and where the Baptists used the modern *Living Bible*, we hewed to the King James Bible. Even our pews were nailed to the floor to prevent unexpected movement.

It was during one of those visits to Old Elam Church that I heard the memorable orator and preacher Reverend Brinkley. A retired Baptist minister, he lived in Madison Park until he died at about ninety-five. He didn't know his birthdate, but he used to say that his mother told him he was born on a Sunday when the flowers were blooming, so he assumed it was in the spring. An earnest man of enormous faith and simple living, Reverend Brinkley owned nothing but the house he lived in and the Bible his mother gave him as a boy when he had decided to take up the cross and follow Christ. He exuded so much concern and love that when he encountered people on the streets of Madison Park, they seemed to light up.

Daddy used to say, "When Reverend Brinkley comes this way, light abounds." It was as though the Spirit of God infused him with a special blessing. Having long ago retired, he had no pulpit of his own and traveled from church to church, often called on to deliver prayer or to read Scripture. He had what I imagined to be the voice of Moses: strong, deep, and resolute, and the presence of a saint. He was blind in one eye, with a cataract shrouding the other, but he still walked erect, without a cane, and had helped to bury more than two generations.

When it came to the Gospel of Christ, he couldn't separate the social from the personal, the temporal from the spiritual, the general from the particular. The love of God was for us all. I still remember the sermon I heard him preach. Holding on to the pulpit, his voice trembling, he spoke about the early Christian missionaries Paul and Silas, who weren't afraid to spread the Gospel, keeping the faith even when they were jailed, eventually leading their jailer to God.

He ended his sermon by reciting a verse from the book of First Thessalonians: "Be joyful always; pray continually; give thanks in all circumstances." Then, with a voice of roaring thunder, startling the congregation, he pleaded, "Lord, I want to be like Paul and Silas. All my life I have tried to be true to You." With tears in his eyes, he took off his glasses and, with no musical accompaniment, sang a stirring rendition of the Negro spiritual "Give Me That Old-Time Religion."

Within the week, he was on his deathbed. A friend keeping an overnight vigil remembered Reverend Brinkley asking, "Is it morning yet? It feels like a new day." With those words, he joined Paul and Silas on the other side. To the residents of Madison Park, the reverend's life and death seemed like part of a grand plan. He was born on a springtime Sunday, and he died on a springtime Sunday. He remains for me one of the greatest examples of a life humbly and completely lived in service to God and community.

Reverend Brinkley was buried at Daggerhole. We all wore black, and even people who weren't part of the funeral procession pulled over and stood solemnly beside their vehicles as the hearse lumbered past. Mr. Bunk was the community's unofficial funeral marshal. Waving his hands in the air like a bald eagle taking flight, he'd direct the cars in the procession forward to the cemetery. Great storm clouds of red dust arose as cars, headlights on, veered off the main road at the bridge and started their descent onto the long stretch of dirt road to the burial ground.

I wish I remembered his funeral better, but we attended so many in my young life that none stands out. Besides the annual church picnic, burials were the only times I remember crossing the bridge as a community.

This intermingling of the churches suited Mama. A woman of strong, Christian faith and a Sunday school teacher for more than forty years, she cared little for strict Methodist doctrine or denominational particularity. She was born a Baptist, but converted to Methodism when she married Daddy. But if she'd been a Seventh-day Adventist, she still would have based every lesson, whether in Sunday school or at the dinner table on Apostle Paul's paean to love, 1 Corinthians 13, which says, ". . . the greatest of these [gifts], is love." She always gave the same answer to those seeking advice on conflict between friend or family: "Show them love." Her class was typically the largest in our church, and pupils over the years generously "showed love" back to her.

Mama believed in the power of prayer and prayed every morning, noon, and night, as though to keep her heart in tune. Besides praying for personal grace and forgiveness, she accumulated long lists of prayer topics and names: friends, neighbors, the sick, shut-ins, prisoners, ex-employers, the unemployed, farmers' crops, and animals. And she had strong views. While Psalm 19:14 was often quoted in church—"Let the words of my mouth, and the meditation of my heart, be acceptable in thy sight"—it wasn't enough by her standards. "God doesn't want to act solo," she said. "He needs feet and hands to fulfill His will of loving-kindness."

Mama lived a pious life. We didn't advertise our abstinence, but I'd never known her to drink anything stronger than lemonade. I knew Daddy had a liking for whiskey, but I never saw him pour a glass at home.

One particularly hot summer day when I was ten, I was on the front porch with Mama. She was shelling peas and dishing out conversation as I tried to read. Mama was a people magnet. As soon as people saw her outside, they'd stop by and sit with us awhile. That day Billie-Marie Perry, Barbara Ann's older sister, pulled her old Pontiac over and started chatting from her car window. Her radio was turned low, and you could just make out Sam Cooke in the background. After a few pleasantries, Billie-Marie started up the car. "Alright, it was nice talking to y'all," she said.

"Where you headed anyway, Billie-Marie?" Mama asked.

"I'm going down here to get a hot fish and pick me up some beers at the filling station, Mrs. Mossy. Can I bring y'all anything back?"

"Well, darlin', I sure wouldn't mind you bringing me a Miller beer. Well, make that two beers—one for now and one for later. Do you mind?"

"No, Ma'am, you know I don't mind. I'll be right back," came Billie-Marie's cheerful response.

If Mama had asked for a loaded gun, I wouldn't have been as stunned. I know I dropped my book. Aunt Prince Ella had indoctrinated me to believe that (a) beer was the lowest, most unsophisticated of all drinks, and (b) it was an invitation to the Devil to come into your body and take control. Right before my eyes, not only was Mama getting *a* beer, she was getting *two*.

Sensing my astonishment, she felt it necessary to explain. "Nothing's wrong with a beer, especially on a hot day like this," she said. "I used to drink beers at least a couple times a year when I first married your daddy. Every now and then you need a cold one."

Confused thoughts flashed through my mind: who is this lady, Billie-Marie? What happened to my grandmother? Surely you won't put the other beer in the refrigerator next to our pure, white, calcium-rich, milk? A travesty! Impurity!

"I know what you're thinking, Bugs," Mama said. "You're thinking Aunt Prince Ella is going to pay a surprise visit, catch me drinking a beer, and that we're all going to be ruined. That's what you're thinking. I know you."

How did she know? I was sure that any minute Aunt Prince Ella would roll up unannounced in her long, cream-colored Chrysler and see Mama chug-a-lugging, dooming us all in the eyes of the neighborhood and, worse, in the eyes of the Lord.

"If she comes, I'm going to say, 'Come on Prince Ella, I have a cold one for you in the fridge. It's sitting right between the milk and the grapefruit juice.' Then, you can pick her up off the floor and fan her until she comes to."

I can remember another hot summer afternoon after work, when Mama's carpool dropped her off at the entrance to Madison Park, Over the Bridge, just off the main road. As she walked home, she spotted our neighbor, a good Jehovah's Witness, watering flowers in her front yard. "Hello," Mama called. "Boy, it sure is a hot day."

Our neighbor decided to "go Biblical," as Mama would sometimes say. "Well, Mrs. Motley, if you're hot now, then you should know that it's ten times hotter in hell. And if you don't know the Lord, that's where you are going to spend *eternity*."

Mama was in no mood to be messed with. She'd just worked nine hours cleaning other people's houses and then walked home in the blistering sun. "If I end up going to hell, one thing's for certain," she told her. "I'm going to tell the Devil I don't want to be your neighbor, 'cause I have already lived in Hell with you once!" With that, Mama moved on, calling out, cheerily, "Okay, you have a good evening, and I'll be seeing you tomorrow."

Our neighbor must have changed her mind about the final resting place of Mama's soul. When she died many years later, Mama spoke at her funeral—at the request of the deceased.

CHAPTER 12

THE BEST "HIND-CATCHER" IN THE NEIGHBORHOOD

I had plenty of friends growing up. Most of our neighbors on Motley Drive were senior citizens, but there were three families that had kids my age. The McCarters, across the street, had two boys and eight girls, with more than a decade separating the oldest from the youngest. All were like siblings to me.

Two teenage sisters, Renee and Sandra, had outgrown our eight-, nine-, and ten-year-old games of dodgeball and hopscotch. Michelle, or Meesha, third youngest, was slender and quiet. Next in line was Pam, a boisterous free-spirit, who didn't countenance seriousness. Tammy, the youngest, noticed *everything*.

Andrew McCarter, or "Brother McCarter," was their father. Brother McCarter worked as a nurse's assistant at the Veterans' Hospital in Tuskegee. After mornings on his tractor, he'd disappear into the house in his mud-caked blue overalls and, in a few minutes, emerge in his spotless nurse's uniform—transformed into an angelic figure clad wholly in white. Gladys, his wife, was a full-time mother. Every hot August afternoon she would set aside her washing,

103

cleaning, or cooking to serve vanilla ice-cream cones—ten cones, *plus one* for me

Four houses down from the McCarters lived the Hendersons and the Simons. The two families shared one large house that had been divided into a duplex. Gloria Jean Henderson, a single mother, and her sons, Roderick and James, lived on the right side. Roderick was ambitious, and could out-talk anyone. His prowess on his dirt bike put to shame all other neighborhood competitors. We knew his older brother, James, as "Man," which we pronounced "Main," a typical Madison Park nickname which seemed to have no origin.

Man and I were the same age, and he was one of my closest buddies. He was big for his age and spoke confidently, though often with a stutter when he got excited. He was fastidious, especially when it came to his prized white high-top Chuck Taylor "All-Star" sneakers. Toothbrush in hand, every morning you could find him wiping away the dirty residue of yesterday's play. He managed to keep them spotless. The only time I saw him ready to throw a punch was when another boy intentionally stepped on one.

I recall pondering with Man, at the tender age of ten, some of the great questions worthy of the ancient philosophers: "What if the base-ball went so high it hit the branch of that tree and jolted that mother bird's nest?"; "What if Johnny Lee's only leg went to sleep while he was driving? How would he stop the car?"; "Where would all the people go to wash their clothes if Jessie Sherman's Washerteria closed?"

Shaking his head, Man would say, "Lord have mercy, what shall we do?" repeating what his mother always said. Then we'd jump on our bikes and careen along the lower paths of Ms. Della's pecan grove, down by Mr. Geeter's Catfish Café.

On cloudy, wet days we savored the sweet fragrance of the rain hitting the lawn and thought how lucky we were not to be city kids, to have the advantage of open space and the sights and smells of the outdoors. We'd talk about what we wanted to be when we grew up. Man would always say, "I want to be just like my daddy, 'Chicken,'"—a nickname that came from a love of fried chicken. Man admired no one more than his father, who worked at a factory, doing what, I can't recall. But I do remember that whenever Mama spoke of Chicken, she used words like *good* and *kind*.

While Man talked about being like his daddy, I'd run through my list of potential professions. I could be a teacher. Even at ten, working in government also interested me. I didn't understand how it functioned, but I'd met the mayor of Montgomery at an elementary school program and seen him on TV and in the paper a couple of times talking about his dream to make Montgomery a great American city. I remember thinking, "I sure would like to help him." First on my list was the ministry. I loved hearing the preacher on Sunday mornings and aspired to win the community's respect as he had, helping people through sickness and officiating at weddings and funerals. I couldn't think of anything more important than bearing the Word of the Lord. In some ways, I suppose this civic-mindedness was in large part due to the example and influence of my grandparents.

Man and I also shared a secret. One day, he promised, he'd help me win the affection of his Detroit cousin, Tammy Harris. Tammy and her brother, Maurice, came to Madison Park for six weeks every summer, fulfilling their parents' desire to stay in touch with their Southern roots. I was fascinated with the way she suddenly appeared each July and then disappeared, just as suddenly, back to Detroit. She was tall and slim, with long brown hair and a wide smile. Her teeth were white and straight, and she bragged about her dentist's handiwork. Shy, I'd stick to Man's side whenever Tammy came out to watch the boys play. My buddy, pumping confidence into my heart and buoyancy into the conversation, would say, "Listen, Tammy, Bugs has more books than you've ever seen. Tell her about your books and rocks and all that stuff you've collected. Go on, Bugs, tell her how many books you have."

I'd break a bashful smile long enough to say, "Over twenty!"

"Over twenty?" she'd repeat in her rounded accent. "You haven't read all those books have you?"

Ah, Tammy. I wonder if she ever knew how attractive she was to me. In the early years, she had a naive sweetness about her. As she got older, she developed the ability to tease, harmlessly, delighting in my obvious enjoyment of her.

Little Joe Simon and his family lived on the left side of the duplex, where the magnolia towered high above the pecan trees. The three Simon boys, Daniel "Boo-Boo," LeRod "Rod" and Joseph "Bimp," were my faithful friends. Their sister, Shalanda "Lady Girl," was too young to join in and played with her dolls on the back-porch steps, where Little Joe gave haircuts on Sundays. His wife, Jean, who kept house, had a high-pitched voice and a high-throttle temper that her sons incited regularly. The Simon boys were hellions. They knew no fear and lived by the words "I double-dare you."

Of the three, Rod had the fairest complexion and the shyest personality. But he was no sissy. He could fight when he had to.

All the girls had crushes on Boo-Boo, the youngest. He was polite and had a radiant, almost pretty, smile. He was also popular among boys. He was brazenly self-confident—a risk-taker who performed more tricks on a bike than any other neighborhood kid would dare. He was the king of "hook-slides," the artful formations you make when, after reaching considerable speed, you slide the back tires of your bike while braking.

The Simons: My childhood playmates and their father, Little Joe, who was my "back-porch" barber. Left to right: Joseph the third (aka Bimp), LeRod (aka Rod), Mrs. Jean Simon holding Shalanda (aka Lady Girl), Joseph the second (aka Little Joe) holding Daniel (aka Boo-Boo) (c. 1978). Courtesy of Joseph Simon Jr.

Bimp was the coolest cat, or at least he thought he was. Packing more attitude than the rest of us together, his skin was as black as night. Short and powerful, he reminded me of an unmovable tree stump. His stare was enough to terrify the well-mannered and gracious McCarter girls, and he went out of his way to intimidate them. On the sunniest and laziest day, he might pick a fight for no reason. If he were having a bad day, we all had a bad day.

I divided my time between the Simon and Henderson boys and the McCarter girls. The girls and I played two games—school and church. I always managed to get myself selected to teach the class or preach a rousing sermon. Only now do I realize how demanding I was of the attention of my childhood friends, always entreating them to listen to my long orations and theories of the universe, proposing a new idea, suggesting a new way of playing an old game, or presenting a ridiculous song of my own composition for them to learn.

The boys had a low tolerance for my cerebral style of play and instead sought me out for action-oriented activities: they tackled me, bruised me, and got me dirtier than I would have been, left to my own devices. They taught me a new, vulgar vocabulary, and their stories and theories raised a curtain just slightly on a previously unknown side of life. We were nine or ten-year-old boys pretending to be men. They wanted me to be on their kick-ball team because I had this uncanny ability to move fast and to kick the ball farther than anyone else. Their cheers still echo in my mind. But no one wanted me on their baseball team. Bimp had no qualms about screaming, "I don't want Bugs on my team! We lost yesterday because of him. He stinks!" Then he'd turn, and, looking directly in my face, say, "Don't mean to hurt your feelings, Bugs, but you're not a good baseball player!"

The group would then negotiate what to do with me as I stood by. Eventually Man, the most diplomatic, would come up with the kindest and most agreeable solution.

"Bugs," Man would cry out, "you're going to be the hind-catcher! You're really good at that, and we need a good hind-catcher. You stand behind home plate and catch anything that comes your way."

There. I had the facts. My best friends loved and encouraged me, but they didn't mince words. Their frankness might have hurt more, but it echoed something Mama had already told me. Not one to shrivel before confrontation, she taught me to stand up for my beliefs. But she was also a realist. Understanding that I was small, with no constitution to whip anyone in a fistfight, she pulled me aside one day and said, "Now, when someone comes along and looks like he wants to fight, remember a good run is better than a bad stand! Run as fast as you can! The life you save might be your own!" It was a blow to my ego, but I knew she was right and she wanted the best for me.

I'll always remember those long summer days when we boys gave ourselves over to play for hours, spending every element of our beings. I often wonder how our young bodies avoided sheer exhaustion. Immortal in mind and spirit, we were having too much fun to allow fatigue or summer's heat to register.

Chasing one another on bicycles, through open fields and around the corners of worn-out houses, we twisted and turned up and down narrow alleyways, pretending to be what we had hopes of one day becoming: heroes. Stopping only to gulp water from the rusty-handled pump next to the fig tree in one of the families' backyards, we played out the high pursuits of Batman and Robin, Superman, Cowboys and Indians, and the Dukes of Hazzard. On this last role play, we were too naive to understand the meaning of the Confederate battle flag emblazoned on the roof of the Dukes of Hazzard boys' souped-up car, and none of our parents, who watched the show, ever told us about the historical implications of Old Dixie.

No matter how vigorous our play, around 6:30 every evening, Man would say, "Y'all, I hear Mrs. Mossy calling. Do y'all hear her?"

Sure enough, Mama's voice would rise above all our noise and clatter. "Bugs," she'd call, "time to come inside and clean up!" It was the signal that our revels were over for the day.

I knew better than to ignore Mama. In our house we didn't deviate from a seven-o'clock supper. My grandparents were part of a generation that held fast to rituals and emphasized the institution of family. Dinner was always just the three of us—Mama, Daddy, and me. Mama decorated the Duncan Phyfe table with fresh flowers from the garden, putting carefully folded napkins and glasses of water and lemonade beside each place.

Daddy, a quiet man, was intolerant of pieties and impatient with long public prayers. When we were seated, he'd prayerfully bow his head, pausing to let the silence seep in and then say, "For these blessings we give You thanks; and make us ever mindful of those who have not. Amen."

People in the country work hard, earning the right to a big dinner. Mama cooked chicken, meatloaf, or pork chops, and three vegetables— some combination of collard or turnip greens, peas, and okra—and fresh tomatoes that she'd pile in serving bowls in the middle of the table. She'd also prepare cornbread, made in a cast-iron skillet on the stove, and sliced thin. Dinner ended with a homemade dessert, usually one of my favorites: apple pie or peach cobbler.

As I grew older, our pre-dinner rituals expanded. Before the blessing, Daddy would say, "Well, boy, do you have a couple of lines from Robert Frost or Langston Hughes you want to give us?" I'd stand at the end of the table as though making a formal presentation and recite a stanza or two of a poem—a different one every night not just from Frost or Hughes but Wordsworth, Shakespeare, or others. He never told me whether he did that because, being a reflective man, he delighted in having a fresh kernel of thought; or whether he thought it set a proper mood for the evening meal. But it showed me that my talents were valued and gave me confidence to speak in public.

Sitting over supper with my grandparents was my favorite part of the day, but I didn't like to think about the meat. My rural environs, where there were no processing plants, meant that the meal was farm to table. I knew the beginning and the end. Like most of Madison Park, my family kept chickens. We ate the eggs but not the birds. When I was seven Bimp and I were playing hopscotch in the backyard when our next-door neighbors Mrs. Bessie and her husband—gentle-hearted Baptists—opened their chicken-coop. We stopped our game to watch her chase and corner five birds. Then, one by one, she held them down as her husband chopped their heads off with an ax. I was devastated by the brutal, bloody sight of all of those headless birds flopping around. I stopped eating chicken for a decade and persuaded my grandparents to stop raising them.

I also witnessed a few hog killings at Nathaniel "Nee-bo" Johnson's, who lived across the street, at 24 Motley Drive. Nee-bo was the eldest adult son of Gertrude "Gert" and Orton "Ort" Johnson, long-time Madison Park residents, whose sensibilities were a bit more "country" than ours. Watching the hog-slaughter made me queasy, but for some reason it was less traumatic than observing the unnatural end to Mrs. Bessie's chickens. The Johnsons kept more than a dozen hogs in a pigsty behind their house, far enough back to be hidden, though in August you could find it by smell. Nee-bo usually killed four hogs a year, timed to family reunions. His brothers and sisters, nieces and nephews, and first and second cousins from Shorter, Alabama, deep in the country, would come up for the day. Every family left with pig parts—feet, ears, shoulders, rump, jowls, and "chitlins"—a southern delicacy made from the intestine. Nee-bo kept us with a deep-freezer full of bacon.

CHAPTER 13

THE MUSIC THAT WOULD CHANGE MY LIFE

Deep down inside, I knew that Man, his brother, and the Simon boys thought of me as a bit of a nerd, but they never called me that, even behind my back. As with the adults around me, I asked questions incessantly. "Who made these rules? Why can't we change them? Were they made just for us? Who else follows them?" I realize now how annoying I must have been, but the only blowback I got was some good-natured ribbing. Once Boo-boo exclaimed exhaustedly, "Bugs, darn it! Why do you think everything's got answers? Just do it, man!"

Even Mama sometimes feared that I didn't joke around or pull enough pranks. Once I got the hang of reading, I couldn't get my fill, but she insisted that I needed "to know at least one board game." The only one she'd mastered was checkers. So one summer she sent Daddy to town to buy a checkerboard with real pieces, so we wouldn't have to use bottle caps, and taught me how. For several years after that, we played every Sunday afternoon on the back porch and, in the winter, next to the fireplace in Daddy's bedroom. I've always been a quick study so it didn't take me long to learn the game or to figure out that Mama hated to lose. She had a fluid sense of ethics when it came to games, occasionally adjusting the rules to claim victory.

"Mama, you just moved that checker in the wrong direction," I said one Sunday. I was polite but firm.

"Oh, did I move that checker way over there? I didn't realize," she said. "Bugs, you know I'm not a cheater. That's not my style." And we both laughed.

One thing Mama passed on to me, without trying, was her love of music. She moved through the curves and motions of life singing. You could hear her sweet, tender voice lifting a note upward as a gift-offering to God, whether she was standing over the stove, washing dishes, or shoveling ashes from the fireplace. Every now and then you'd also hear her whistling. "What song are you whistling?" I'd ask. "What are the words?"

"There are no words," she'd say. "Bugs, you know every tune doesn't have words."

I'd joined the Melody Aires, our church's children's choir, at an early age. The minister's wife was our director and had one of the loveliest mezzo-soprano voices I've ever heard, even when she was only humming. The whole congregation would turn out to hear her sing at Christmas and Easter. Tall and light complexioned, she was as elegant and eloquent as her voice. She wore bright, colored turbans, beads upon beads around her neck, and what seemed to be hundreds of bracelets around her nicely shaped arms. In 1980s rural Alabama, this was as glamorous as it got.

Most people in Madison Park had no formal music training. The choirs were volunteer corps—and part-time at that, made up of people who'd alternate between the pews and the choir stall and were often referred to as "First Sunday Choir," "Second Sunday Choir," and "Third Sunday Choir." They were distinguished not only by the ages of their respective members—the First Sunday Choir was for the senior most members of our congregation, the Second Sunday Choir was for the young adults, and the Third Sunday Choir was the children's choir. We distinguished choirs also by the color of the robes—white for the First, maroon for the Second, and blue for the Third.

No matter where they sat or when they sang, no one in the choir knew how to read a scale, yet somehow, everyone was always on cue and on key. Music flowed forth from these working people, making them forget their troubles for a moment. Subscribing to Aunt Shine's and Mrs. Bertha Winston's memorization theories, Mama was convinced that the hymn book hindered more than it helped. "Learn the words by heart, and they'll never leave your mind," she'd say. "Open your mouth and your heart, and the words will come easily."

They always did, and even now I have thousands of words—and hundreds of songs—etched in my mind.

I enjoyed singing in the choir so much so that I wished for other musical outlets. I longed to take piano lessons like the white kids at Dozier Elementary, although no one else I knew in Madison Park could afford lessons. I daydreamed about what it would be like to perform in the church hall, on a Steinway piano. I also imagined myself wearing a long white robe, like the men in the First Sunday Choir, taking a bow at the altar, the spotlight beaming down on me.

Such visions weren't implausible, even though I had no training. We were one of the few families in Madison Park to own a piano, and it was practically new. My grandparents told me that fifteen years earlier, they'd scrimped to buy an upright piano for Barbara Ann, who took lessons for only a year before giving up. That story of unappreciated sacrifice made me cringe, and I never pressed Mama and Daddy for lessons. I knew how great the financial strain would be.

My strategy was to borrow sheet music from the church organist, Dr. Hagalyn Seay Wilson—mostly introits and postludes by classical composers such as Bach, Beethoven, and Handel—and teach myself how to imitate and repeat what I heard, at the keyboard. I assumed that my passion would stand in for my lack of knowledge. But I quickly discovered that a good ear didn't automatically give me the ability to read music. In a desperate attempt for instruction, I visited Mrs. Sarah Pearl Coleman, who not only owned a piano but whose son, Silva Jo, served as one of the church's part-time pianists. In her time, she'd known a great deal about music, but as I soon discovered, she was now so old she'd forgotten nearly everything. Her instruction was gracious, but useless. So, after two lessons, I lied to her and said that my interest in the piano had faded. Not one to give up easily, I sat at the piano in the living room every day for nine years, attempting to play. How Mama and Daddy put up with the cacophony, I do not know.

Mama worked for Mrs. Gretchen Peabody, a well-to-do white woman in Old Cloverdale for more than twenty-five years and loved her with her whole heart. The feelings were reciprocated. Mrs. Peabody adored her "dear Sweet Mamie" and "her little boy at home who dreamed of going to college." Mrs. Peabody was always sending home books, magazines, and other things she thought I'd like. Whatever she offered, Mama took, even though, Daddy would always remind her, "We already have enough stuff at home."

Mrs. Peabody thought the best writers wrote for the *New York Times*. Twice a week, she gave Mama her old papers, insisting, "Your little boy will learn how to write well if he reads the *Times*." And I still am reading the *Times*.

One day after cleaning out her parlor, Mrs. Peabody asked Mama, "Mamie, do y'all have a record player? If you do, take these records home to give your little boy something to listen to."

Mama lugged her ten records home in a wooden vegetable crate, some still unopened. It was summer, and I took my time uncrating my present. I examined each record one-by-one until I found two or three whose covers I really liked. Daddy, as curious as I, brought the record player out to the back porch and plugged it in. "What are you going to play, son?" he asked, reminding me how much he also liked music. I turned the volume up as high as it would go, and the three of us waited.

I didn't know that what I had decided to play would forever change my life. Out came the most transcendental and wondrously strange sound. It was the voice of the soprano Jessye Norman singing Richard Strauss's "Four Last Songs."

I'd never heard such a voice—it enveloped me. The dogs and chickens seemed to hush, and the clanking of tractors plowing faded to the background. Even my normally voluble grandmother said nothing. The look on my face must have stopped her. I was transfixed. Norman's voice was so refreshingly different and new to our surroundings that in minutes Bimp, Boo-Boo, and Rod raced across the yard, landing with a thump on the porch. "What you listening to, Bugs? What is it?"

They weren't ridiculing me or scoffing at the music but expressing wonder. How could the human voice create such a sound? How could it sway back, turn curves, and climb so high? I played that record at full volume every day for the whole summer, and no one complained.

Eventually I played all of Mrs. Peabody's records, but the Norman album touched me most. It wasn't until years later that I learned that she was black, grew up in Augusta, Georgia, and got her start singing in the church choir. After many years of listening to that album, I truly appreciate what enormous range she possessed, what impeccable control and phrasing she exercised in her singing. But sitting on the back porch with my grandparents, I never could have imagined that one day I'd receive an invitation to dine with Ms. Norman in Aspen, Colorado, and tell her the story of how I came to love opera.

THREE QUEENS: ROSEBUD, MAMA, AND MAYES

Mama and Daddy had always restricted my bike riding to the one hundred-yard stretch of Motley Drive. But at the mature age of thirteen, when I entered sixth grade, I was finally allowed to venture past the stop sign at the corner of Motley Drive and Old Wetumpka Highway and head onto the roads of Madison Park. I was desperate to explore, but my old road bike, passed down to me by the Grants, one of the families that employed Mama, was old and rusted.

So in late November, we drove to a Western Auto store that sold automobile parts, accessories, and bicycles in Wetumpka, where Mama was born and grew up. I nervously paced the bike aisle and eventually settled on two or three that I liked. Then Daddy, who seldom expressed preferences, said to the salesman, "I like the silver-dime-colored ten-speed." That was good enough for me.

That bike opened up a world of travel. This Side of Madison Park had 343 pecan trees, 25 stop signs, and no traffic lights. I know, because that summer, I set out on my bike to take inventory. I rode it 365 days a year, developing what I called my "afternoon route." I'd stop in and spend a few minutes with the ladies who had tutored me in my earliest years—Frankie Lee Winston, Prince Ella Madison, Carrie Madison Seay, and Sarah Pearl Coleman, who'd tried to teach me piano.

I kept up this routine for five years. Aunt Prince Ella's and Mrs. Winston's houses became second homes to me. No matter whom I stopped to see, I was offered cookies, a slice of cake, or a bowl of ice cream. Out of courtesy, and a commanding sweet tooth, I'd say yes to them all. I'd usually do a few chores—changing a light bulb or carrying out the trash—but my friends and I spent most of the time sitting and talking.

I would stay until it seemed like a good time to move on. Seeing me to the door, Mrs. Winston would lean her eighty-plus-year-old frame against the door.

"Motley," she'd call as I started down her graveled driveway, "may the angels watch over you!"

As I enjoyed their company, I watched the gradual decline of these lovely women. My daily visits kept me attuned to their needs, which in turn increased my desire to see them as much as possible. Over time I added other elderly people to my roster, visiting Mrs. Gretchen Jenkins, Mrs. Julia Hendricks, and Miz Cheney's brother Mr. General Yelder, who lived behind the old Madison Park School.

Another of Madison Park's elderly women, Mrs. Rosebud Hall, was synonymous with red velvet cake. People, including me, stood in line at funerals and wedding receptions just to taste her pecan-filled cream-cheese icing, but she was busiest at Christmas. Every December for at least a quarter century Mama commissioned her to bake us two cakes—red velvet and coconut. Mrs. Beulah Byrd, equally famous for her blackberry pies, once knitted Mrs. Hall a red-velvet cape to wear during the holidays.

Apart from her cakes, growing up I'd had little association with Mrs. Rosebud outside of church. This changed when I was a young teenager. After years of fish fries and baby pageants, the annual conference of black Methodist churches in Montgomery decided to try a new fund-raising idea. Ms. Clara Mae Ivory—a bold and enterprising missionary leader—had just returned from a meeting up north and believed she possessed one of the most entrepreneurial and lucrative schemes to raise money ever employed by a church: the Fruit Tree Queen Festival.

The way it worked, she explained one Sunday, was that every registered church in the Central Alabama Conference, including Union Chapel Church, would elect one female contestant, each representing a different fruit. The festival pitted parish against parish to see which could out-fundraise its competitors. Each contestant would have to demonstrate knowledge of her particular fruit, with the winner crowned Fruit Tree Queen. Word came straight from the presiding bishop that this was to be taken seriously.

Reverend Washington asked for candidates to represent Union Chapel Church and bring the crown to Madison Park, but it took a lot of persuasion from the pulpit before Mrs. Rosebud, the sole volunteer, raised her hand. The minister called her before the congregation and praised her for putting herself forward.

Mrs. Rosebud was not shy. With one hand resting on the rails of the altar, she cleared her throat and began to speak, "Well, I was sitting there listening to the reverend, and no one answered the call. I felt, and I truly do believe I did, the presence of God calling me to represent my church family. You see I remember Isaiah in the Bible, answering the call and saying, 'Send me. I will go.' So how could I not volunteer? Please send me."

Her statement evoked a small rising of "A-mens." But Mrs. Rosebud wasn't finished. "I've decided to represent you as Mrs. Pomegranate."

Reverend Washington, refusing to allow the weight of this moment to be lost, said, "Let the church say, 'A-men.'" The parishioners did.

After the service, Mama congratulated Mrs. Rosebud and then asked, "Rosebud, how come you chose a pomegranate? We all thought sure you'd be a lemon, because everybody knows how much you love lemons."

Mama had a point. Mrs. Rosebud suffered from a chronic sore throat, and seldom did you encounter her without a lemon in her hand wrapped and tucked neatly in an iron-pressed handkerchief. A good singer, she was called upon from time to time to take the solo part in the choir, and she'd suck on the lemon as if it were a lozenge.

The minister had now to fulfill Rosebud's only request of him: to find her an escort for the festival. Rosebud, not too long after having been widowed, felt it inappropriate for a woman of her grace and maturity to seek out a male escort on her own.

Two weeks passed and Reverend Washington had failed to find Mrs. Rosebud a willing prince. The festival was only two weeks off. I was waiting in line for the men's room nearby when the minister approached Mr. Frank Hutchinson. "Please answer the call and join Rosebud in her bid to become queen," he said. "All you have to do is walk her down the aisle, Frank, that's all."

Mr. Hutchinson was an old man, and I'd never seen him move as quickly as he did leaving the line. Waving his hands in the air as if batting away the suggestion, he declared, "Reverend, God is not calling me to be a king, and I don't want to be Rosebud's prince either."

I gulped down my laughter. Reverend Washington turned to me. "How about you, young Motley? You'd make a fine prince for Mrs. Rosebud."

I met his request with a long silence. Lost for excuses and fearing lightning would strike if I lied to a minister, I accepted.

Mrs. Rosebud took the process more seriously than I ever imagined, requiring me to come to her house three separate times to practice walking her down the aisle. Walking back and forth through her kitchen, she held a lemon in her right hand as if it were an orb or scepter, while I trailed politely at her side. "I'm using a lemon for now, but on the day of the real event I will have a pomegranate, a nice large red one," she explained. "I'll be wearing an evening gown, so you'll have to walk a lot slower," she added.

During one practice she asked me to retrieve a handkerchief-wrapped lemon from her pocketbook. I discovered, to my alarm, I'd selected the wrong bundle; I picked up the white handkerchief wrapped around a full set of false teeth. She heard me scream and explained that she always liked carrying an extra set, just in case.

After weeks of anticipation, the festival came and went like a firefly in the night. It was a beautiful evening and the church was packed from front to back, with the overflow crowd pressed along the walls.

Spectators were talking excitedly and cameras flashed as the contestants and their escorts crowded into the vestibule in the rear of the church, waiting their turn to be announced. Miss Watermelon preceded us down the aisle. In a moment of heightened anticipation, as she tried to settle her nerves, she said, "There's nothing sweeter than being Miss Watermelon."

Then our moment came. Mrs. Rosebud was resplendent in a long, golden gown, with dangling red earrings and a three-strand pearl necklace at her neck. I knew that all eyes would be on her. I was just for decoration. But not wanting me to be upstaged, Mama had found me an all-white suit with a powder-blue shirt and a white bowtie. I looked like a black miniature of the writer Tom Wolfe. Mrs. Clara Mae Ivory's voice blared over the amplifier, "Ladies and gentlemen, I now present to you Mrs. Pomegranate, being escorted by Master Eric Motley."

This was probably the biggest moment in Mrs. Rosebud's life. We walked down the long aisle as the organist played "There's a Sweet, Sweet Spirit in this Place." Mrs. Rosebud as Mrs. Pomegranate never glowed so brightly. She carried the pomegranate as if it were the Holy Grail, lifting it high as an offering to God. She was proud, I was proud, the minister was proud, Mama was proud, all of Madison Park was proud. As the contestants were lined in front of the audience to announce the results, each ceremoniously had to surrender her fruit in anticipation of the ultimate prize, the crown.

Alas, the title of queen was bestowed on some ordinary fruit, but Mrs. Rosebud was awarded Honorable Mention. Later she confided to Mama that her walk down the aisle with me was almost as good as her wedding to Harvey fifty-odd years earlier.

As we stood around taking photographs and greeting friends, Mrs. Rosebud gently pulled me aside and whispered sweetly, "Hurry over to get my pomegranate off that table before someone else does. I paid over two dollars for that thing."

That year I was captain of the safety patrol, a position of honor for a sixth-grader at Dozier Elementary. I'd first been elected a safety-patrol officer in second grade. I'd served so faithfully for four years that I was awarded Outstanding Patrol of the Year. The honor entitled me and the other county winners to a weeklong trip to Disney World, underwritten and chaperoned by the Montgomery County Police Department.

Up to that point, the only other time I had left Montgomery was to visit Barbara Ann in Atlanta with Mama. Disney World seemed so exotic to me, like Venus.

I had never stayed at a hotel. I had never seen a showerhead with more than one setting, the assortment of tiny soaps and shampoo, or enjoyed the splendor of a free breakfast buffet. Because I had grown up in a church-centered environment, I assumed that the Gideon Bible in my bedside drawer meant everyone everywhere read the Bible before going to sleep at night. Its presence in the drawer, instead of out in the open, disturbed me somewhat, but I thought "to each his own."

Even though the trip was all expenses paid, we had to have our own spending money. I had been frugal with mine. I resisted the temptation to scoop up mouse ears and buy Mickey T-shirts and went easy on the caramel popcorn and candy apples available for sale around the park.

Although the ride "It's a Small World," with hundreds of singing dolls representing nations from around the world, is known for driving many people nearly insane, it was my favorite. I liked the idea that the world was greater, grander, more diverse, and yet more connected than I had known. Important influences appear from the most unlikely places.

As the week came to a close, I realized I had one day to find a gift for Mama. Surrounded by souvenir shops I'd studiously avoided, I now studied the merchandise and prices closely to find a special token of my "World" exploits. Since I'd spent so little all week, I could splurge.

I didn't realize that the jewelry shop carried only costume trinkets; I'd never purchased a piece of jewelry before, so I didn't know the difference. It all sparkled and shone, and that's all that mattered to me. Mama wore only a wedding band, and I decided that anyone so jewelry-deprived would be sent positively over the moon by the pearl ring encircled with a band of small diamonds that was on display. The fifteen-dollar purchase was one of the best buys of my lifetime. Mama loved the ring so much she wore it until she died, minus half the diamonds and the pearl re-glued to the band multiple times. Vastly transcending its monetary value, the ring served as a constant reminder to her that she meant the world to me and I to her.

I started seventh grade at Capitol Heights Junior High School in Montgomery, and like my neighborhood friends, Boo-Boo, Bimp, and Man, my Capitol Heights classmates bolstered my confidence in all things unathletic. I joined the yearbook committee and was elected president of student government and Junior Honor Society and head of the theatrical society. Could life get any better?

My tenure at Dozier Elementary, though rocky at the start, had transformed me into a serious student. I was on track to live up to my potential but didn't understand how much guidance I'd need to reach college. I had to become more driven than I thought possible.

John Steinbeck once wrote, "I've had many teachers who taught us soon forgotten things, but only one . . . who created . . . a new attitude, a new hunger. I suppose that to a large extent I am the unsigned manuscript of that teacher." Until junior high, I'd had a flock of hardworking teachers, yet until I met Susan Mayes, I hadn't encountered the one who would change my life. She took me on as a special project in her seventh-grade speech class, and my "new hunger" was born.

Mrs. Mayes required us to deliver a "demonstration speech" at the beginning of each semester explaining step-by-step how something was made or operated. I demonstrated the art of making a straw broom, as I had often seen Mama do. I showed how she cut the straw to size, firmly braiding and tying thin wire and widely cut ribbons together to make individual stalks of straw strong and unified. For me, that was a routine task, much easier and less messy than showing how to bake a cake, plant a tree, or trim a shrub. I was surprised that I was the first to choose that presentation topic. I received an A and offered Mrs. Mayes the broom. I was beginning to understand how much a good orator could achieve.

Mrs. Mayes quickly recognized my passion for giving speeches. Knowing I would need scholarships for college, she helped me enter every speech competition possible during seventh and eighth grades. My teacher, who was white, drove me around as though we were reversing the roles in *Driving Miss Daisy*, although I sat in the passenger seat next to her, not the backseat. Almost every Saturday, she would pick me up in her green Mercedes and then glide down country roads to competitions sponsored by Optimist Clubs, Lions Clubs, American Legion Posts, and Boards of Education.

One Friday evening found us at a speech event at Garrett Coliseum, in Montgomery, during the Annual 4-H State Fair. Having little room to accommodate wildly different events, the organizers placed us in a pavilion, where our competition would immediately follow the Invitational Youth Dairy Cattle Judging Contest. As soon as the cattle judging finished and the cow dung, though not the odor, had been cleared, the emcee called for the oratorical competition contestants. I was announced first. Looking out from my hay-bale platform, I made eye-contact with every member of the audience, just as Mrs. Mayes had taught, and began the opening lines of my speech, "Destiny: A Matter of Choice, Not Chance."

The room was packed, and the spectators included not just fellow contestants, but parents, teachers, family members, interested onlookers, and a few doleful cattle grazing in the back. There were no "boos" that night, but there were a few "moos." I did all I could to keep a straight face, remembering Mrs. Mayes's lesson: "You do not always have complete control of the speech situation."

Once my grandparents accompanied me to a competition held

in the chambers of Montgomery City Hall. We arrived nearly thirty minutes early, and a guard allowed us to enter the hall before our appointed time. As the three of us waited in silence—Mama in her gloves and hat, and Daddy dressed in his Sunday best—I watched their eyes wander to the inscriptions on the wall. The quotations, expressing sentiments like "Equal Justice for All" weren't profound; they were typical of governmental buildings. But to my grandparents, this was the people's government in all its marble majesty, and I was a part of it.

Mrs. Mayes had a way of demanding the best, and with her help, we won almost every speech competition. The two we lost were followed by long, quiet rides home. I felt guilty for letting her down. Only as an adult have I realized what she imparted to me, that tall, skinny black kid with untested hopes: her confidence, a sense of worthiness, her standard of excellence and expectation that I would benefit from competing with others as ambitious and driven as I. She did it for no extra pay and no personal gain. If she cut me slack because I was black and most of my competitors were white, I never felt it. Twenty-nine years later we remain friends. Someone once said that good teachers are with us for a lifetime; certainly the lessons they teach us are, and in some instances the teachers are as well.

First Place: Seventh-grade speech competition (c. 1986). Left to right: Mrs. Jean Mattox (biology teacher), Mr. Thomas Bobo (Montgomery County Public Schools Superintendent), and Mrs. Susan Mayes (seventh grade speech teacher and life-long friend)
The collection of Eric L. Motley

CHAPTER 15

THE BOOK OF KNOWLEDGE

My twelfth year, in 1984, had been a momentous "gift" year, with big rewards—the bike—and big trips—Disney World—that I'd never dreamed possible. So I didn't expect much would come my way at Christmas. But two weeks before Christmas and one week before my birthday, on a cold night, the winter wind roaring across the fields, the kindling crackling in the fireplace in Daddy's bedroom, and silver-foiled sweet potatoes baking in the ashes, an unfamiliar knock at the door interrupted our quiet evening. Daddy rose to answer the door, and like his shadow, I closely followed. A young blond-haired man stood at the screen, the porch light illuminating his profile.

"Good evening, sir," was all he got out before Daddy, with the urgency of a man who had no intention of heating all outdoors, invited the unexpected stranger in and led him to a chair by the open fire and into our family circle. Daddy reached up and switched on the light bulb dangling from a single wire, then offered our guest a hot sweet potato. Our house smelled wonderful, the delicious aroma of Christmas coming from the decorated tree in the corner.

Mama took his brown coat with a fuzzy lining. The hot potato flipped from one cold hand to the other as the stranger peeled back the foil. He was red faced from the wind. His Northern accent left no doubt that he was not from our neighborhood.

As he worked on the sweet potato, the stranger revealed that he was a college student who'd traveled almost two hours from the University of Alabama in Tuscaloosa, to the rural outskirts of Montgomery, selling books to finance his education. I remember thinking maybe I could sell my way through college someday. Our little community saw a lot of traveling salesmen who peddled jewelry and bed linens, vegetables from the backs of pickups, and, once, even extra car parts. But we'd never encountered a book salesman. To me, this was a most noble job. He had a bag of books that with Mama's permission he spread out on the bed. His display arranged, he started talking, looking at my grandparents, fully aware that he had my attention.

"Is this your son, sir?" he asked.

"This is our grandson. We're raising him," Mama and Daddy replied in unison, as if they'd rehearsed it.

"Well, I hope he likes school, because I have a lot of books that can help him with his studies. I'm selling a lot of encyclopedias and dictionaries this Christmas." Mama confidently told him our home already had a dictionary, though she didn't tell him it was two decades old. We didn't have a full set of encyclopedias, only random volumes.

"What else is in your bag?" Daddy asked, looking to hear the whole spiel.

"Well, sir, I also have a book of knowledge," the stranger replied, as if saving the best for last. He artfully pulled from his bag a large red leather book, embossed with gold letters and decorated with speckled leaves.

"Knowledge?" I asked, moving closer to the bed to inspect this treasure.

"Yes, the *Basic Knowledge* is kind of like having twenty encyclopedias in one book. It covers everything you want to know about the world—American history, science, technology, art, and music. It contains the knowledge of the world."

"The whole world," Daddy asked politely but skeptically, "in that one book?"

"Yes, sir," came the response. Turning to me with all the expertise of one who had done this many times before, the salesman asked, "You want to look at it?"

I reached my hands out and reverently held the book up to the light. Its red-leather binding felt sacred, as if it were Scripture. I'd never seen such a book—so full of facts. My grandparents reminded me of their aspirations on my behalf almost every day. I was smitten. In that uninhibited way that children blurt out their desires, I said, "Boy, this is a mighty big book, and it could really help me with school!"

Only one thing could spoil the deal. Daddy asked the dreaded question, "How much does a book like that cost?"

As though apologetic, the young man said in a low but firm voice, "Sixty dollars."

I was stunned. Sixty dollars was a lot of money in our household, especially so close to Christmas, when gifts had been purchased and the turkey was in the freezer. As Mama motioned to Daddy to follow her into the kitchen, the young man confided, "I really wish it were less." He realized that sixty dollars would be a sacrifice for us, yet at the same time, he wasn't offering to reduce the price.

Moments passed with hushed whispers coming from the kitchen. Then my grandparents returned smiling, knowing they were about to make two young men happy. Daddy reached into his pocket and carefully counted out two twenties, two fives, and one ten. Stuffing the money in his pocket the student salesman handed over the book gratefully. I felt a surge of joy at the prospect of life with all that knowledge. Mama held in her little wrinkled hands all the knowledge of the world: "A gift for you, dear Eric," she'd said. "Now the future is yours."

Years later I learned that Mama and Daddy had used seed money for the spring's planting and money reserved for the annual church picnic from the family savings jar to pay for the book. It was an affirmation of their hope for what I might become.

To further feed my appetite for knowledge, Daddy now began driving me to the city every week to check out books from the library—a simple act that changed my life. The fifty-minute round trip provided a refuge and bound us more closely. We sometimes drove past the Dexter Avenue Baptist Church, where the Reverend Dr. Martin Luther King Jr. had once been pastor and the spot where Mrs. Rosa Parks refused to move to the back of the bus. I'd learned about these two figures in school but didn't fully comprehend their courage and sacrifice, along with many others, white and black, who called the nation's attention to the tragic injustice of racism. Daddy never talked much about that, or about his role ferrying bus boycotters to and from the city for 381 consecutive days, but he called them "our heroes" who, despite being ordinary people, found the strength to be courageous. He raised his chin, and looked into the distance as if gazing at something invisible, fighting back tears. I learned early to sense when he reached his emotional limit. I would retreat to find the answers on my own, either from printed sources or from the more voluble Aunt Shine, always there to remind me of those who'd made strides for our race. I didn't see it then, but now I can appreciate how she filled in the blanks that Daddy had left open from his inability to summon up remembrance of pain and suffering caused by racism.

Daddy kept the faith despite the prejudice he had encountered. He seemed never to divide the world into black and white—good and bad—his conscience was too large, his heart too generous, to reduce the issues of life to skin color. We never had one of those father-to-son talks where he told me to watch out for people different from me, or to stay in my place, or to protest, if anyone sought to take advantage of me.

The weekly trips to the library about which I was speaking were pure joy for me. By my childish standards, the old Montgomery Public Library downtown rivaled the great Library of Alexandria—my intellectual holy of holies I'd learned about in school. The Montgomery Library was a magnificent cathedral of information, a grand temple of imagination and story. Since my grandparents had been forced to make do without an abundance of books, they taught me to appreciate their worth. Daddy, and occasionally our kind neighbors who drove me in his stead, didn't understand why I loved books as much as I did. But my own delight was sufficient reward. Daddy must have believed that the library was to me what a playground was to most kids.

I don't recollect Daddy ever getting out of the car, although he and Mama had graduated from high school and were highly literate. Perhaps he didn't enter the library out of shyness, or maybe it stemmed from his memory of the not-so-distant past when the library was off limits to him because of his race. As he'd pull into the circular curb drop off, he would ask in his slow, deliberate tempo, "How long will you be today?"

"A little over an hour," I said—my standard reply—even though I almost always stayed longer.

"There's no rush. Take as long as you need. Read every book you can till closing."

Only the Lord and the librarians know how often I tried to take him at his word!

I never knew what unusual fact, what teasing photograph, whose quaint story I might stumble onto. I'd begin in Poetry and select arm-loads of books by familiar authors, often to the librarians' whispers: "There's the Motley boy." They knew I had a mental map of the shelves and often turned up in esoteric sections such as Medieval History and Classical Greek Mythology, where few others went. I'd then park my satchel and a stack of unread books on a long wooden table—the same one every week—establishing "the Motley boy's" place, as comfortably as if it were our family room.

One Saturday, after rambling about on the third floor, I found my way back to my table on the main floor. Situating myself with a note-book and pencil to copy passages, a dictionary and thesaurus, I began to read one of the several dozen books I'd piled up. Suddenly my concentration broke. My eyes were drawn from the page to an older, fragile-looking white man, seated at a table across from me. He was in a wheelchair, with a black attendant at his side. We three were the only ones in the main floor reading room. He moved delicately, as though to avoid a provocation of pain. With bright, piercing eyes hooded by heavy brows, he struck me as a man bearing heavy burdens.

I returned to my reading. But sneaking a glance now and then, I'd find Wheelchair Man flipping pages casually, as though he didn't know what he was looking for. Our eyes met awkwardly several times. I knew him from somewhere! Once, nodding, as if to say, "Good day," he seemed as curious about me as I was about him. Perhaps he saw in me, Nameless Black Boy lost in wonder at the library, the embodiment of a time that was no more. Maybe he thought of me as the future's promise. Maybe he was pondering poet John Greenleaf Whittier's lines, "Of all sad words of tongue or pen, the saddest are these: it might have been."

As closing time approached, the loud reshelving of books at the circulation desk gradually ceased. The silence added a reverential quality to the nonverbal rapport that had developed between the Wheelchair Man and me. Suddenly I knew why he seemed so familiar.

As I gathered my books and walked to the circulation desk, we nodded—a parting benediction. I was so eager to tell Daddy, I took the stairs two at a time, and headed to the car, where he'd been waiting for two hours. At the sight of me bounding down the steps, he flashed one of his rare smiles and stubbed out the cigarette. I opened the door to his usual questions—"What have you been up to in there? Find any good books today? Any Robert Frost?"

"Yes, sir," I answered.

I was struggling to keep the lid on my surprise. Finally, unable to hold back any longer, I laid my satchel on the rear seat and blurted out, "You'll never guess who was in the library; who kept looking at me today."

Wanting to share in my excitement, Daddy managed a dramatic pause before asking, "Someone special?"

"Yes, sir," I said emphatically. "It was Governor George Wallace!"

"Do you mean *the* George Wallace?" he asked.

"Isn't that something? You just came face to face with one of the most notorious former segregationists in the country."

"Some people believe he learned that he had to get the support of black voters to win elections," Daddy said. "But I think he changed his mind about black people after a gunman tried to assassinate him in 1972 when he was running for president. It put him in a wheelchair for the rest of his life and made him understand suffering for the first time."

"Do you realize," Daddy asked, "that if you'd been born ten years earlier, at the start of Wallace's first term, you wouldn't even be allowed in this library? Now, you can sit at the same table with him. Sometimes justice comes slowly, but it always comes."

It was probably the most he ever said to me about racism.

I'm not certain how Daddy passed the time on those long Saturday afternoons while he sat in the car. He brought nothing to read and never turned on the radio, worried that it would run down the battery of our old Pontiac LeMans. I imagine he sat, smoking Winston cigarettes, thinking and watching. Whenever I asked him how he'd passed the time, he'd say in his quiet voice, turning the key in the ignition, "Just thinking—a lot to think about, you know."

The older I got, the more this time at the library took on greater significance than satisfying my curiosity. It's quite likely that as he waited in the car, he was pondering my future. Deep within Daddy was this abiding conviction that we are saved by hope, an idea affirmed by evidence at major turning points in time. He took advantage of opportunities to educate me about the inexorability of historical change as long as those who yearned for it kept the faith. As with his talk about Wallace, he didn't erupt into an angry diatribe about the nefarious acts of a former segregationist or gloat over the fact that Wallace came to suffer as he had caused others to suffer. Instead he used the occasion to celebrate the fact that now I could freely use the same library from which Wallace would have banned me. As I came to adopt that same hope, my grandparents' dream for me to go to college became my mission.

CHAPTER 16

BLESSED INTERVENTIONS

Besides my trips to the library, I also got involved with the Montgomery County YMCA youth development programs downtown. As important as these weekly trips were for me, they were an extra stretch, effort and moneywise, for my grandparents. Daddy drove me to Montgomery three evenings a week, which added up to sixty miles for him behind the wheel. Mama didn't drive, so the burden of late-night pickups fell exclusively to Daddy, who, although his eyes weren't as good as they used to be, refused to ask the neighbors to fill in for him. A good many, including our neighbor Ray, who was retired and readily available, had already begun volunteering their time—and a seat in their cars—to take me to town to get books.

One evening I looked out the screen door and saw Daddy and his longtime friend Alan Salery sitting under the chinaberry tree in our backyard talking, as they regularly did—passing the time in the cool of late evenings, covering a regular array of topics: farming, weather, old times, and friends who had already "climbed up the old sycamore tree to glory." Few people brought as much sheer delight and satisfaction to Daddy as Alan Salery. People in Madison Park spoke his first and last name together: AlanSalery. For reasons unknown he was never "Alan" or "Salery" or "Mr. Salery."

Everything about him was unpretentious, unvarnished, and seemed to belong to an earlier, simpler time. About twenty years older than Daddy, he wore overalls splotched with a multitude of colored patches without apology or comment. Mama would say that he had "more patches than overalls." Speaking in an old-time, deathly slow meter, he would have made a fit subject for anthropologists or psycholinguists researching nearly extinct speech patterns. He drove a weary old Chevrolet, once a taxi—every scratch and dent from the forties to prove its antiquity—which he nursed back to health every time it appeared terminal. Since he lived on This Side, Alan Salery told Daddy that he found his way home after dark only because his old car had memorized the way. There was something unmistakably authentic about him, which must have been a large part of what Daddy found so appealing in him.

He relied on an old-fashioned anti-theft device: every night he took his battery out of the car. Having no keys for the doors or ignition, he would "arc" the wires to start the engine. "Alan Salery," Mama would tease, "stealing your car would be more trouble than it's worth." And, "You never need worry about finding it, because there is no place on earth that car could hide."

He would always say, "Never mind, Mossy, it's paid for."

More than that, it was his most prized possession. Without the car he couldn't have visited with Daddy under the old chinaberry tree.

In any case, the car seemed in pristine condition compared to his house. One of the last sharecropper shacks left standing in Madison Park, it really belonged in a museum. Consisting of one tiny room, it was held together by rusted nails, loosening their grip on the old wooden planks. Unstable on its footing, the house would shimmy when you stepped on its rickety floor. Fearing its collapse, Alan Salery wouldn't allow more than two guests at a time. The little hovel's centerpiece was an open fireplace, which functioned as both radiator and stove. He slept on a pallet in front of it at night, and, during the day, cooked rabbits, squirrels, potatoes, chicken, corn, and some unknown, perhaps unclassified, flora and fauna.

Everyone in Madison Park, except perhaps Alan Salery himself, knew that he had little. But he was rich in love: the whole community embraced and valued him.

That spring night that I looked out the screen door, I heard Alan Salery raise an objection: "George, isn't that taking up a lot of gas going back and forth like that to town?" He was referring to the expense of transporting me back and forth to the Y. Daddy, in his modest way, set the question aside. "It's not all that bad," he said quietly. "God will provide, as He always has."

Over the next three months, as Daddy went out early in the morning to warm-up the car to take Mama to clean houses, he discovered, somewhat regularly, that what had been a near-empty gas tank the night before was miraculously full. Daddy, too amazed to know what to say, never said much. But Mama, who always had an opinion, offered it up as God's "blessed intervention." Adding to the mystery, the timing coincided with my YMCA meeting days. Looking for an explanation beyond what I considered to be Mama's dubious hypothesis, I concluded that the car's fuel gauge must be defective and sporadically showed incorrect readings. Whether divine or not, the intervention lasted until spring, when a Y staffer agreed to take over my personal carpool.

Not until about fifteen years later, after Alan Salery had "climbed that old Sycamore tree to glory," did a Madison Park street peddler, Nelson Young Jr., reveal the secret. "Old Man Alan Salery," as he called him, would pull his old car into our driveway in the late-night dark, park it alongside Daddy's car, take a length of garden hose from his trunk, and siphon gasoline from his car to ours. He who had a lot less than we did made an unheralded investment in my future through his quiet generosity. "Old Man Alan Salery was worried that your daddy didn't have enough gas to get you back and forth to town for those meetings," Nelson said.

"How did you know?" I asked, my emotions betraying me. "Why didn't you ever tell us?"

"Old Man Alan Salery gave me a dollar to push his car out of your driveway and start the engine so it wouldn't wake you up. And he gave me an extra quarter to keep quiet."

So it turns out that Mama had been right. We had a "blessed intervention." The unidentified instrument of the Lord was Alan Salery.

In ninth grade as part of my list of odd jobs I was hired to replace a negligent janitor at Union Chapel Church, who'd apparently never found use for a broom. My first Saturday on the job, I rode my bike and stopped off in the sanctuary—my custom whenever I entered the church. I was kneeling in silence when I noticed that the two tall gold-plated candlesticks on the altar were missing. I looked in the closets, the pastor's study, even the kitchen cabinets, but the candlesticks were gone.

After I called for backup, Aunt Prince Ella, Dr. Winston, and Reverend Washington showed up to help, but a second search turned up no more than the first. The precious objects must have been stolen. Although it was our practice to handle problems internally, both at church and in Madison Park at large, we called the Montgomery police, because we needed to file a complaint. To everyone's surprise, the police concluded that it was an inside job. Word spread quickly through the community. If someone could steal from God's house, then we all felt vulnerable.

The Sunday sermon that week, titled "The Cross without the Lights," revolved around what was noticeably absent from the altar. Reverend Washington told congregants that the candles represented the belief that Jesus is the light. "When we gather to worship the Lord," he said, "the Light is with us, it means that God is at home. As bearers of Christ, we must illuminate the darkness." Then he asked us to pray for the thieves.

Unwilling to follow the pastor's directive, Mama, in her outspoken way, turned to Mrs. Franklin, sitting in the pew behind her, and in a stage whisper said, "The thieves should burn in hell!"

Daddy asked her to tone it down, but she just said, "Anyone with the gall to steal from God is sure to be damned."

Her outburst embarrassed me, but I was used to her volatility, even in a worship service. Also, although I couldn't condone Mama's public rebuke of the thieves, in sharp contrast to the conciliatory tone of our pastor, I privately agreed with her.

Reverend Solomon Snowden Seay Sr. was a giant of a man who stood tall both physically and spiritually to all who knew him. He had been a great preacher in the pulpits of the South, a committed advocate for the poor, and an original organizer of the American Civil Rights movement that began in Montgomery. He lived one street over from us on Old Wetumpka Highway. His wife, Carrie, who was on my afternoon route, was among the retired teachers who taught me to read as part of Aunt Shine's volunteer brigade. Reverend and Mrs. Seay believed in the ethic of hard work and shared my grandparents' faith in the transformational power of education. More important, they believed in me.

Reverend Seay had to have his left leg amputated because of diabetes. His daughter, Dr. Hagalyn Seay Wilson, a noted doctor, had warned that the effects of the disease on his other leg would be severe if it wasn't exercised. Daily therapy was required to keep up the circulation.

Reverend Solomon Snowden Seay—
Montgomery Civil Rights Leader (c. 1985).
The collection of Eric L. Motley

In his seventies and relegated from standing tall to sitting in a wheelchair, Reverend Seay was slowly losing control of his faculties—only his mind remained sharp. Mrs. Seay, also a septuagenarian and somewhat frail, called me to their house one October evening. They'd already hired me many times to clear brush and gather broken limbs in their yard after storms. This time, Mrs. Seay explained, she was proposing a different job, one that would require more of me: I was to drop by the house every evening to help Reverend Seay do leglifts. The exercise would prevent further deterioration of his leg muscles and prolong his life. The idea left a considerable impression upon me.

It seemed simple, but the impact my work could have on his health was intimidating. The job was more hands-on than any I'd ever had. Even with Mrs. Nellie, I'd never been that close to someone sick. I accepted and started the next day: up-down, up-down, up-down, until we reached the required twenty-five lifts. I received a penny for each one, and at the end of every session Mrs. Seay would place a quarter in my palm. It was a simple way to earn $1.25 a week.

The strength Reverend Seay had developed in his lifetime of faith enabled him to face his last difficult and painful days with serenity and dignity. But over the next year, his strength diminished and his wife's health began to fade. They hired a day nurse, but there was a gap between her departure each evening and their doctor-daughter's arrival. Mrs. Seay asked if I would fill in.

Taking it meant I either give up some of my jobs or radically rearrange my schedule. It wasn't an easy decision. Mama, Daddy, and I sat at our kitchen table to talk about the pros and cons, concluding that school came first, and if my grades declined I'd have to quit working.

Without discussing the pay, I accepted the job with the Seays. Even today, I believe that at fifty dollars a week, I was overpaid. Relieving the nurse at 4:30 p.m., I would set up shop at one end of their dining table, laying out my books and assignments and start in on my homework. I exercised Reverend Seay's leg, took in laundry from the outdoor clothesline, kept the water pitcher on Mrs. Seay's bedside filled, distributed medication according to schedule, greeted visitors, and provided as much comfort as I could to the Seays until their daughter arrived at 6:30, often after dark.

Dr. Hagalyn Seay Wilson, who entrusted me with the care of her parents (c. 1994) Courtesy of William Winston family archive

At first we'd sit together—Mrs. Seay and I at the table and Reverend Seay in his recliner—talking, laughing, and reading aloud to one another. Sometimes Reverend Seay would commence to preaching a sermon, often retelling his favorite story of Paul and Silas in jail.

I don't know whether or not he imagined standing in a great pulpit with hundreds of people listening, but he never seemed discouraged by his audience of two. We'd conclude by singing his favorite hymn, "A Charge to Keep I Have."

Gradually, those days became fewer, as did the visits from former parishioners and clergy. I was perplexed at the paucity of visitors to see folks who'd invested so much of themselves in others. Where were Mrs. Seay's former students or the Madison Park children she'd tutored? Where were the men and women Reverend Seay had baptized in infancy or those he ministered to Sunday after Sunday?

My childish eyes saw for the first time the signs and ways of on-coming death. I learned to place pills on tongues, maneuver straws in tall cups so the Seays could drink water, massage swollen shoulders, and soothe them when they cried out in pain.

At times I felt unfit for the task. Even as I poured over homework I listened to their labored breathing and choking coughs. I had never facilitated toileting for someone, nor suffered the varieties of odors that follow the sick. But the grace the dying couple showed me gave me courage. They never ceased to encourage me, to speak with love and affection, to gently correct my grammar when I misused a word, to teach me the names of flowers in the front window boxes.

I managed each new hurdle in their care by pretending that none of it was unusual to me. Daily, I learned about the strength one can find within and the ability to pray aloud, even when the body is racked with pain. I listened to solos, often sung with meager voice from darkened rooms, meant only for the ears of God.

During the two years I spent with the Seays, as their health declined, I saw a particular joy: Reverend and Mrs. Seay never stopped living even as they were dying.

CHAPTER 17

1,002 USES FOR A PIE PAN

Being a teenager raised by my grandparents meant that waking up at 7:00 a.m., even on Saturdays, was considered oversleeping. My idea of a celebrity was Charlton Heston, not Michael Jackson. I knew more about the laws governing Social Security, Medicaid, death, and taxes than I did about skateboarding, video games, and moonwalking.

Mama and Daddy were all about preparation. While other people spent their money on baby showers for the advent of a child, my grandparents saved up for life insurance and took out a burial policy in my name before I hit my one-month birthday. They'd seen too many people of their station laid to rest in potter's fields, and this possibility preoccupied them both. Just as they made sure that our neighbor Ronnie didn't end up in an unmarked grave after he died in a house fire, they made certain that everyone in my family would be given a proper burial, with a casket and headstone, when the time came. Mama would say, "You know if you come into this world you may get sick and need to go the hospital, but one thing is for certain—you are gonna sure leave this world. You are gonna one day die, so you might as well prepare yourself by getting your affairs in order." Daddy had hammered three long nails—primitive hooks—into the wall to the right of the fireplace in his bedroom—one held a key to the church, the second, a key to the barn, and, on the last, hung a large envelope containing the medical and burial policies for each of us.

In those days when money was tight and working-class-families' insurance policies often lapsed, most people I knew had "policy-man" visits. Every two weeks, a little after 4:30 in the afternoon, a white gentleman drove up to our houses in his white Ford sedan, took the dollars we offered, and checked our names off his list. Paying in these small increments meant that we didn't have the anxiety of saving up to meet a large monthly or quarterly premium.

Besides giving me a lifelong relationship with death, Mama modeled for me the relationship between economic thriftiness and good stewardship of the environment. Her notions about thrift and reuse would put Al Gore to shame. At the end of every summer she cleared the pantry, making room for a fresh battalion of mason jars. If it grew and could be canned, she had plans for it. She preserved whole tomatoes, peaches, okra, and more, transforming the blackberries I had spent hours picking into jam, and the cucumbers that she grew in her garden into relishes. The pantry provided us with delicious surprises, even in the middle of winter.

Mama may have been among the earliest recyclers; people of her generation survived the Depression by scrimping and avoiding wastefulness. Theirs was a time when everything cost a nickel and banks could not be trusted. You worked hard to get by, and every penny counted. In our house we counted every penny into columns of fifty and rolled. Mama saved every newspaper and every grocery bag and stored them in the pantry. She even slotted away the Styrofoam trays that meat comes in at the grocery store, though I never saw her pull one back out.

I remember once opening the hall pantry and having what seemed like a hundred butter and Cool Whip containers tumble out—not trash, but useful vessels saved for future picnics, leftovers, and sharing with neighbors and friends. I don't know how we acquired so many aluminum pie pans and plastic bowls, because she never used store-bought whipped cream, and she made her own piecrusts. But their mere presence comforted Daddy and her, who both envisioned 1,002 uses for whatever objects might come their way. They repurposed them to store nuts and bolts and needles and thread and to double as flowerpots. "There's always a second use for everything," Mama lectured. "Remember that, young man."

We used plastic milk jugs for water and sweet tea. Daddy opened them up to mix paint and to suspend from trees as bird feeders. I can see Mama now, holding up an empty egg carton and thinking, "Now what could I do with this?" Even if she didn't have an immediate answer, she kept it until she did. We had drawers of plastic forks and knives washed and preserved, "just in case."

At our house we had outside and inside drying lines. The one just beyond the back screen door was for clothes. The one that stretched "inconspicuously" across the kitchen sink was for drying reusable aluminum foil and resealable plastic bags: Mama washed and reused pieces of aluminum foil like they were dishes and hung them to dry. When I was in high school, I decided to make a BLT sandwich. After I finished the last bites, I started to clean up. As I was pouring the bacon grease down the sink she walked in and yelled, "Stop! What are you doing, Bugs? Don't throw that grease down the sink. Boy, that's good stuff. We can use that again!" And she did, carefully siphoning it into an empty Cool Whip dish and bringing it out as lard for her next frying project.

One day I complained, "Why, why, please tell me, do we have a thousand aluminum pie pans, hundreds of plastic butter containers, and drawers of used plastic forks and knives?"

"Well, you never know when things might go wrong and you need all of this," Mama explained. "Plus, you never know when someone else might need it."

She wasn't just talking about pie pans. She was trying to teach me the important lesson that we never know what the future holds—not just for ourselves, but for others.

One of Mama's greatest gifts was her self-confidence. She looked at a complex situation and rendered a straightforward opinion as if Right and Truth were her personal possessions. She was able to speak with such self-assurance that she was rarely questioned even though, objectively, she was correct only about three-fourths of the time. That never mattered to her. She measured the world by her own standards, in which she was never wrong.

In truth, her memory seldom failed her. She had an ability to call forth times of day, dates, and rare genealogical data that eluded others, flaunting her total recall to anyone listening: "No, I remember it well," she'd say. "That boy Nelson was born to Julia in 1945, on July 15, in the afternoon, at about three o'clock. Now his sister, Sue Ellen, came into the world on December 13, 1942, at seven o'clock in the morning. It was two days after her cousin, Little-Bro, had a heart attack. He was up in New York, still driving that green Mustang that had the broken tail light George told him to get fixed, but he never did. We thought Little-Bro was going to die, but he lived a long time and had seven kids, the first born in 1949, in June, and the last in 1954, I think it was April. Well, I know it was April."

She was so good at details, even ones that pertained to the lives of other families, that friends and even acquaintances often came to our house for Mama to explain their family tree when they needed to write an obituary that listed decedents and survivors. "Do you just want me to write the obituary for you?" she'd ask. And she would.

But one day we argued about the date that Robert Kennedy was killed.

"I remember that day like it was yesterday," she boasted.

"But Mama," I corrected her, "you have the date wrong by a day. It was June 6, not June 7. It says so right here." I pointed to the book in my lap.

When confronted with evidence of her mistake, she refused to yield. She asked me with an air of doubt and contempt, "Where did you get that book from? How do I know it's legitimate?"

"Because it's large and red and has *Encyclopedia Britannia* in gold on the cover," I answered, in a snippy tone verging on back talk.

Instead of accepting the unlikely possibility that her memory might be imperfect, Mama protested. "I was thrown off, because 1968 was a leap year," she explained impatiently "The extra day interfered with my sequence of events."

An only child, Mama never had siblings to remind her of her faults. So it was upsetting to be challenged by her grandchild and bruising to her sense of self to be wrong. Even though as a devout Christian she would openly acknowledge her flawed state as a fallen human, she—humanly—had difficulty accepting her imperfections. She could accept the mistakes of others but not her own.

My passion for being correct often collided with Mama's. I sometimes felt a need to push back against her unbreakable spirit to assert my own identity. The clash of wills between us continued as I got older and the educational advantages I enjoyed over my grandparents became more apparent.

The skirmish between Mama and me scarred both of us. We recovered, but the guilt I felt for knowing more than she did—of surpassing the people who'd sacrificed so much for my welfare and education—never left me.

That afternoon I selfishly gloated to Daddy that I'd bested Mama in an argument. Daddy and I were sitting together on the back porch, abiding by an unspoken rule in our house that no one should ever sit on the porch alone. He was usually not one to provoke conversation. Since he didn't need it, he assumed no one did. But that day Daddy cleared his throat and spoke. "Be gentler in victory next time, son," he coached. "Your grandmother dishes it out boldly, but she hurts easily." From the incident I learned to value life experience as much as book learning.

He had a quiet, almost subterranean way of imparting wisdom. I remember sitting on the porch one evening when I was younger as he patiently allowed me to describe how I'd just reconfigured my carrot and strawberry garden—I'd taken up gardening as a result of Mama's influence. I painstakingly described how I'd laid six rows, cultivating them with mulch, and how I buried the seeds with my bare hands into the earth.

"Are you pleased?" he asked, turning to look at me with his piercing green eyes. "Is there any more you could do, or are you satisfied? Are six rows enough? Did you plant some to share?"

But the answers were embedded in the questions—and by example. He made clear every day that life was about doing your best and planting enough to share. His convictions sustained him; they would sustain me too.

CHAPTER 18

KEEPING IT REAL FOR ME

Since she was an only child, Mama needed to care for others who were alone. Preserved in her soul was the desire to be the "Big Sister." In my childhood, she constantly ministered to neighbors, old friends fallen on hard times, spouses who had lost their mates, and victims of tragedy and illness. For more than two years, while Mrs. Della Young was dying of cancer, she cooked three hot meals a day for Mrs. Della to sustain her strength as long as possible. She washed another neighbor's clothes every day. He was elderly, a widower, and had no family. She wanted me to understand how to help those whom Jesus called "the least of these." She'd say to me, "Always remember that everybody is your neighbor. We must be family to one another."

Her generosity extended to every living creature. Mama believed in the Ten Commandments, and she took "Thou Shall Not Kill" literally. In our house the flyswatter wasn't used to smash flies, only to gently shoo them away. She had a soft spot for all animals. When stray cats and dogs wandered onto our back porch, she'd say, "They're just passing through for an extra meal."

Mama loved dogs in particular. When the dogcatcher's van would pass through Madison Park, friends would phone so she could hurry outside to call the strays, feed them, and lock them in the barn until the danger passed.

I imagined that our house was a destination on an "underground railroad" for dogs—dogs helping out other dogs in distress, pointing them to the right house for immediate relief and assistance. I concluded that there must be a special symbol clawed into the tree in our front yard, something that all animals recognized as a sign: "Come in for a free meal and a bed in the barn."

Some canine guests had no intention of leaving after lunch—or ever. A beagle-hound stopped by our house for an afternoon snack one day. He had no collar, and we'd never seen him before. Afraid he was someone's pet, Daddy had me post signs, advertising "A Missing Dog Who Answers to the Name 'Bear.'"

Fourteen years later, Bear the beagle was still with us.

We always had one dog, and sometimes two. And every one was called Bear. As soon as one Bear died, we'd get another. When I protested against naming yet another dog Bear, Mama said, "They always answer, and that's all that matters!" It was a note of contention between us that Daddy wisely refused to comment on. Besides the beagle, the other constant was our black Labrador retriever, also confusingly known as Bear.

One scorching-hot July afternoon, years after the beagle came to stay, Michael Galloway, the young grandson of Gladys and Brother McCarter, came running over to the house. He banged on the back door, calling out, "Mrs. Mossy! Mrs. Mossy! A man hit your dog, and he kept going." He led Mama to our dog—Bear the Labrador—who'd dragged himself from the middle of the road to Mrs. King's front yard, two doors down form the McCarters. Bear was still alive, but barely. When he heard Mama's voice, he did all he could to lift his head.

"It's going to be all right, my little Bear. Mommy's here," she cooed. Then, by herself, and he wasn't small, she picked up the dog in her arms, cradling him like a baby, and brought him back to our house, laying him gently on the back porch. Both his hind legs were broken.

Country folk didn't take dogs to veterinarians. The expense could never be justified. Most people could hardly afford to go to the doctor or dentist themselves. Mama called Daddy out of the house and as soon as he sized up the situation, he brought out the large, greasy jar of Kerosene and a couple of old T-shirts. She began to cradle Bear as Daddy tore the shirts into strips. Mama, who put her faith in old-time remedies, poured Kerosene over the dog's hindquarter, massaged it in, and bandaged him with the shredded T-shirts strips. She poured castor oil down his throat and washed it down with cool water from the pump.

Next she got the wheelbarrow out of the barn, stuffed it with old pillows and coats to make it soft and comfortable, and, with Daddy's help, lifted Bear into his make-shift bed, whispering a prayer: "Dear Lord, Bear needs you tonight. Bless this dog. This is a good dog. Have mercy on him."

And God must have. Bear made it through the night and the next night and the night after that. I was away at college at the time, but Daddy told me, "Bear was sure enough dead, and Mama brought him back to life."

Bear stayed in that wheelbarrow for more than three weeks. Every afternoon Mama would pull him around the yard just in case he got bored. She'd say, "He needs his exercise." Then she would pick him up in her arms and sit down in the back-porch swing to rock him.

If a dog could talk, that dog would have a lot to say. Since he couldn't, he demonstrated his love for Mama as abundantly as he could.

Bear never walked the same again. He had a bad limp the rest of his life, and everywhere Mama went he limped right behind. From the day he got out of the wheelbarrow, he became her shadow. When she crossed the street to visit Gert and Ort Johnson, Nee-bo's parents, Bear would follow, sitting outside their front door until Mama was ready to return. On Sundays, he followed the car to church, climbing the steep steps to wait at the front door until the service ended. People used to tell her, "That dog sure enough loves you."

She'd smile and say, "That's my Bear."

After eight years Mama woke up one day to find Bear wasn't there. She walked up and down the street calling him and enlisted the neighborhood children to look for him. He was gone forever. She was distraught. Our old neighbor Mr. Yelder called out, "Mossy, that dog loved you like he never loved anyone before, and when a good country dog knows he's about to die, he doesn't want to die at his master's side. He doesn't want grieving. He wanders into the woods and dies on the other side of the creek. That dog loved you so much that's what he did. Isn't that something?" That was all that needed to be said. Mama seemed consoled by those words.

The respect he showed her was mutual.

Mama retired the name Bear, and that was the last dog we owned.

As good as my grandparents were, neither was sanctimonious. Describing an old friend who'd given up on an active life and spent most of her time in prayer, Mama would say, she was so "heavenly minded that she was no earthly good." Being of "some earthly good" was vital to Mama. She often reinforced this lesson, never more effectively than the summer I was fourteen, when she assigned what I considered an especially onerous set of chores to my already long list of responsibilities: I had to take all of the glassware out of the china cabinet that no one ever used, wash it, and reline the shelves with paper. The shelves were irregular so that I had to trim the edges with a pair of scissors.

Mama and Daddy seemed to understand better than me that the gift of "grace" could not be repaid; it could only be extended to others. Yet individually, if Daddy's legacy to me was his gentle spirit and upright character, Mama's was rooting me firmly to the ground. The small successes I'd had in my young life could easily have left me puffed up and narcissistic, but she wouldn't allow that. She never let me forget where I came from and why it was important to remember my heritage, even as I got older and my opportunities to experience the world outside of Madison Park increased. She worked hard to "keep it real" for me, often to my great embarrassment.

The summer I was fifteen I had a summer job as assistant to the director of a local summer program for teachers. At four dollars an hour, it paid more than I'd ever made. It was rare that I was able to try to match the gifts that my grandparents had bestowed on me with one of my own, but I had a firm plan for what to do with that cash besides save for college. A severe spring thunderstorm had blown several shingles off our roof, causing it to leak, and insurance wouldn't cover the considerable repair cost. Replacing it would strain our family's slim savings. But Mama and Daddy refused to let me contribute. My earnings, they insisted, were for my education. They didn't even want me to contribute bonus money I'd won. But in the end, I won the debate.

The next summer I had a more eye-catching gift in mind. I wanted to buy Mama a riding lawnmower. As long as I could remember, she'd insisted on mowing the lawn herself, and, at seventy-two, she was still cutting more than an acre of grass with a push mower.

One of the happiest days we spent together was when I took her to Lowe's Home Improvement Center to pick out a riding mower. It reminded me of the day that Mama and Daddy bought me my bike. She selected a bright red Craftsman, and as we made our way to the checkout counter, she told every customer and salesperson we saw, "This is my grandson, and he has just bought me my first riding lawn mower. I'm so happy—and I am so proud of him!" It was one of those days memory will never give up. I think it was the greatest gift I've ever given.

The mower was delivered to our house that afternoon. Our neighbor, good friend, and barber, Little Joe Simon, who had his own riding mower, came over to give Mama a few operating instructions. She knew how to drive a car but failed the driver's test five or six times before she gave up on getting a license. "It's the parallel parking that gets me," she reckoned. I'd seen her behind the wheel only once when she moved the car to clear the way for a tractor to get into the back garden. She hit the corner of the back porch, knocking out a support pillar and causing half of the porch to collapse. Daddy repaired the damage but never allowed her to live down the incident, or drive his car again, for any reason.

Her relationship with the riding mower was more successful. She continued to cut the grass twice a week until she was eighty-eight. To the displeasure of our retired neighbors, Mama always started cutting the grass at 6:00 a.m. "I start early to beat the heat," she'd explain to anyone who'd listen. She would mow the entire lawn by the time most people got out of bed in the morning. One miffed neighbor once informed me that his idea of retirement was not to be awakened at dawn by a rumbling sound reminding him of a freight train. His love and respect for Mama kept him from complaining directly to her.

One of the greatest, yet most obvious, gifts the people of Madison Park gave me was transportation. Part of the ethos of Madison Park was that no one went alone to community events. With relatively few cars and drivers, everyone almost always took someone to church meetings, picnics, voting rallies, garden shows, backyard barbecues, weddings, birthday parties, and baby showers. Mrs. Olla, Madison Park's wealthiest citizen, used to say that if you bought a small car, "it was a sign of selfishness; a way of looking out only for oneself and family."

As customary as it was to ferry friends from place to place, it was as great a gift to me as anything else Madison Park bestowed on me. I'm certain that I would have been put at a disadvantage had the friends, neighbors, and friends of friends not been willing to take me to the interesting and educational activities that took place in Montgomery. As I got older and learned to drive, this was one investment I was able to repay. And the most immediate and costly repayment, in time and patience, was to drive Mama and her friends to funerals.

Funerals weren't like our weddings. Instead of mailing individual wedding invitations, one was delivered by hand to the church secretary, who read it aloud during the announcements on Sunday, inviting all within earshot—and all attended. It was a sign of your family's good standing in the community to have a full church on your wedding day. Yet when someone died, too often, folks were memorialized with the church sparsely filled. Mrs. Sara Pearl, one of my former tutors and piano teacher, would say, "It's an awful thing to be all alone on your last day on earth, even if you're lying in a casket."

Mama and her good friends came to attach great importance to funerals. They'd wake up in the morning, call each other to assure themselves that they were all accounted for, eat breakfast, and then study the obituaries in the *Montgomery Advertiser.* There wasn't one in Madison Park that they didn't attend.

Of Mama's friends, only Mrs. Bea Davis and Aunt Prince Ella drove, which made them the designated drivers for all church-related and community events, that is, until I got my driver's license at sixteen (although Daddy taught me how to drive at thirteen by sitting in his lap and driving up and down abandoned dirt roads). I became the official chauffeur, and I took great delight in driving Aunt Prince Ella's large, cream-colored Chrysler—it was one of the finest cars in Madison Park, and I'd admired it since I was little.

Aunt Prince Ella had moved me to the front seat years before so I could read road signs to her. Speeding down I-65 South to Greenville, Alabama, she'd call out, "Look, Motley, there's a sign—a green sign coming up on your right. What does it say? Read it for me."

My head poking out of the window, I'd scream back, "It says Greenville, 25 Miles!"

"Okay. Thank you, Motley, but here comes another sign. What does it say?"

"55 MPH."

"Okay, that means 'miles per hour,' Motley."

Aunt Prince Ella asked these questions not just because her eyesight was failing but because, ever the teacher, she wanted to engage me in conversation.

I can't begin to count how many times I drove the ladies during my high school years. I always drove Aunt Prince Ella's car, as it was large enough to accommodate almost everyone, and Mrs. Bea would take her car if there were "extra" people to be collected. Upon arriving at our destination, I would deliver the community's mourners as close to the front steps of the church as possible, park somewhere in an open field under a shade tree, and run to join them in the church. I would not have dreamed of asking to stay in the car; my place was there in the church with the other mourners.

I once asked Aunt Prince Ella, while walking her to the car after one of these funerals, how well she knew the deceased. Her answer was like a memorized, often-quoted passage from the book of Genesis, detailing a long lineage: "You see, her grandfather's sister was married to the brother of Wilma Jean's daddy's child by his first wife, who died in her sleep; but before she died she bore a son, and that son was a good friend of your grandfather, George, and my late husband, Eli, who was named for his grandfather, who happened to be the founder of Madison Park. We all lived here in this community of Madison Park."

When I look back I realize how much I learned about life and death, about loved ones and how they cope and move on after loss. As much as these experiences prepared me for Mama and Daddy's declining health, more important they showed me how a community comes together to support one another in their times of need.

CHAPTER 19

STEVE URKEL AND BOYS STATE

In 1989, on my first day of tenth grade, I passed the tall, bronze statue of the Southern Civil War General Robert E. Lee, standing sentry at the entrance to the high school that bore his name. Just a little over two decades earlier, in 1964, three black students had been the first to integrate Lee High. Much had happened in Alabama in the intervening years, confirming that we had come a long way. Among other things, George Wallace had been elected to an unprecedented fourth term as governor in 1982. His apologies for his past actions had helped him capture a majority of the African American vote in that election. Both his changed attitude, and the change in African American perceptions of him, showed that racism had lost some although far from all of its vicious hold on our Deep South state.

I had never attended so large a school as Lee, whose approximately one thousand students came from different communities. Black kids from the local housing project, Trenholm Court, and poor white students from the neighboring Chisholm community, rode city buses. Students from wealthier communities were chauffeured to school by parents.

Those of us from Madison Park took the classic yellow county school bus every day. Each weekday morning for three years about six of us from Madison Park gathered at the same pickup point, the Washerteria, at the corner of Motley Drive and Old Wetumpka Highway. Altogether, more than a hundred students from Madison Park attended Lee.

I arrived at the school academically confident. We didn't have grade-point averages at Capitol Heights Junior High, but I was an honor-roll student and elected president of the Honor Society by my classmates. What I failed to anticipate was how much more demanding the work would be in high school, with more classes and considerably more homework. Mastering these new academic challenges now stood between college and me.

Socially, I had a few problems. The kids of Madison Park *always* had my back, and I had theirs. It was the other thousand-plus students who worried me. How would they accept and treat me? Could I persuade them to give me the leadership roles to which I had become accustomed? Would I easily make friends among the kids I was meeting for the first time?

As it turned out, I was already widely known among certain groups at Lee High. The gossip on me ran like this: "There's this new kid named Eric Motley who's smart and equally eccentric." I'm not sure the people who referred to me as "eccentric" knew the definition exactly, but it was a convenient word and, to me, a lot better than "weird." "He walks very fast. He loves ginger ale and doesn't drink alcohol or smoke. He always sits on the front row. He hasn't missed a day of school in his whole life. He alternates between cordovan penny-loafers and white Reeboks, looking more reminiscent of the fifties than the nineties. He carries a briefcase and a can of Lysol everywhere he goes."

Teachers helped perpetuate this reputation. My theater teacher,

Mr. Flynn Murphy, identified me as "unique" and encouraged me to become more eccentric, or, as he might have put it, to stand out more in every way. On one occasion, Mr. Murphy was bragging about me to a group of upperclassmen when one of them chided, "You make it sound like that little nerd can do anything."

Mr. Murphy's response was something like, "Yeah, that little nerd does anything he sets his mind to—if he was interested he could become the fastest quarterback at Robert E. Lee!"

Within a few days, this absurd prognostication about my potential as a football player had become an urban myth—except that people took it seriously! One day as I was getting a corndog in the cafeteria, my history teacher, Ms. Ernestine White, introduced me to the famously successful football coach, Spence McCracken, who kept repeating, incredulously, "So you're Eric Motley? I hear you were a fast quarterback back in junior high?" Suspiciously sizing me up, he added, "You don't look like one to play football." Never having stepped foot on a football field, I could tell he was having a joke at my expense.

Holding my briefcase in one hand and the corndog in the other and having no idea where he'd gotten the ridiculous notion that I could succeed at football, I replied as politely as I could: "No, Sir, I am pretty good at T-ball and kick ball."

I've never seen a grown man laugh as hard. That was the beginning of the McCracken-Motley friendship.

I never set out to be a nerd. Some things come naturally, or they somehow get ascribed to you. I carried the briefcase because I preferred it to knapsacks and because it had sentimental value. It was "lent" to me by my seventh-grade teacher, on the eve of a Model UN conference. I walked fast because I hate being late and learned from Mama that the speedier I moved, the more I could accomplish. We used Lysol liberally around the house, and so I brought the practice with me to school. It must have worked, because I never caught a cold or flu—hence my perfect attendance record—and I don't remember my grandparents getting sick, either.

My first year at Lee happened to coincide with the 1990 release of the sitcom *Family Matters*, featuring Steve Urkel, the quintessential nerd with thick glasses, colored suspenders, and a cardigan sweater, who quickly became famous as "Urkel." I didn't even know who the character was until a jealous upperclassman branded me "Urkel" when I wouldn't let him copy from my test. For the next two years, I remained "Urkel" to those who loved and loathed me.

In my second year, the Motley-Urkel phenomenon reached new heights. Coach McCraken asked Mr. Murphy if he would design a few skits to open up the pep rallies held before Friday-night football games. I regarded the pep rallies at Robert E. Lee as high-octane events, with the high school band in the balcony, the cheerleaders stretching across the bottom apron of the stage, and all students and faculty packing shoulder-to-shoulder into the auditorium.

But the upperclassmen had been complaining that the pep rallies were losing some of their "oomph" and that maybe a few theatrics could reenergize the required assembly. Flynn Murphy never turned down an invitation to put his students on stage. When he asked me if I would help him out, stage fright almost made me say no, but I stepped up for the cause. As devised by Mr. Murphy, I played Urkel, defender of the Robert E. Lee Generals! And overnight, I became a high school "sports" star.

Wearing suspenders, pocket protector, pants cuffed-high, plaid shirt, and large black-framed glasses, and carrying my briefcase and Lysol, I would appear on stage on my bicycle in a great puff of white smoke and fight off the opposing team. Five other nerds, also on bikes, followed me on stage, and we crashed our bikes into one another.

After we untangled from the wreckage, I alone would confront people representing players from that week's opposing football team. Making exaggerated karate gestures in the air, I'd shriek, "Yah, Yah-Ozzz!"

The "quarterback" of the opposing team would yell, "This guy is crazy! Let's get out of here!" and one of my nerdy sidekicks would then chase them from the stage.

The routine was a smash hit. The audience came unglued with laughter. After my histrionics, the band played, the cheerleaders jumped up onto the stage and catapulted me in the air, and the football players stomped as the chant broke out "We Will, We Will Rock You!"

And the rest, chronicled in the Lee High Generals' yearbook, is history. After six pep-rally appearances, the Generals captured the state championship. I had secured my place forever, at least in my role as Urkel. The playacting allowed my classmates to see me as someone who was willing to sacrifice some dignity to be a team player. If there were ever a nerd voted most popular, I would have won. And I *did* have a lot of fun.

Playing Urkel, all hilarity aside, was an important distraction for me; a chance to feel like other kids and offload some of the pressure of the looming goal of college. But I continued to excel and wouldn't be satisfied unless I pursued every endeavor with everything in me.

The summer of 1991, just before my last year in high school, the faculty named me to represent Lee High at Alabama Boys State. Boys State and Girls State are summer leadership and citizenship programs, sponsored by the American Legion, for high school seniors across the country. That June, I was one of more than three hundred Alabamians who descended upon the campus of Samford University (not Stanford in California but SAMford), a well-respected, private university in Birmingham, about ninety-five miles from Madison Park.

I'd been on several university campuses, including Alabama State, Tuskegee Institute, Auburn, and Troy State, all in or near Montgomery, but I had never seen a place like Samford. It had everything I believed a university should—classical cupolas and columns, uniform redbrick, colonial-style buildings, and an imposing front entrance. Coming to that campus as a soon-to-be high school senior energized my aspirations. I was truly excited about attending college. I had prayed, saved money, and prepared academically, but no great plan had been revealed. I hoped that God's intervening hand might make my next steps a little clearer that summer. One of the privileges of Boys State was the opportunity to hear from some of Alabama's greatest minds. Two speakers from that transformative week left an indelible impression on me: the Reverend John Claypool, then minister of St. Luke's Episcopal Church in Birmingham, and Dr. Thomas E. Corts, then president of Samford.

Their messages urged us to live out a great, God-directed destiny; we were needed to lead, to bring *principled* leadership to the issues of our time. I sat listening to them, looking around Samford's vast concert hall, contemplating my future and wondering where I would fulfill my dream and desire for higher education. I wondered too what my life could become. Then I had a eureka moment. My next step needed to be at Samford. Even though it still remains unexplainable, I had a deep-down assurance that this was the place I was meant to be.

A prominent feature of Boys State each year was the election of a mock slate of state officials, including the governor and the governor's cabinet. After about two-dozen fellows gave me a standing ovation for my talk on the need for the state to better support education, a handful of delegates urged me to submit my name as a candidate for governor. "Think about it," one friend joked, "you could be our first black governor in Alabama!"

I campaigned hard, shaking as many hands as I could and making as many promises as I felt I could live up to, and I won the election.

I remind myself that this was a mock election. Though its cities have some prominent black mayors, all these years later Alabama still has never elected a black person to a senior executive position in state government. Neither has it elected anyone who supported spending more on education. Such support would require an increase in property taxes, and most Alabamians have no interest in giving up their standing as the state with the lowest property taxes in the country.

My victory was cause for a celebratory collect call home. My grandparents, while pleased with my accomplishments, never overdid their praise in an effort to keep me humble. Their restrained exuberance this time was further tempered by their less-than-total understanding of the nature of Boys State. "If it's a good thing, and you believe that you can deliver, then we're proud of you," they said. That was praise enough for me. It was an exciting time, and it would ultimately lead to a new and loftier goal none of us could have foreseen.

Mama wasn't as pleased when she realized that with my election came the honor of a trip to Washington, D.C., as one of the two Alabama state representatives at Boys Nation.

I had traveled beyond Alabama's borders as an active member of National Methodist Youth conferences, which were held in a different city across the country every December. But I'd never travelled with a group outside of the authority of my church—without church chaperones.

Mama had never been so anxious about my travel. She had read about crime in Washington and New York, and from her vantage point the two cities were the same. And the idea of my going so far without knowing anyone on the trip unsettled her. "Do you think they would allow Aunt Prince Ella to go as a chaperone?" Mama asked.

"No, I don't think they will allow *Aunt Prince Ella* to go as a chaperone," I answered in a tone that left no room for doubt.

It was a great trip. I met fellows from across the United States, who came from places I'd never heard of. And I never will forget seeing the marvelous marble—the Lincoln Memorial, the Vietnam Wall, and the White House—for the first time. All one hundred of us stood outside the White House gates, peering in, not knowing the front of the house from the back. It was a once-in-a lifetime opportunity crammed into one short visit, each of us wondering what it would be like to pass through those gates to the other side.

Toward the end of our stay, we held another round of mock elections. While in real life the U.S. president makes cabinet appointments, we held elections for each top position in the federal government. I threw my name in for president, but after someone else won, some of my friends pushed a ballot forward with my name for secretary of defense. I don't think I was particularly well suited to defense and will never know why my friends chose me for this, yet I clinched it.

What we didn't know was that, as secretary of defense for Boys Nation, I was to spend an afternoon with my counterpart, the real secretary of defense, Dick Cheney. We were invited into his office at the Pentagon, where I received special attention. Secretary Cheney showed me around his executive suite and invited me to sit at his desk, use his stationery and fine fountain pen, and make calls from his personal telephone.

When you're eighteen, in one of the world's most prominent cities and most distinctive buildings, in the seat of the man who controls the greatest military might, whom do you call? I thought about calling Man, my buddy from Motley Drive, but I knew that he'd be out playing ball, and it seemed pedestrian to squander a momentous opportunity on a friend.

Or, I thought, I could call one of my teachers. Sensing my uncertainty, Secretary Cheney encouraged me to call Mama to let her know about my latest electoral victory. Blushing, I refused his kind offer several times, until, too embarrassed to decline again, or attempt an explanation, I succumbed. Before I had left home, Mama, already wary of my trip to the big city, had made it clear that under no circumstances did she want me to go wandering off from the "boys," and I was not to speak to strangers, no matter how tempting the circumstance. I promised to comply.

Knowing how little she knew about the program and how apprehensive she was, I thought it best not to excite her with a midday phone call.

But with Secretary Cheney, one of the most powerful men in the world, standing over my right shoulder being persistent, I didn't see a way out.

Secretly I hoped Mama wouldn't pick up. But she did—on the second ring.

EM: "Mom, it's me, Eric."

Mama: "Bugs, is that you? Where are you? You better still be in Washington! Are you with those boys?"

EM: "Oh, yes. I'm great! Thanks for asking. Yes, I am still here in Washington."

Mama: "Why are you phoning me? Is this call collect? Are you with those boys?'"

EM: "Yes, I am with the boys, and we're having a great time. And you'd never believe where I am now!"

Mama: "You better be in Washington, D.C., with those boys. You aren't with some stranger are you?"

EM: "Yes, yes. I am at the Pentagon."

Mama: "Where? Where is that? Are you still in Washington, D.C.?"

EM: "Yes, the Pentagon. I've been elected secretary of defense, and I'm spending the afternoon with Dick Cheney!"

Mama: "Who? Who?"

As Mama's volume rose, I pressed the phone to my ear trying to prevent Secretary Cheney from hearing.

"Dick who?"

EM: "Yes, Dick Cheney . . . I know . . . I am so honored."

Mama: "I don't know who Dick is, but you better find your bottom back to Washington, D.C., and get with those boys as fast as you can! You hear me, Bugs?"

EM: "Yes, well, it's great talking to you too. Yes. I love you too. Okay. Bye-bye."

I hung that phone up as quickly as I could, fearing that Secretary Cheney might ask to say hello to Mama and that she just might give him an earful. It was one of the briefest conversations I ever had with her.

I made the call only months after the first Persian Gulf War, when almost everyone in the country had heard the name Dick Cheney. It was an important lesson: being important in Washington doesn't make you important everywhere. Mama didn't measure a person's worth by possessions or access to the rich or mighty.

Neither of us could have foreseen that one day I would have the opportunity of standing in *Vice President* Cheney's office, reminding him of that event, and telling the full story.

The collection of
Eric L. Motley

Déjà Vu: Sitting in Secretary Cheney's chair at the Pentagon in 1991, I could not have imagined that twelve years later I would be visiting with Vice President Cheney, in his White House office, as a senior advisor to President Bush.
Courtesy of the Office of the Vice President of the United States

CHAPTER 20

EVOLUTION

To graduate with honors, as I planned, I had to take advanced chemistry and biology. Despite my fondness for botany, science courses had always been challenging for me. As luck would have it, I ended up with Mrs. Susan Foster for AP Biology. She was an equestrian, and teaching biology was her second calling. She looked like a woman who could not only breed horses, but round them up too. She taught biology as if she were present during the seven days of Creation, although she had little use for rest on the seventh day, and I don't think she gave much credence to the idea of creationism preached by Reverend Washington. Once while lecturing she used the word *evolution*, and the devout Southern Baptist classmate sitting next to me, Jeremiah Reed, leaned over and whispered, "I don't believe she used that *word*. We all going to go to hell now."

The closest thing to hell for me, at least during that semester, was possibly failing that class. Since I never wanted to endure that heat again, I passed the class with a B+. I still remember Mrs. Foster as being not only one of the hardest teachers I ever had, but one of the best, especially at helping to open my mind to new ways of thinking.

Even before I took Mrs. Foster's class, I was beginning to reexamine some of my deep-seated presumptions. Reconciling my faith with everyday life had always been a serious preoccupation, but for the first time, during that biology course, I encountered a scientific theory that challenged my religious beliefs. My upbringing had made little accommodation for science, yet Mama's fascination for how living things in her garden grew, mutated, multiplied, and declined linked her to Darwin. Had the similarity been pointed out to her, she would have been horrified. While I talked to her and Daddy about biology in general, I never felt emboldened to broach the subject of evolution, let alone try to explain it.

Mrs. Foster taught evolution by subtly and thoughtfully introducing aspects of natural selection, in a manner that did not overtly challenge our inherited belief in creationism. She never posed the matter as an either/or proposition between creationism and evolution. Perhaps she believed this herself, or she might have suspected that a frontal assault on religion would have led to her firing from a school in the Bible Belt.

Her careful approach aside, magnifying glass always in one hand, the concepts she put forth suggested that everything in our existence could be explained in biological and physical terms, at the expense of faith. But because her teaching allowed space for religious belief, from that moment onward I felt, even more confidently, that scientific truth and religious faith could exist harmoniously. I later encountered the same harmonious blending in Saint Thomas Aquinas's synthesis of matters of faith and matters of reason.

I wasn't much stronger in math than in science. The night before every algebra test, I'd make the rounds of Mama's friends, calling Aunt Prince Ella, Mrs. Bea Davis, lovingly known as "Aunt Bea," our church's designated head cook, and Mrs. Frankie Lee Winston on the phone and ask them to pray on my behalf. The end results were always favorable and compounded my belief that with a lot of work and a few prayers anything was possible

Unlike science and math, my classes in history and government came naturally to me. The semester I took government, in the fall of 1991, Clarence Thomas was undergoing the confirmation process to become a Supreme Court Justice. My teacher, Ms. Ernestine White, a lovely, tall, and slender black woman with long grayish hair, used the confirmation hearings as an excellent real-world example of government at work. Against the backdrop of what became one of the most acrimonious and contentious confirmation hearings in modern U.S. history, we talked about the positives and negatives of judicial review and how one branch of government exercises checks and balances over another.

At the end of the term, I wrote a paper on Thomas and the judicial process. It was sympathetic—my reaction to the blistering accusations of sexual harassment that he had endured during his confirmation hearings and the tenacity he demonstrated to defend his name. What most attracted me was his personal story. Regardless of the venom directed at him, here was a fellow Southern-born African American who had been surrendered at an early age by his mother and had seen his father only twice by the time he graduated from law school. Though poor, he had learned the value of education at an early age and was reared by his grandparents. I could identify with his life, and I wanted to know how he overcame obstacles and financial uncertainties, how he persevered and eventually escaped the snares of poverty and low expectations. There were too many similarities between our stories for me to be distracted by what his alleged shortcomings might be.

Word of my fascination with Justice Thomas reached Dr. Thomas

Bobo, Superintendent of the Montgomery County Public Schools. The supervisor at my summer job was having lunch with Dr. Bobo and told him both of my interest in Justice Thomas and my plan to attend the National 4-H Young Leaders Conference in Maryland, my second trip to that part of the country within a few months. Without my knowing, Dr. Bobo contacted Senator Richard Shelby of Alabama and asked him to help me meet the newly confirmed Supreme Court justice.

Two days later I received a telephone call from Justice Thomas's secretary, inviting me to meet the justice in his chambers after the conference in Maryland. I made plans to arrive at the Supreme Court a full five hours before my scheduled departure at Washington National Airport (now Ronald Reagan Airport) so that I could spend the maximum amount of time with him.

I lugged my large cassette recorder and tapes, that would serve as the basis for my report to Mrs. White's class, up all those steps at the imposing Supreme Court building. Having already checked out of the hotel, I was further weighed down by my hand-me-down green suitcases. At the door, baffled security guards looked me over cautiously, as if I planned to spend the night in the building. To their surprise, a phone call verified my appointment on the third floor, beyond the brass gates of the Great Hall that evidently separated the public space from the private chambers of the chief justice and his associates.

The first things I noticed in Justice Thomas's chambers were a placard on his desk bearing the message "Old Man Can't Is Dead—I Helped Bury Him" and an imposing portrait of the formidable nineteenth-century abolitionist and former slave Frederick Douglass that hung over the mahogany-framed fireplace. I asked him to explain the meaning and significance of the placard and his reason for selecting the Douglass portrait. He explained that Douglass's self-reliance and purposeful style of life inspired him and influenced his intellectual development.

"Aunt Shine, one of my childhood educators, often quotes Douglass," I said. "She says he's a model for how to face an uncertain future with conviction strengthened by education."

The motto on the placard, he told me, was an admonition passed down to him from his grandfather that only a "can-do" attitude conquers life's obstacles, no matter how formidable. It was a common refrain in my household as well, and I came to appreciate how we'd both been taught that the future doesn't have to replicate the past, that through perseverance one can overcome any obstacle.

Justice Thomas spent almost two hours with me. He struck me as extremely serious, even a bit somber, as he prepared to assume his new duties, which moved me enormously. But for all that he'd endured over the past few months, especially during the confirmation hearings, he was remarkably gracious. To my amazement, he told me that I seemed like a younger version of him. "Always look ahead, but never forget home," he said, advice that I still cherish.

Although it didn't come from as high a pulpit as Justice Thomas's, I received a lot of well-placed advice in my final years of high school. Cameron and Stanley Seay, sons of Reverend S.S. Seay and Carrie Madison Seay, the couple whom I'd helped care for after school, had made lives for themselves elsewhere but moved back to Alabama to support their parents before they died. Stanley was a chemistry teacher, who helped me with my science projects, and Cameron was an engineer, who encouraged my intellectual growth.

Cameron was one of the warmest people I knew, with a seemingly unlimited capacity for encouragement. Pushing me intellectually and creatively, he helped me grow as a reader, writer, and thinker. We often read together, and when I decided to conduct an exhaustive study of David's psalms as lyrical poetry, Cameron discussed each psalm with me. He read and edited my poetry and urged me to keep a diary, which I do to this day. When I came up with a movie idea, he offered to help me create a treatment. In a small, rural town where often my intellectual curiosity was tolerated good-naturedly, I was fortunate to have Cameron take my ideas as seriously as if he were my thesis adviser and teach me how to explore them with intellectual rigor.

Like many seniors at Lee High—but few from Madison Park—my senior year was consumed not only with classes, extracurricular activities, and afterschool jobs but with applying to college. From my "eureka moment" at Samford forward, my only goal was to apply and gain admission. Mrs. Joan Watterson, my junior year English teacher at Lee High, knew that I wanted to attend college, and agreed that Samford, from which her daughter had graduated in the 1980s, would be a great choice. She encouraged my interest in Samford partly because of her family's connection to the university. Her husband was an acquaintance of Dr. Corts. I'd always wanted to go "far off" to school, and in those days ninety-five miles fit that definition. Samford had a small minority population, yet I felt I could thrive there. Unfortunately, the tuition, as I came to find out, seemed astronomical at the time.

Mrs. Watterson coached me on my university application and essay. While working with me, she also worked over her poor husband, who kept telling President Corts how desperately I was needed at Samford, that he would forever regret the decision if Samford missed Eric Motley. After much effort on my part, of talking to everyone I knew who had some Samford connection, and even more persistence on the part of

Mrs. Watterson, in the spring of 1992 Samford offered me admission with a full presidential scholarship.

I accepted without hesitation.

Friday night, May 29, 1992, was my high school graduation. Daddy, in his brown Sunday suit and black shoes, drove Mama and me downtown to the coliseum, the very same venue where I gave a speech before an audience of cows in junior high. Feeling fragile in health, he stayed outside, sitting and smoking on the hood of the car. He was proud of my achievement. That was clear. But he couldn't compete with the crowd. Mama took her place inside among Madison Park friends and neighbors. Photographs from that night reveal how proud she was— her face was beaming. I realize now what I couldn't fathom then. Her sacrifice had been enormous and burdensome but still an immeasurable blessing. Raising me didn't just mean that she'd gotten me from birth to age nineteen. She had *lifted* me up.

I was proud too, but at the same time, I felt somewhat fearful of the future. Would I be able to live up to the dreams and achieve the goals set for me by those who had so strongly believed in me and invested so much? Another concern was financial; even though I had a full scholarship, how would I pay for books and the one-hundred-eighty-mile round trip to visit my grandparents? I had always had my own room. Now I would need to adjust to having a roommate. What if I met a girl I wanted to date? I had never dated in high school.

The issue of race loomed over me too, notwithstanding the fact that I had attended integrated schools in Montgomery. Samford had a well-earned reputation as a solidly white, upper- and upper-middle-class bastion. Would the color of my skin or my modest family background be a handicap?

Four weeks after graduation, I embarked for Europe as a Lions Club International Fellow on a generous scholarship. This first trip abroad launched me on my great voyage beyond Madison Park and presaged the vistas, thanks to my education, that would be opening up to me. Mama had never been abroad. Daddy had served in the European theater in the aftermath of World War II but hadn't returned to Germany since. Yet they were ecstatic that I would have the opportunity to travel. They wanted me to test out all I'd learned.

At nineteen years old, and just a day before I was to leave for Paris, my friend and high school classmate, Alisa Roberts, was tragically shot to death in Montgomery as she walked to her car after work. She died from crossfire as two teenagers senselessly argued over a pair of boots. Who could have known on the night of our graduation that one month later she would lay dying on the ground in a parking lot. For my high school group, it was our first serious encounter with our mortality. It was a sober lesson for me that even in youth, life is a fragile possession. All these years later, I often leave fresh flowers on Alisa's grave when I am in Montgomery.

There was another sad thought for me that summer: soon I would have to say goodbye to Mama and Daddy, a moment that would be hard on me, and even more difficult for them. They'd been my constant support, so I did feel some pangs of guilt at leaving them, especially at their advanced ages. Then there was that unsettled feeling that comes to college freshmen, naturally unsure at an awkward time of life about how well or poorly they might be accepted by peers. Having been a large fish in a small pond, would I still thrive in the turn-about of being a smaller fish in a larger pond?

Evolution

A backward glance over my personal odyssey to that point shows that I had stood on the shoulders of a great number of people. Theirs was a collective act of grace. Together they formed a gigantic account-ability circle, helping me focus on higher things, such as the liberation that an education could afford and the guiding principles that would keep me true to my course. Going forward, my success would be on my shoulders alone.

At church the Sunday before I left for school, Reverend Washington announced that I would leave Saturday morning for Samford University in Birmingham. I had left home many times: summer camp, YMCA leadership meetings, church youth conferences, and school trips. But this time I had the feeling that I was leaving Madison Park for good. I was about to cross that great chasm that separates high school from college, to live on my own, manage my own affairs, and choose my own friends.

In that week of August 1992, before I left for Birmingham, a sense of melancholy set in, and as I began packing on Thursday night, real sadness took hold. Earlier that day, my late-in-life, self-appointed godparents, Frankie Turner and her husband, Thomas, had taken me to the PX at Maxwell Air Force Base in Montgomery to buy necessities. I came home and sensed that Daddy, knowing Saturday was only two days away, was more taciturn than usual.

I didn't approach him, afraid that any encounter would be awkward. Instead, he pulled me aside. Since I had a lot of packing left to do, I took my seat on the back porch impatiently for what I knew would be more silence than conversation. Handing me a few neatly folded pages from an old magazine—I think it was *Life*—he said, "This is pretty important, and I would like for you to read it now!"

I began reading it aloud, as was the practice at our house. A defense of nonviolent protest, it had been written by Martin Luther King Jr. I quickly noted that it wasn't a speech, the genre I associated with him, but a letter.

So as Daddy listened I read "Letter from Birmingham Jail," including the famous line "Injustice anywhere is a threat to justice everywhere" for the first time. After I finished we both sat in silence. I needed no words to understand how deeply Daddy had been moved. Only on rare occasions had I seen him cry, but now he quietly wiped away tears.

I carefully refolded the pages, tucked them into the envelope, and handed it back. I didn't know then how widely the missive would resonate in my life. A year later, I wrote my own letter from Birmingham. Writing it from the relative luxury of a college dormitory room, I told Daddy that earlier that day I had driven into downtown Birmingham, from Samford's suburban campus, with my classmate Ovit. The jail had been torn down, but I stood on the spot where King had penned his powerful missive in 1963. Weeks later Mama replied to me in a return letter that Daddy was "so happy that you remembered the jail in Birmingham."

How could I forget? I have read Dr. King's letter every August since, and altogether I must have perused it more than a hundred times.

On Friday, my next-to-last morning at home, Daddy got up surprisingly early. A few days earlier he had bought a burgundy 1988 Mercury Grand Marquis from his brother, Dot, so that I'd have a nice, reliable car to get me to and from Samford. Together the two of them drove it to a certified mechanic, Mr. Cottrell, in the city, to make sure that it passed muster. We'd always relied on our friends and neighbors who were "backyard" mechanics to keep our cars running. But on this occasion Daddy wanted assurance from a professional that the Grand Marquis would make it up Interstate 65 North to Birmingham. Mr. Cottrell gave it a clean bill of health, promising Daddy that it had miles to go before it slept forever.

My last night at home seemed never to end. It was as though God had inserted some extra hours, stretching the day out of compassion for Mama, Daddy, and me. For more than twenty-seven years of their life together, they'd had someone in their home requiring nurture, care, and provision—an adopted daughter and an adopted grandson. Barbara Ann had left. Now I was going too.

Mama made my favorite meal—fried pork chops, creamed corn, collard greens with homemade cornbread, and her famous peach cobbler. In honor of the occasion, Daddy asked me to "offer up a prayer" and a poem. As I began to pray, Mama interrupted, almost as if offering her own prayer. "All I ask of you is to never forget home," she implored. "Always remember us."

She must have been afraid that I would lose touch like Barbara Ann had, but we never talked much about that; it was too painful.

We enjoyed Mama's cooking but strained for conversation under the sense of heaviness that hung over the table. After dinner we sat on the back porch and stargazed. "Look at that one, it's moving so quickly!" Mama exclaimed. I smiled, not wanting to correct Mama, who had just mistaken an airplane for a star.

On Saturday, as we ate breakfast together, we pretended that nothing was out of the ordinary. Just before nine o'clock, as I'd almost finished loading the car, a stream of friends and neighbors began arriving. With more than twenty people gathered in our backyard, Mrs. Rosebud burst into "Blest Be the Tie That Binds" and Reverend

Washington led us in a prayer for my safety. When the last goodbyes were said, hugs shared, promises made, "little Motley" set off for Birmingham and the future.

Never having driven such a distance before, I listened to the radio the whole trip to be sure not to doze off. It was a long ride, almost two hours. As I made my way up that road, I reminded myself to pay close attention to where I was going because I sure wanted to remember how to find my way back home.

CHAPTER 21

BEYOND MADISON PARK, BUT STILL A PART OF IT

On a fine August morning in 1992, I drove through the Georgian colonial gates of Samford University, as triumphantly as Napoleon returning to Paris. With a pocketful of scholarships and the money hoarded from a lifetime of neighborhood jobs, I felt rich as I cruised slowly up the hill in my four-year-old Mercury Grand Marquis. Others might have zipped around campus in a shiny, top-down Miata or BMW, but no one could deny that my burgundy sedan, only slightly smaller than a Bradley tank, made for a commanding presence.

I didn't know enough to be embarrassed driving such an uncollegiate car. I don't necessarily recommend it to others, but I don't deny that my off-to-college, '88 Grand Marquis became a part of who I am.

My Napoleonic pretensions masked my fears of the unknown challenges that this new world would pose for me. I had decided, before leaving Madison Park, that I would throw myself into college completely and in every conceivable way, holding nothing back. I was determined, in Thoreau's words, "to live deep and suck out all the marrow of life."

My boat of a car wasn't the only thing that differentiated me. My presence at Samford mystified many students who had never had a black classmate. I baffled still others who had seen a black man but had never seen anyone behave as I did. In my desire to make new friends right away, I greeted and shook hands with my fellow students as they entered the classroom. I also shook hands with my entering professors as people stood around and watched. In contrast to the standard college uniform of blue jeans and T-shirts, I wore starched button-downs and creased pants—part of the new wardrobe my grandparents had bought for me.

I'd dash to the cafeteria at 7:00 a.m. for breakfast, which eliminated candidates for roommates in the double occupancy room I had managed to get assigned to. I did all that I could to disseminate the information. I ironed my shirts and pants, dispensed Lysol in the communal shower after an outbreak of athlete's foot, and listened to Bach on full volume every morning. I met and made friends by holding afternoon tea in my dorm room, but the practice became so popular that I had to issue invitations.

Although the other students were not exactly *like* me in terms of race, background, and upbringing, we quickly bonded. Samford introduced me to friends who helped me come to appreciate the lighter side of life. Five friends in particular—freshmen on my hall—helped me loosen up and learn to enjoy myself. These were the first peers with whom I had ever shared living space. As with my friends in Madison Park, they coaxed me out of my comfort zone, were critical of me without invitation, and catapulted me into their athletic pastimes. It was to them that I began referring to George and Mossy Motley as my grandmother and grandfather to explain why they were so much older than other parents.

Neil, Michael (who went by Kael), Ovit, Wayne, and Dennis were outgoing and hilarious. Each had grown up with siblings and experienced childhood rivalry and contested space. I had not. Since they knew that I had grown up as an only child, they were always playing pranks, like hiding in my closet to scare me, rearranging my furniture, turning off the hot water for my early morning showers, and penning fictitious love letters from nonexistent female admirers.

Kael was the most unusual white person I had met up to that time. He was tall, with Italian features, but he fancied himself the white Michael Jackson, who could out-moonwalk his idol—and he could. Kael introduced me to gospel rap—religious lyrics adapted to a hip-hop beat and style—which was unheard of at Samford in the early 1990s. One morning, to my total astonishment, he came up to me in the hallway and began to rap "The Lord's Prayer."

When my buddies learned that I wanted to ask out a particular classmate, Lisa Beck, they rallied behind me but nixed my Oxford button-down shirt and Duckhead khakis as too unfashionable for my first college date. I also lost the argument to wear a suit, even though I had an extensive wardrobe of fine suits, thanks to Mrs. Sarah Pearl Coleman's son, Silva Jo. Any time he gained weight, he gave up a good number of his "outgrown" Italian and English hand-tailored, pinstriped suits, with waistcoats and cuffed trousers. In the end Kael led us on a shopping spree. I appeared date-ready with a denim shirt, Polo khaki pants, a leather rope belt, penny loafers, and Kael's personal stash of Calvin Klein cologne.

For all of their pranks and japes, their warmth and joviality helped me adapt to my new surroundings. I was able to pursue my academic endeavors knowing I had a new family by my side.

From my first days at Samford I was confronting differences among people—differences I had never known before. I couldn't wait to get up every morning. University advisers told me repeatedly that no one at Samford was getting more out of the four years than I did.

Following the advice of my high school YMCA counselor, Angela Williams, I sought out professors based on their reputations for excellent teaching and mentoring. Dr. Rod Davis, the dean of the College of Arts and Sciences, was white and grew up in Jim Crow Alabama, but he refused to live a segregated life. When he left graduate school in the 1960s, he devoted his early years to teaching in historically black colleges in the South, where students were economically and educationally disadvantaged. At Samford he made it his aim to seek out every black student and discuss his or her future and the importance of education.

As I was walking across campus on a cool October afternoon during my first semester, he flagged me down, saying, "I've heard about you, and I've been dying to talk to you." He then introduced himself and invited me to drop by his office. I did, that afternoon.

Dr. Davis opened the intellectual doors for me at Samford. He introduced me to National Public Radio (NPR), *The New York Review of Books*, and *Christianity Today*. He was the most liberal intellectual figure I'd encountered and wasn't afraid to affirm it in an overwhelmingly conservative Southern Baptist milieu; we frequently argued about politics, culture, and Christianity.

He was a devout Christian, of a left-leaning variety, which was novel. After all, even in the Bible Belt, scholars tend to be a bit more conservative. Most important, he wanted his mostly staunchly right-wing students in the college to analyze viewpoints different from their own. He constantly challenged them to establish their own arguments based on facts and their faith, not just what they had learned at home and in their churches.

At the end of the year, just before the summer break, he called me into his office and handed me a stack of books with a note that read: "These are books that you should read. They are important."

The urgency of his tone reminded me immediately of Mrs. Peabody who had insisted that Mama take the records "to give her little boy something to listen to," which had led me to my love of opera. In the stack were James Baldwin's *The Fire Next Time*, William Faulkner's *Go Down Moses*, an edition of Emily Dickinson's poems, and a collection of Langston Hughes's short stories. I was familiar with the authors, but I hadn't read much of their work. He didn't offer his opinions but made sure I understood he expected me to read them over the summer.

When I returned to Samford in the autumn, I visited his office almost immediately. "What's next?" I asked, ready for my next assignment.

"What did you think of Baldwin?" he asked, ignoring my question and drawing me into a discussion about the power of the written word and its relationship to our lived reality.

Although Dr. Davis hadn't shared my experiences as a black male growing up in the Deep South, he knew that exposing me to *The Fire Next Time* would feel familiar and help prepare me for the challenges I would face, as an adult member of a racial minority in America. Likewise, reading Emily Dickinson carried me to the other end of the spectrum, seeing life from the perspective of a privileged yet cloistered white American female who, like me, felt uncertain about her identity and role in the world.

Not all of my professors were quite so eager to befriend me. My practice of dressing up for class, sitting as close to the door as possible and my handshaking routines struck some as peculiar. Professor Steven Epley taught the first class I took, English 101. I didn't know that he was fresh out of Columbia University's graduate school, and I was in his first class. He had just started his teaching career, and I almost drove him from it at the outset.

Dr. Epley told me years later that before he entered the classroom on the first day, he had spied me shaking hands with one startled classmate. He remembered thinking to himself, "I've got to watch out for that kid."

Sure enough, I extended my hand to him as he entered and said, "I'm Eric Motley, and I'm pleased to be in your class." Dr. Epley took it in stride and shook my hand.

At some point during his lecture, he was describing the writing process by means of diagrams that he had sketched on the chalkboard. Pointing to a series of circles, he explained, "This first one represents the invention phase of writing, when you come up with ideas, and the next one corresponds to the drafting phase, when you begin writing out your thoughts." Overcome by enthusiasm and the desire to help Dr. Epley make these concepts more relatable to my classmates, I jumped to my feet, stepped up beside him, gently snatched the chalk from his hands, and began drawing my own flow chart.

"This reminds me of what I studied at 4-H camp this summer," I beamed. Dr. Epley stood next to me in stunned silence. He later told me, as he watched me scribble with his chalk, that he thought, "I learned a lot in graduate school, but not what to do when the student takes the chalk out of your hand." He gently managed to get me back away from the chalkboard. "Eric, that's very interesting and helpful," he said, "but let's return to the writing process."

Despite our unorthodox beginning, Dr. Epley was a forgiving man, and we eventually formed an extremely close bond. Among other interests, we shared a love for debate. I had always been a student of politics, and the 1992 presidential election—Bill Clinton, George

H. W. Bush, and Ross Perot—was particularly meaningful to me since it was the first national election in which I was eligible to vote. I watched all the debates and followed the issues carefully. The week after the vice-presidential debate, Dr. Epley announced in class that, using the debates as our study tool, we would be exploring the topic of persuasive rhetoric.

When he asked for a show of hands of those who had seen the debate on TV, only mine shot up. I hadn't only watched the debate; I had taken notes, which for some reason I had with me. In front of the entire class, paying no mind to the fact that no one else was participating, I had a rousing discussion with Dr. Epley on the debating strengths and weaknesses of the sitting vice president, Dan Quayle, and the soon-to-be-vice president, Al Gore.

Just like Dr. Davis, Dr. Epley made me think differently about books and authors I had read but never really considered before. One was Ernest Hemingway. On a random day during office hours, we struck up a discussion about Hemingway. He recited one of his favorite passages, from the end of *A Farewell to Arms*, when Lt. Henry recalls saying goodbye to his dying lover, Catherine Barkley: "But after I got them to leave and shut the door and turned off the light it wasn't any good. It was like saying goodbye to a statue." Henry, in an attempt to achieve some form of closure, performs one final act of affection and kisses the face of his dead lover. Unfortunately, the kiss fails to requite his grief and serves as a timeless reminder of the permanence of death.

Dr. Epley didn't look at me but stared into distant space, as if pulling words from the air. I listened quietly as his eyes filled with tears in remembrance of his own loss.

CHAPTER 22

REMEMBER, WE'RE STILL IN ALABAMA

In a society where so many people lack passion, at Samford I was surrounded by people fired by their zeal for education and their teaching careers. They held the same ideals as Mama and Daddy, prizing community, caring for others in need, and seeking rewards that weren't just material. I might have left Madison Park, but its values flourished in my new surroundings.

The greatest of these mentors was Dr. Thomas Corts. When I first met Dr. Corts at Boys State the year before I entered Samford, I was an eager, enthusiastic eighteen-year-old prospective student and he was a fifty-year-old university president. In our dramatic age and experience gap, we resembled James Boswell and Samuel Johnson—the impressionable Boswell was twenty-two when he met the fifty-four-year-old Johnson. And like Boswell, I found myself breathing the equivalent of "Johnsonian ether" around Dr. Corts, trying to absorb the essence of the man. In Boswell's diaries he recorded Johnson's words, gestures, and inflections, producing what some scholars call the greatest biography ever written, *The Life of Samuel Johnson*. I would likewise try to capture

Dr. Corts in my journal entries, as if I could recreate him on the page, though I never would have dared expose my thoughts in a public forum.

But unlike the fiery and disheveled Johnson, famous for his raw outbursts and nervous tics, Dr. Corts was a study in Stoic self-control—rather reminiscent of Daddy. Of average height and build, he was dressed immaculately, and students used to say he must have slept in his tie. Legend has it he greeted students at the London Study Centre, in Kensington, London, at all hours of the night dressed in a suit.

Dr. Corts had studied classical rhetoric at Indiana University and had a sonorous voice. He spoke in measured cadences and a steady, unhurried tempo. Yet this was the same man who had grown up delivering newspapers before daybreak, painting houses, and washing hearses at the local funeral home. Unashamed of his upbringing as a Midwesterner raised in Ashtabula, Ohio, he encouraged me to claim my story and fashion my own identity.

Beginning as a freshman at Samford, and for the next seventeen years, I enjoyed a close relationship with Dr. Corts. He was my university president and ultimately my friend. Privately, he began to mentor me and helped me appreciate the nuances of language, along with the profundity of silence.

He taught me how small, day-by-day decisions add up to great consequences and that every thoughtful and educated decision I made about my life would eventually lead me to a clear and more satisfying understanding of my calling. He shared some of the thoughts that had captivated him as a young man, with the hope that I might discover the wonders he had. Quoting Isaiah 30:15, he advised me, "In quietness and in confidence shall be your strength."

I observed how he spoke as gracefully to secretaries and cleaning staff as to a chaired professor or a $30-million donor. Even as university president, Dr. Corts insisted that he didn't need a reserved parking space, and he believed that every Samford graduate—twelve hundred each spring—deserved the president's signature on their diplomas. He held firm to the belief that the *student* lay at the heart of education. He once wrote: "Watching students move into the dormitories, I found myself deeply touched by their long farewells—the hugs, the well-wishes, the reminders to phone home, the tears at the last driving away. It is a poignant scene that I have seen before, but it still moves me, even after thirty years' repetition."

I've always considered myself as Dr. Corts's adopted son.

Every year during winter break two Samford professors offered a two-week course in the humanities for twenty-five students at the university's satellite campus in London. Dr. Corts believed that such an educational opportunity abroad would not only stretch me intellectually but contribute to my cultural enlightenment. Aware of my straightened finances, he wrote a modest check to help me cover the trip during my junior year. When he found an article or poem that he thought I might like or benefit from, he sent it to me with a personal note attached. Although Samford was, and is, overwhelmingly white and upper middle class, Dr. Corts took great pains to make sure that I met influential African Americans to build my self-esteem and provide assurance that I could, like them, make a difference and succeed.

Dr. Corts introduced me to Stephen Carter, the prominent African American academic, and invited me to Sixth Avenue Baptist Church to meet its pastor, Dr. John Porter, former assistant pastor at Ebenezer Baptist Church, in Atlanta, under Martin Luther King Sr. When Odessa Woolfolk, founding director of the Birmingham Civil Rights Institute came to campus, Dr. Corts sent his administrative assistant to find me so I wouldn't miss the opportunity to talk with Ms. Woolfolk.

With Dr. Corts's encouragement, I ran for freshman class senator of the Student Government Association and won. All of a sudden, I found myself becoming increasingly interested in matters of governance. The next year I was elected president of the sophomore class, and in my senior year, I was elected president of the entire SGA—the first African American student to hold that position.

One of the happiest days of my life: receiving my Samford degree from Dr. Corts (c. 1996). Courtesy of Samford University

Dr. Corts's contributions were not limited to my academic or student government achievements. He knew of my love for the fine arts and poetry, so when he noticed my admiration for his fountain pen, an *objet d'art* I had never seen, he showed me how to fill up the inkwell with India ink, and then swept the pen effortlessly and gracefully over the page, demonstrating the varied calligraphic effects the pen could produce. As I watched, I vowed I would learn to write my name as impressively as he did.

Dr. Corts had a formality that often masked his deep affection for people. His wife, Marla, was far more outgoing. I became so comfortable with them that I often stopped by their house unannounced. After Dr. Corts passed, she invited me into her home to grieve with the family and gave me several of his personal items, including a limited press, six-volume edition of Boswell's *Life of Johnson*.

By my sophomore year, I had become at ease in my surroundings. Yet, so far from Madison Park, I was still learning how different the world was outside of my hometown. Birmingham was only six miles from Samford's campus and, with a population of one million, afforded me an opportunity to meet a much more diverse group of people.

One of my greatest friends and most important influences in Birmingham was local businessman and philanthropist Hal Abroms, whom I met during my sophomore year. We began having lunch twice a month. Until then, I had met but never known anyone who was Jewish. I knew little about the history of religion, and most of what I had learned was from my Sunday school classes, which lacked depth. The Southern Christian culture I grew up in often criticized Judaism as a pale forerunner of Christianity, and I had never thought to reexamine that criticism. Mr. Abroms's profound insights into human nature and Judaic faith began to reshape my understanding of my faith in relation to his. He introduced me to the work of Jewish theologian Abraham Joshua Heschel, a colleague of Christian theologian Reinhold Niebuhr. In reading about how strongly they supported one another's work, I realized that Judaism and Christianity are compatible after all.

But just as I was experiencing the excitement of urban diversity, I discovered just how unenlightened the world remained. With the naive anticipation of any undergrad, I decided to rush a fraternity and received a quick lesson in old-fashioned Southern racism.

Until my sophomore year, I felt neither excluded from anything at the school nor eager to belong to an exclusive club. I had been president of my freshman and sophomore classes and sufficiently filled my extracurricular dance-card with little time to spare. But close friends who had decided to go through rush convinced me to join them.

By the time I was a sophomore, though, many of my good friends had joined, and I wanted to do the same, setting my sights on one, in particular. I had rushed as a freshman, as part of my strategy to meet as many people as possible. But since I was simultaneously running for class president, I gave little thought to being rejected by any fraternity.

Growing up in Madison Park, I had been largely sequestered from the harsh realities of the world; everyone in my community was black, Madison Park was mostly self-sufficient, and my grandparents didn't speak much about the injustices that they had faced. But I hadn't handled racism well the few times I had encountered it. It was hard for me to comprehend how one person could be cruel to another based on the color of their skin or their gender.

Since Samford was a Christian school with no black Greek organizations—the university didn't have the minority population to support them—I assumed a good number of my close friends in the "white" fraternity of my choice would accept me. This time the stakes were higher because I had set my mind on one house. I was naive, because I didn't realize that the selection process in social fraternities was entirely subjective. I also had no plan for how I'd pay for fraternity membership. But I knew that I was every bit as impressive and credentialed as other rushees and saw myself as a strong candidate for Sigma Chi, especially since I had friends on the inside pulling for me.

It wasn't until a friend and fellow African American student, Leo, joined me for lunch one Sunday after church that I came to realize the serious roadblocks that lay ahead. Leo was active in the Black Student Union (BSU), and our friendship dated back to the first week of freshman classes. He was widely respected by all students and faculty and was known for being intellectually capable.

We had similar tastes and backgrounds, and unlike most minority students at Samford at that time, neither of us was on an athletic scholarship. We both were working hard to keep our academic scholarships. But we were of different minds on a number of issues. Though

I understood the sentiment and purpose behind the BSU's founding, I'd decided the year before not to join. The university was heavily committed to Christian values and thus to racial equality. I thought Samford's student body was too small to be racially segmented. Instead we all should be working toward a full integrative experience. I hoped to perpetuate and nurture community in the fullest, rather than in any narrow sense.

Leo appreciated my thinking, but he felt that I was unrealistically progressive and unable to appreciate the need of some black students to be part of "a more secure community." Over lunch that Sunday, we sequestered ourselves in a private corner of the cafeteria, and he poured out his feelings about my going through rush. He said that he was proud of me, the BSU was 100 percent behind me—in fact, many black students thought I was going through rush to make a statement, an idea that hadn't occurred to me. But he was concerned for me, because, if I were serious about joining a fraternity, I was bound to be hurt. No black had been offered a bid in Samford's 153-year history, and he knew of two instances in which blacks had rushed but had been rejected, primarily because of race. "I think you're great, and you're one of the most exceptional people I know," he said. "But don't forget you're black, because *they* haven't forgotten. Remember, we're still in Alabama."

His comments hurt me, though I tried to disguise the sting I felt. Lunch ended, we hugged, and though our eyes were filled with tears, I parted with my optimism intact and my mission undeterred.

As the weeks passed, I detected a chilliness from several members of Sigma Chi—although my friends there continued to encourage me. In retrospect, perhaps they were as naive as I was. But by the time the fraternity voted, I'd begun to think like Leo. I was discouraged and nervous as I waited for the call to let me know whether I was in or out. Some nights of my life have seemed to stretch on interminably, but that one registers as the longest ever. Finally, as I sat reading in my room, the phone rang. A low muffled voice said, "I like you, but the time has not come for a black to be in this fraternity. You need to know that."

I was too overwhelmed to answer and still can't imagine what I would have said. But there was no time. The caller had already hung up.

I sat, dumbfounded. For some reason, I remember all the details of that night, except what I was reading. The phone rang again, and I didn't answer. I was too emotionally charged and, to be truthful, too scared. When the phone rang a third time, I thought, "What would Daddy do?"

I picked up but said nothing. "Are you Eric?" a voice asked.

"Yes," I answered.

"My name is Jeff," he said in a pleasant but nervous voice.

He told me that he was an alumnus of Samford's Sigma Chis and that though we'd never met, he had heard a lot of good things about me through mutual friends. "I'd like to meet you one day," he said.

Then there was a long pause.

"I know this night was important to you," he said. "I couldn't vote, but I support you. You're great, and you don't need any group to validate that. You've already proved it."

And that was the last call I received that night.

The next morning, on a bright spring Alabama day, all of the fraternities lined the coliseum-like steps of the Davis Library for the ten o'clock "Call-Out," when each fraternity announced its new initiates. More than a thousand students had gathered on the lawn to watch. And whether or not it was true, it seemed that every black student at Samford was present. I woke up that morning feeling conflicted as to whether to attend, but in the end, I knew that regardless of the outcome, I needed to be present to face whatever the outcome was. I tried to hide in the crowd, but that proved impossible. Then I heard Sigma Chi shout, "Eric Motley."

I was stunned—and elated. Friends congratulated me and reached out to hug me. I'll never forget the joy on Thad Franklin's, Chris Corts's, and Russ Hovater's faces. Another friend, Brad Heifner, said, "I hope you know I've always considered you my brother"—a simple reminder that our ties were stronger than fraternal brotherhood. A week later when my pledge class elected me president, Leo was one of the first to congratulate me. We were too happy for tears. I was now—well almost—a Sigma Chi.

But not every happy ending is as happy as it seems.

Six years later I learned the background story, which, as much as the selection, forever changed my life. Leo proved to be a prophet. He had correctly sensed that at the time I rushed there were those at Samford—as there will always be everywhere—who needed to protect themselves from "the other," no matter how "the other" is defined.

According to the friend who told me the story behind my bid, eight members of Sigma Chi, having decided it would be best that I not become a Sigma Chi, sought to persuade the other members why I wouldn't make a good "brother": I was too nerdy, uptight, and aloof, and insufficiently clubby. Most important, I was black.

One evening, feeling confident that they had secured enough votes to blackball me, the eight men gathered in the fraternity house's den and started singing a crude, sophomoric song that one had set to the tune of "If you're happy and you know it, clap your hands."

Walking in unannounced and hearing the new lyrics, which included then N-word, Brad reprimanded them for their outrageous behavior. When the fraternity met two nights later to vote, the odds seemed heavily stacked against admitting me. But ten respected fraternity brothers, all seniors, stood tall and challenged the moral complacency of the other fifty members. They pressed their brothers to decide, "Whose side are you on?"

They bore the cost of their convictions.

They'd left an out-of-town basketball tournament to make it back to Samford to vote. A few of them received hostile calls from the Alabama state fraternity headquarters, and one, returning to his room in the Sigma Chi house, walked in to find his roommate's parents helping their son move out. That family could not have their son living with a "n–– lover."

Years later their son apologized to me, not realizing how much I already knew. Even more remarkably, his mother phoned me unexpectedly on the morning of President's Obama's first inauguration. The message she left on my voicemail acknowledged how far we had come, how much we had learned, and how proud she was of me. I have never erased that message.

I recently spoke with a friend, one of the seniors who defended me. He recalled that night with pride; it was one of the most important moments of his life. Until then, he had never stood up for anything that was so important to him or had challenged him to be true to his moral compass. Nothing, until that moment, had ever caused him to call his beliefs or his friendships into question. He said in that one moment, "I was willing to lose the whole fraternity for what I believed to be right."

Wrangling over fraternity membership is inconsequential in the larger scheme. But to me, any time an individual heeds the summons of conscience and takes a step forward, it's a landmark moment.

As Dr. Martin Luther King Jr. wrote in his Birmingham letter: "We will have to repent in this generation not merely for the vitriolic words and actions of the bad people, but for the appalling silence of the good people. We must come to see that human progress never rolls in on the wheels of inevitability."

Although the episode was searing at the time, I can't look back on it with total equanimity. I've never regretted my decision to pledge. My fraternity brothers came to see me as more than a token of a minority group. We became true brothers.

CHAPTER 23

THERE'S A PART FOR EVERY ONE OF US TO PLAY

In autumn of 1994, amid this year of life lessons, I was invited to represent my hometown church, Union Chapel Church, at a national Methodist youth rally being held at the Old Ship AME Zion Church in Montgomery. This one-time weekend gathering was intended to be a spiritual retreat, culminating in a beautiful service of praise and thanksgiving featuring the Right Reverend Cecil Bishop, the presiding bishop of the AME Zion Church.

The Right Reverend Bishop was one of the most intellectually inspiring black ministers I've known. In sermons that cited Tennyson, Saint Augustine, and the apostle Paul, he seamlessly combined theology and literature. Growing up, I could listen to him for hours whenever he would visit local parishes. He knew of my love for language and liturgy and always made an effort to speak to me about what I was reading.

But I had mixed feelings about attending the retreat. Friends and acquaintances from around the country would be there, and it would be one of my last opportunities to see them together. However, four months earlier I'd lost the election to become president of the National

Christian Youth Council, and I was plagued by embarrassment and frustration. I still felt that I should have beaten out the young woman who won. She could preach well, but I was the most qualified candidate. And she didn't seem to have a plan for where she wanted our organization to go.

Something else I couldn't articulate then troubled me even more. I perceived among my black Christian youth peers a lack of appreciation for my individuality. I'd never lost an election, mostly in predominantly white academic environments. So it was ironic that my black Christian contemporaries seemed to reject the same passion and dedication that were valued elsewhere. They seemed to favor rhetorical skills over organizational vision. But I put it behind me and made plans to come home from college to attend the weekend conference. It took no time for Aunt Prince Ella and Mama to ask to join me at the Sunday evening service.

The church was standing room only that night. Reverend Bishop delivered his homily, followed by a few rousing hymns sung by the combined choirs. Then the Reverend returned to the pulpit to make his closing remarks: "Instead of offering the closing prayer tonight, I'd like to ask a special friend of mine to come to the front of the church to offer our prayer," he began. "I've known Eric Motley since he was a boy on the other side of town in the little place of Madison Park. We met one summer when he was twelve, and I've kept my eyes on him all these years. While he has grown in mind and body and wisdom, he has also grown in the understanding of our Lord. He is now in college and like most of you has come here for this special conference. Eric, will you pray for us?"

Flabbergasted at what was happening, I made my way through the crowded aisle of Old Ship Church and found myself standing next to the Right Reverend Bishop at the great altar. I was shocked. I looked over the crowd of hundreds of people as I mounted the pulpit. Then I took a deep breath, and prayed:

"O Lord, Awaken us to this moment.
Frighten us from our hiding places
Lest we lose sight of you.
Awaken us to the awareness of who we are—
Help us to know ourselves more fully and wholly;
Help us to never forget from whence we have come;
And all those who have transported us.
Awaken within us the desire to know you,
To know your will, your way for our lives.
Help us to seek you in all that we do,
And to follow you more nearly as we leave this place tonight.
In your name we pray.
A-Men."

My grandmother recorded these words on the back of a funeral home fan and later transferred them verbatim to our family Bible.

As people departed, I heard goodbyes from all sides, when suddenly a small, dark-skinned woman seized my hands. "Your prayer was beautifully prayed," she said. "Who taught you to pray?"

Before I could answer, she continued, "You sounded like Reverend Thurman up there. Do you know who he is?"

My expression must have conveyed my ignorance, because she quickly added, "Rev. Howard Thurman was Martin Luther King's teacher at Boston University. He had a great influence on Dr. King."

Years later I realized what a compliment that was. I had never heard the name Howard Thurman until Mrs. Johnnie Carr stopped me. Since then his writings have greatly influenced my thinking and spirituality. I'd heard Mrs. Carr's name spoken admiringly by Daddy, who told me how she helped organize carpools during the Civil Rights boycott in Montgomery. She helped orchestrate the Monday-night mass meetings that Dr. King addressed, and encouraged her childhood friend, Rosa Parks, to take her magnificent stand when she refused to move to the back of the bus.

Mrs. Carr invited me to visit her in her Hall Street home the next time I returned home. When I did, I realized I sat with a legend. On one visit she spoke to me about sacrifice and playing my part. "We can't all be the drum major," she said, perhaps sensing my disappointment that my grandparents hadn't played a more prominent role in the Montgomery struggle for rights. "I could not preach like Reverend King, yet I did my part. Your grandfather wasn't a marcher or a public face, but the bus boycott succeeded because of people like him. He used his car to take people from Madison Park to work when they weren't riding the buses. Never forget that there's a part for everyone to play."

During my years at Samford, my mind stretched to increase its capacity and reach into subjects and fields I had never known. My faith, which had been based primarily on the heart rather than the head, was enriched and inspired by the example of people I admired. As I encountered new ways of interpreting Scripture, I began to ponder theology more deeply and call earlier beliefs into question. No ideas had a more significant impact on my intellectual, spiritual, and social attitudes than those of twentieth-century theologian Reinhold Niebuhr. I read his magnum opus, *The Nature and Destiny of Man*, in a philosophy of religion class my junior year. Niebuhr's observations on the human condition—with his emphasis on its social and political aspects—changed my way of thinking about my own moral obligations to society.

Niebuhr said: "Nothing that is worth doing can be accomplished in a lifetime; therefore we are saved by hope. Nothing that is good, true or beautiful makes complete sense in any immediate context of history; therefore we must be saved by faith. Nothing that we do, however virtuous, can be accomplished alone; therefore we are saved by love. No virtuous act is quite as virtuous from the standpoint of our friend or foe as it is from our standpoint; therefore we must be saved by the final form of love, which is forgiveness." To me, this simple yet profound statement spoke to the humility of the quest for enlightenment, and the limitation of our knowing.

That same year, I took a political philosophy class with Dr. William Collins, renowned as an eccentric but powerful lecturer who kept his classes spellbound with his encyclopedic knowledge and wide-ranging witty anecdotes. He required us to read *On the Nature of Things* by Lucretius, a first-century Roman poet and philosopher. Lucretius argues that everything in the universe is composed of tiny atoms moving about in an infinite void. His central idea about order in the universe, including our individual, atomistic role and responsibility in society, was mind expanding.

Hoping to clarify some incomprehensible passages, I knocked on Dr. Collins's office door one afternoon. He was preoccupied with his writing, and we wasted no time in getting to the text. As we sat in his office, an exhilarating sound seemed to pour from the speakers on his bookshelf. I asked him about the music. "Mr. Motley," he replied, without much more than a pause in our discussion, "you have been distracted by Bach's *Goldberg Variations*."

At that moment, two things happened to me: Lucretius started to make sense, and I experienced a musical epiphany.

Since then, "the Goldbergs"—and pianist Glenn Gould's playing of them—have become a prism through which my senses are reawakened. Whenever I hear them, I'm reminded that there remains an abiding sense of order and beauty in this often complex and confusing world.

When I'd entered Samford University's gates, I had sought only an undergraduate degree. I didn't think my love for ideas, history, music, and art would grow as they did. I had studied political theory and philosophy, and as I began to think about what would come after college I knew that I somehow wanted to play a part in helping the wider world move toward achieving justice. I was just beginning to understand that one person, in one lifetime, could wrap his mind around so many different facts and thoughts, and still have a capacity for only a minuscule fraction of the total. I'm reminded of a quotation from the Quran: "Why do you want to know what you do not know, when you do not know what you know?"

I didn't have to contemplate this riddle for long. During my junior year, I had taken Dr. Wilson's class on the history of the Vietnam War. He had served as an Air Force colonel in Vietnam and brought his wartime experiences to life, transporting us to the theater of war with its pain and agony on one side and humane acts on the other. Dr. Wilson, who had followed my progress at Samford and wanted to help me in any way he could, nominated me for the Rotary International Fellowship—an academic scholarship administered by the Rotary Foundation to encourage and support international study.

One day during the winter of my senior year I raced from my mailbox to Dr. Wilson's office to share the news that I'd been chosen to be a Rotary Ambassadorial Fellow. Then I went to see Dean Davis, Professor Epley, and President Corts before visiting the University Chapel to offer prayers of thanksgiving. I had so much to be thankful for. Once again, while wondering, "What next?" a way forward had been revealed. I had been invited to attend the University of St. Andrews in Scotland.

But as big an honor as this was, I was uncertain about what to do. Over the past few years my role in my grandparents' lives had expanded. As their only caretaker, I'd begun to help make more decisions about their health, investments, long-term care, and, from time to time, even how to fill in economic gaps. The ninety-five-mile distance between Samford and Madison Park had assured me that I could come home quickly in case of a family emergency.

If I went to St. Andrews that would no longer be true. It wasn't only a problem of distance. Accepting the fellowship created a financial strain. Affording college two hours from home had been daunting enough. Living abroad with only enough funds to cover my academic life seemed impossible. And I couldn't imagine a year without seeing my grandparents.

Then Mr. Pete Hanna stepped in. The owner of Hanna Steel and a former Samford football player, Mr. Hanna was a tough-but-fair-minded business man. An unembarrassed Christian and proud American, he had performed many kind acts for people, though few are known. During the height of civil rights tensions in 1960s Birmingham, he delighted in moving the ropes on segregated buses to allow more African Americans to claim seats. Many of his enraged fellow white citizens would have liked to either throttle him or have him arrested, but no one dared challenge him. An imposing figure he was also the son of a famously pugnacious U.S. Army General, "Crack" Hanna. Under his command federal troops had cleaned up the notoriously corrupt and crime-ridden town of Phenix City, Alabama, ten years earlier.

I had met Mr. Hanna during my sophomore year. Fundraising for the SGA, I'd reached out to him with no formal introduction, and he'd agreed to meet me in his office. When I arrived, I presented him with my proposal for "an intellectual renaissance" at his alma mater under the auspices of the SGA and asked him to help underwrite a $10,000 capital campaign by giving $1,000. To my surprise, he seemed amused. That wasn't the reaction I had expected.

It was an odd meeting in other ways too. He repeatedly asked me, "Hey, son, do you believe in Jesus?"

"Yes, sir, I do!" I responded each time.

Finally, in near-total exasperation, I asked him, "Sir, are you at all interested in supporting the academic program that the SGA is trying to start with your help?"

"Do you believe that God has a purpose for you?" came his non-answer.

"Yes, I do, sir, and I believe that part of that purpose is raising money for this program," I boldly replied. "All I need is a thousand dollars from you."

Throughout the meeting he had called his subordinates into the room to witness my unease, making me feel like the butt of a joke I didn't understand. Then he summoned his assistant and scribbled something on a piece of paper that he handed to her. Ten minutes later she returned with an envelope. "Consider your work done," he said, passing me the envelope. "You can go home now and take a nap. You've earned your pay. Open the envelope."

Not knowing what to expect, I followed his instructions and, to my amazement, discovered a check, not for $1,000 but for $25,000. I went to him behind his desk and shook his hand.

"I can't believe this!" I said.

Mr. Hanna took a long look at me and said, "Son, if you said that God has a purpose for you, then you should believe this."

That unusual initial meeting turned out to be the beginning of a wonderful friendship, unimaginable to me as I sat squirming in his office waiting for a straight answer to my plaintive request for help. Despite our extreme differences in background and temperament, Mr. Hanna took a liking to me and would help me out financially whenever he perceived I was in need. When he learned that I'd been elected president of the SGA, which required me to remain in Birmingham the summer before my senior year, he offered me a part-time internship at Hanna Steel headquarters in nearby Fairfield so I would have spending money.

One day, while I was sitting at my desk, Mr. Hanna's secretary phoned to ask if I'd like to fly with the boss in the company helicopter to Tuscaloosa, about fifty miles away, for a lunch meeting at the Hanna plant near the University of Alabama campus. It was my first helicopter ride, and sitting next to the pilot did nothing to settle my nerves. When we landed, a lanky, broad-shouldered, deeply tanned man greeted us. Mr. Hanna shook his hand and turned to introduce me.

"Coach, let me introduce you to my newest friend, Eric Motley, a student at Samford University, who's working for me this summer."

Before I could speak, the man replied, "Son, I've been hearing about you ever since Pete met you a year ago. Tell me about yourself."

Unable to identify this tall figure, I said, "Well, sir, it's a pleasure meeting you."

"Don't you know who you're talking to?" Mr. Hanna asked

incredulously. "This is Gene Stallings, coach of the Alabama Crimson Tide."

Not knowing what to say, I blundered, "Coach, glad to meet you." Later I found out he was the coach of the 1992 Alabama national championship team.

"Pete told me that you don't know anything about football. So what type of sports do you play?"

Mr. Hanna laughed. "Does it look like he plays any sports? He needs to protect his mind."

Six months after I met Coach Stallings, I received word about my Rotary fellowship. When Mr. Hanna heard the good news, he knew that the distance between Scotland and Alabama would present a financial dilemma for me. He insisted on covering my trans-Atlantic travel expenses, lifting an enormous burden. I could accept the scholarship and leave Alabama knowing that I could come back to visit Mama and Daddy.

But I was still anxious about who would take care of them if one should fall ill. "Uncle" William Winston, a long-time family friend, son of one of my cherished childhood tutors, Mrs. Frankie Lee Winston, and brother to my childhood hero Dr. John H. Winston, must have felt my aches from a distance. While I was at home visiting one weekend, Uncle William called and asked me to meet him at the Madison Park cemetery. "Oh, and Eric," he added, pausing for affect, "you should come by yourself."

It was an unlikely meeting place, even though I knew it well. We met on a warm March afternoon, and when I arrived he was walking the length of the graveyard. Beckoning me to join him, he said he'd learned I had received an important scholarship that would take me away for a while.

Before I could answer, he pointed across the cemetery and said, "There are a lot of people who are here, including my mama, Frankie Lee Winston, and my aunts Carrie Madison Seay and Emma Bell [Aunt Shine], who spent a lot of their time and love on you, because they believed in you. Their investment is paying off. Since you were a child, you've cared for the people of this community. I want you to know that my wife, Myrtis, my daughter-in-law, Karen, and I will take care of your grandparents when you leave."

I immediately felt relieved of my guilt. I knew I couldn't do right by my grandparents if I were in Scotland. Uncle William's promise also assured me that I wouldn't be alone even after their eventual deaths. With tears in his eyes he said, "I give you my word and my life. I'll take care of your grandparents, so don't you worry. You go and finish what we've all started in you."

Toward the end of my senior year I learned of an internship at the Carter Presidential Center in Atlanta, and at the urging of a university friend's mother, Mrs. Paula Hovater, and with her help, I applied. I got the internship and lived with the Hovater family on their farm just outside Atlanta. I commuted into the city every morning, alongside thousands of cars making their way to the 1996 Summer Olympics.

I never met President Carter one-on-one, but one afternoon, fresh from a meeting with a visiting head of state, he made his way down the main corridor to chat with us interns. We held this unpretentious former president, who dressed in penny-loafers, made his own coffee, and famously carried his own bag aboard aircraft, in great respect. His casual style, I quickly learned, was accompanied by an intense seriousness and dedication to the causes he valued.

Standing in the auditorium, without manuscript or notes, President Carter presented a list of world problems, such as untreated disease, tribal enmity, and rape and brutality, which he attributed to nonresponsive governments and citizens all over the world. His purpose was clear. "We do our best to meet these challenges here at the Carter Center, and we need help," he told us. Then he issued a challenge: "Unless you start thinking about these challenges now, working to find solutions, they will not go away; they will multiply."

We applauded thunderously as he departed. Not one of us moved. We sat in silence, as though the world's problems had just been transferred to our shoulders—as, in effect, they had been. The problems he had listed were urgent. I hadn't been willingly callous, but at twenty-three, my experience hadn't made me fully aware of the overwhelming magnitude of these problems. Working for the causes that he advocated gave me a new perspective on human rights and issues of social justice.

The Carter Center dealt with everything from election monitoring in the Third World to treatment of river blindness, malaria, and AIDS in Africa, to medical intervention in battle zones around the globe. By the end of the internship, I was acutely aware of the pain and injustice that were pervasive in our world and inspired to use my gifts to take on these problems.

CHAPTER 24

SCOTLAND

The only way to get to St. Andrews, Scotland, is to make it your destination. Over two days, in the fall of 1996, I flew from Birmingham, Alabama, to Atlanta, Atlanta to London, and London to Edinburgh. Ahead of me still lay a one-and-a-half-hour train ride, to Leuchars, and a twenty-minute car trip, from Leuchars to St. Andrews.

The road to St. Andrews winds up around the grassy hills of Strathkinness, a small village just three miles west of St. Andrews, with purple and browned heather stretching as far as the eye can see. Everywhere sheep were grazing on the lush greens, quaint cottages sat in picturesque surrounds, and gray stone walls meandered until they dissolved into the horizon. Beyond this was the encircling North Sea and its tributaries. I would have traveled this far for no other reason than to see its breathtaking beauty; the vistas that I encountered that day were the most wonderful sights I had ever seen.

Just as I reached the highest point on the country road, where nothing else could be seen but the sky, there in the distant air, almost afloat in the clouds, was the town of St. Andrews. The square tower and pointed spires of the ruins of the old cathedral—surviving tokens of medieval learning—stretched like a painting on a canvas of blue sea.

The long white beaches where the movie *Chariots of Fire* was filmed pulled me into the scene. Even the residence hall for postgraduate students, Deans Court, which dates back to the mid-1500s, seemed etched into the landscape, standing as a witness to time and fortitude against the great winds of the North Sea.

I felt, even at first sight, the steadfastness of the community, where the ageless joy of learning in a remarkable atmosphere had ruled supreme for almost six centuries. A former principal of the university used to say that it's not easy being Scotland's first university and the third oldest in the United Kingdom. "But being first is not enough; St. Andrews has to be foremost."

A woman with red hair and smiling eyes greeted me at the Leuchars rail station. Barbara Sibbett, a transplant from Northern Ireland, with her husband, Professor Wilson Sibbett, had volunteered to be my official Rotary International host family. Their job wasn't to put me up but to help me acclimate.

During the drive to St. Andrews, I could barely understand Barbara— she had a pronounced Irish accent that she spoke at a rapid-fire tempo. She could have been reciting Gaelic poetry for all I could tell. To compound my anxiety, I learned that Professor Sibbett was head of physics at the university, no light task, as St. Andrews has one of the leading physics programs in the world. He is one of the world's top laser experts—a likely candidate for the Nobel Prize. Didn't Rotary understand that I was a man of letters who'd intentionally avoided all advanced math and physics? What would this man think of my scientific shortcomings?

I'd traveled before but never this far from Madison Park and never with the intention of staying away for such an extended period. Now I was on the other side of the world for a year, without friends or mentors except this family. How would these light-skinned northern

Europeans, who lived on the promontory of the North Sea, relate to a dark-skinned African American from the rural South? I was a full-time student without employment plans or prospects. What about the food? I dreaded the prospect of being served haggis—a spiced pudding containing sheep's heart, liver, lungs, and oatmeal, all traditionally encased in sheep's stomach—instead of the creamed corn, collard greens, barbecue, and pecan pie I'd eaten all my life.

Greater than all of the other concerns put together, though, was the fear that my intellectual capacity wouldn't rise to the challenge. I'd graduated from Samford, the largest private university in Alabama, but in Europe that distinction might seem as irrelevant as saying that Moe is the most intelligent Stooge.

I soon realized that my worries were needless. The Sibbetts and their daughters, Ruth, Hannah, and Rachel, embraced me for who I was. Every time Barbara saw me, including the first, she wrapped me in an Irish bear hug and said, "Oh, Eric, it's so good to see you. So happy you're here. You're just going to love it." As time went by that became, "You're just loving it here, aren't you?" Her warmth equaled anything I'd experienced in Madison Park.

I began to fall in love with the place. But my time at St. Andrews would be brief. The Rotary Ambassadorial Scholarship was one year—just enough time to earn a master's degree in international relations, if I worked long hours.

St. Andrews, the town founded by royal and papal decree, and Madison Park, the town founded by emancipated American slaves, have both survived because of commonly shared values grounded in faith and a spirit of shared responsibility. Every day, these Scots reminded me of the importance of community, which evoked my own hometown four thousand miles away.

Unlike Madison Park there were only about a dozen black people in St. Andrews, counting the Africans and Islanders, so I stood out. But my uniquely American style—quick stride, gregarious engagement of strangers, and relentless can-do attitude—distinguished me more than my skin color. I enjoyed being Eric Motley; but even though I became instantly recognizable among the locals, the same wasn't necessarily true of visitors.

One day, just as I was returning from a long walk on the beach, wearing a fleece jacket and baseball cap, I ran into a group of Japanese tourists getting off a bus. They started screaming, "Look, it's Tiger Woods!" and then, "Tiger! Tiger!"

I turned to look, only to realize that, yet again, I'd been mistaken for the famed golfer, a frequent visitor and competitor in the British Open held at St. Andrews Old Course, the world's oldest golf course, located just under a mile from the university. If only they knew that of all the people here I probably knew the least about golf.

During my time there I met eccentric scholars and townspeople, including one who made pâté from the livers of dead, washed-up seals, and served it, along with roadkill (the classy kind, like pheasant) at formal dinners. One student in his sixties, whose father had invented the turbojet, ate meals every day in my residence hall and collected academic degrees as others collected classic cars. He'd already earned ten, in fields ranging from dentistry to metaphysics to Mandarin Chinese. Among this assortment of geniuses, eccentrics, royals, and rascals, I played croquet, sipped afternoon tea in their drawing rooms, and enjoyed their hospitality at elaborate dinner parties.

I first met Mrs. Anne Tynte-Irvine as we both stood at the local stationery shop perusing the greeting card selection. Her properness reminded me of Aunt Prince Ella. Her house, at number 54 South

Street, furnished with antique treasures and curiosities, was one of the town's oldest continuously inhabited dwellings. It seemed that everything in St. Andrews was rare and older than those who possessed them. I was often invited to a five-course meal on Sundays in the Tynte-Irvines' second-floor dining room, where the candlesticks dated from the 1600s, the plates from the 1800s, and the wine from the ancient cellar. "Nothing belongs to us," Mrs. Tynte-Irvine would say in her rarefied English-Scottish accent that indicated a bygone elegance and nobility. "We're only caretakers of what is."

Mrs. Tynte-Irvine cheered me on at all the significant events during my time at St. Andrews—talks I gave, parties I threw, and dinners hosted in my honor for my contribution to "town-and-gown" relations. When her husband died, she asked me to ride with her and her son to the service and burial. She's probably the only person, other than my advisor, to have read my dissertation word-for-word—and I'm not sure my advisor read it as thoroughly. All these years later, I stay with her on my return trips to Scotland, and it fills me with pride when I spot my photograph on the mantel alongside those of her family. She possessed a love of history and never missed an opportunity to provide historical and cultural context on all things St. Andrews and Scottish. But she was equally fascinated to learn about the place I'd come from and the characters that had been formative in my development. With the same zeal, I was always eager to share with her reports from home, issued by Mama, about all of Madison Park's happenings. With time, Mrs. Tynte-Irvine became just as familiar with Madison Park as I became with St. Andrews.

Another widow, Mrs. Kathleen Noble, and I met at a town-and-gown poetry reading, where she stood and recited "The Lake Isle of Innisfree" by William Butler Yeats. Mrs. Noble's recitation was so eloquent and emotive it reminded me of the words of Reverend Washington, my childhood minister, who'd say, "Sometimes, the heard word is better than the read word."

I approached her after she finished and said, "You just recited one of my favorite poems."

"I know," she said. "I could see it in your eyes. Is your name Eric? I live across the street from Anne Tynte-Irvine, and I asked her, 'Who is the tall, handsome young man who comes and goes from your place once a week?' I always notice your upright walk."

"I've also noticed you," I told her. "Please pardon me for saying this, but you remind me of my grandmother in so many ways."

Her floral print dresses, tam, pearls and matching earrings, and, mostly, her hurried pace were familiar. Upon her death, I discovered that she was born in 1920, the same year as Mama.

"What's her name, and where does she live?" she asked.

"Alabama," I said.

"So far away from her. I guess I'll now have to become your Scottish grandmother."

She did.

At our weekly lunches at her home we read poetry to each other and discussed British history. But our relationship was not centered purely around academics. I confided in her my attraction to various St. Andrews women, and over each meal our prayed grace would include a petition that God would assist me in finding the "right one." Like my grandparents, I'd always kept matters of the heart private, but her persistent questioning drew the information from me. "Have you seen Yasmina today?" she'd ask. "When will you ever ask out Pascale? I think you've chosen the best. You must act soon. Let's pray about it." She had them all over for soup and did her best to help win them over for me. My friends came to embrace her almost as much as I did, and on several occasions she would join us all out for dinner.

At the same time that I was forming indelible relationships with the townspeople of St. Andrews, I was fortunate enough to develop equally rewarding relationships with my classmates and members of the faculty and staff at the university. Sir Kenneth Dover was a unique soul whose attitude and intellect had a profound effect on my view of "knowledge." Sir Kenneth had retired to St. Andrews from Oxford University where he'd been president of Corpus Christi College. Modest and a bit disheveled, he was one of the world's preeminent Greek scholars. He'd written commentaries on Plato and translated countless texts, notably *The Frogs* by Aristophanes. He also bore the distinction of having written the seminal work on Greek homosexuality that is still widely used by scholars today who seek to understand the ancient world.

He was polite and courtly but never stood on ceremony. In his mind and manner, he lived in ancient Greece. His way was the Greek Way—his attitude and philosophy of life and his traditional values of duty and civility were of a bygone era. What impressed me most about Sir Kenneth was his ever-present sense of humility. He understood that brilliance does not have to be pre-announced, and certainly not self-announced. His genius resided quietly, gently, and unassumingly—a rare attribute. We became such close friends that I organized his eightieth birthday celebration. Asked for remarks at the end of the evening, the great, titled scholar said, "A friend once told me she thought I always solved my problems. On the contrary," he added, "a number of unanswerable problems had remained vexing, unable to be answered." He identified five such problems:

"In Herodotus [485–425 BC], wherever two epsilons are brought

223

together by inflection, which happens often, they are written separately: $\varepsilon\,\varepsilon$. Yet in the Ionic dialect—and Herodotus wrote in Ionic—they are contracted into a single ε. Who first unconstructed it, and why was it done? If we knew the answer, we would learn something about classical Greek attitudes to literature."

He went on. "Problem number two, is there a Hell? Three, how did my mother make her short-crust pastry always turn out perfect? Four, is free will always an illusion? And five, what was going on in philosopher and writer Roger Scruton's head when he spoke of the 'unctuous narcissism of Cesar Franck's piano quintet'?"

CHAPTER 25

THE LIMITS OF KNOWLEDGE, THE UNLIMITED NATURE OF FRIENDSHIP

I met Professor Struther Arnott, C.B.E., Ph.D., Sc.D., D.Sc., L.L.D., F.K.C., F.R.S.E., F.R.S., principal at the University of St. Andrews, at an informal gathering not long after I arrived in Scotland. The long trail of abbreviated titles after his name makes clear that he was no ordinary chap. Along with his many academic degrees and accomplishments, he had the fortunate timing of being a graduate student in the labs of Dr. Maurice Wilkins, the molecular biologist who shared the Nobel Prize in 1962 with Watson and Crick for their famous experiments with DNA. Dignified and respectful of ceremony, he was the perfect person to lead the university. He was also right for the time. At no sacrifice to scholarship, he was the first to manage the university like a business, with a focus on results.

Professor Arnott, whom I called "the Principal," played a role in my life at St. Andrews and beyond similar to that of Dr. Corts. Both were meticulous and displayed a rich command of the English language. In other ways, they couldn't have been more different. Dr. Corts was of above-average height, trim and angular, while the Principal was short and squat, with a ruddy complexion.

Each one shaped me in a distinctive fashion. Dr. Corts was concerned with my spiritual and intellectual development, while the Principal had little interest in matters beyond the temporal. Dr. Corts frequently engaged my attention in poetry or history, but for the Principal, scientific reason and logic transcended all else.

He was brilliant, erudite, and possessed a transcendent awareness of life. Space absorbed him; with just the two of us in a room talking, he'd often look into the middle distance, as if birthing an unrelated thought. Never one for small talk, he'd extract himself from a conversation as soon as he became bored.

I'm sure the awe I felt for the Principal created a distance between us. His wife, Greta, and I were more informal friends. The Principal must have known from our first meeting that his wife and I were kindred spirits. We shared an interest in music, art, and literature and a love for nature. A voracious reader, she often amazed me at afternoon tea when she talked about her recent readings—William Boyd, Thucydides, Dante, Boswell, Wordsworth, Hopkins, Shakespeare, Vikram Seth, Walker Percy, Henry James, and she even made time to read chapters of my dissertation so as to fully engage and challenge my own thinking, which I found to be immensely valuable. Greta spoke with a grammatical correctness that was eloquent and poetic—managing never to be pedantic. Gaiety filled her eyes. She possessed a robust appetite for life; everything was to be explored and experienced. The vastness of her appreciations opened my eyes to new wonders.

The Arnotts: An evening of Shakespeare at Stratford-upon-Avon
with Struther and Greta Arnott (c. 1997).
The collection of Eric L. Motley

After Sunday lunches the Principal and I often strolled through the mansion's gardens to talk about life, all of its beautiful ideas, and the wonders of nature. Emerson once said of Thoreau, "It was like a pleasure and a privilege to walk with him . . . because he knew the country like a fox or bird."

The Principal offered observations about everything we came upon, making visible so much that ordinarily went unnoticed: "Still yourself, there's a red-breasted thrasher resting on the lower branch of the cherry tree," he'd say, pulling me into his observation.

He also asked questions that drew me out: "Do you know this flower? It dates back to the Greeks." Then he'd explain the importance of classical symmetry in Europe's great gardens.

My interest in botany was rekindled. I felt the same warmth I'd felt as a child when, working alongside Mama in her flower garden, she would name various species of flowers and have me record them in my flower book.

One day after a long walk in the garden, five months before my Rotary year was up, he invited me to stay for a cup of tea in the sun-house. He must have felt my anxiety about next steps beyond St. Andrews.

"So, you will have become a master of knowledge, of sorts, during your one long year here at St. Andrews, which seems all too short. What are you thinking, Eric Motley? What's next? I assume you're still feeling rather incomplete?"

When I didn't respond immediately, he urged me on.

"Well?"

"Education has always been my enduring aspiration," I replied, "and I've come to enjoy the pursuit. I hadn't anticipated how much my appetite for learning would grow—the more my curiosity is fed, the more it seems to demand."

He listened, nodding and waiting for me to explain myself. I hesitated, taking a deep breath. It wasn't easy for me to acknowledge my future goals; they were filled with fear of the unknown.

At Samford and St. Andrews, I was beginning to learn something of the magnitude of what I didn't know—perhaps the truest measure of education. I wasn't taught what to think, but rather, how—how to ask questions, how to reject assumptions, how to seek knowledge—in short, how to exercise reason.

While learning the limits of "knowing," I'd also begun to acknowledge to myself that the only way I could continue to grow intellectually was to examine opinions, attack prejudices, and apply reason. For the first time, as I sat at seminar tables with classmates from around the world, I began to reconsider many of my long-held but little-examined opinions of American foreign policy and the implications of power politics on justice.

One professor who had a strong influence on my intellectual development was Nicholas Rengger, who taught political theory and international relations. Although his lectures primarily dealt with the history of intellectual thought, he ranged broadly over his scholarly concerns. It was in one of his seminar courses that I began to question the ways the United States unilaterally projected its military power around the world. Up until that point, I had possessed a rather simplistic, naive, and moralistic view of realpolitik.

I had studied the American theologian Reinhold Niebuhr at Samford, but it was only under Rengger's tutelage that I fully appreciated Niebuhr's critique of moral complacency relative to my own country. In his application of Christian philosophy to the realm of politics, Niebuhr brought into greater focus the contradiction that exists between the personal ideals, which govern our conduct as individuals, and the political realities, which dictate our national foreign policies. In unanticipated ways, my own ethical beliefs, intellectually speaking, came into greater focus as I became better able to comprehend how my faith should inform my political and social philosophy. I increasingly became aware that Madison Park had transported me to new places and different experiences, no more valuable than previous ones, however more expansive in the range of intellectual pursuits that they afforded me. I had progressively moved beyond the pragmatism of learning—so often dictated by the necessity and demands to read, write, and demonstrate proficiency in exams—to a more persistent and deliberate quest to acquire knowledge as an end in itself and to understand ideas in their fullest context.

I didn't say all this to the Principal sitting in the sun-house. I merely said, "I've decided a master's degree isn't enough. I'd like to pursue more graduate study, maybe even a Ph.D., when I return to the States."

Pouring more tea, he leaned forward, "You don't have much time to decide, so it's best that you start thinking *now*."

It was a gentle reprimand. He didn't know that it was the issue preoccupying me most. His look was disconcerting and yet quite revealing of his disappointment. "You have been poor; you are poor, and in an education lies your prospect of wealth. Do not return to America as a freeloader, expecting a place at the table because you think it owed to you. Expect a place, because you deserve it and have the credentials to verify that you deserve it. Get your Ph.D., and get it at a reputable university. Get it here at the University of St. Andrews, and no one will question you."

For a moment I felt as if I were back in high school, and Aunt Shine were admonishing me to take advantage of every available opportunity. But I was pleased that the Principal thought highly enough of me to keep me at St. Andrews.

Weeks later, when Dr. and Mrs. Corts paid me a visit, while they were in the U.K., the Arnotts hosted the Cortses at lunch, and the Principal asked Dr. Corts to speak to me about staying on for a Ph.D. I didn't need much persuading. I applied to pursue a Ph.D. in international relations, starting that autumn. I was selected for a scholarship, which generously covered the cost of tuition, room, and board.

Professor Rengger became my doctoral supervisor as I sought to explore the ongoing relevance of Niebuhrian thought to contemporary world politics. At issue was whether Niebuhr's brand of political realism, which was rooted in Christian faith and just war theory, could function as the basis of foreign policy in a world where the perennial existential struggle is not one between opposing economic systems, as during the Cold War, but one where environmental degradation, economic contagion risk due to globalization, and the security threats posed by terrorist organizations and other transnational non-state actors, pose an ever-present risk to global stability. Given that Niebuhr's political philosophy was rooted in the Western, Judeo-Christian tradition, how relevant was his thesis in a world where conflict was increasingly defined along religious and civilizational lines, where our foes do not share our values, despite how fervently we assert their universality. As we entered into a new age in global interaction, with the emergence of new power centers and fault lines, which aspects, if any, of traditional paradigms could we depend on as we forged into the fast-approaching unknown. While I found these questions to be daunting at times, I was grateful for Professor Rengger's guidance during my knowledge quest.

Professor Rengger would invite me for a drink at Ma Bell's, a popular pub in St. Andrews, often to talk about Niebuhr. While I drank ginger ale, he would down a half-dozen—or more—Johnny Walker Scotches, never losing clarity of thought. He'd ask questions and expect answers from me. The best doctoral theses, in his opinion, were written by passionate people searching for answers to difficult, probing questions, such as "Can Jamesian pragmatism coexist with Niebuhr's existential idealism? Can the ethical claims of love and justice be reconciled?" All of this and more poured from his lips, which all the time were busy making way for more Johnny Walker.

As the months and then years went by, there was no shortage of intellectual experiences at St. Andrews that challenged me and expanded my universe of thought. I belonged to study groups, reading clubs, and helped to found the St. Andrews Symposium, which was an interdisciplinary forum that monthly presented a speaker and open discussion, with over two hundred students in regular attendance. I developed relationships with countless scholars and academicians who treated me to great discussions as well as extended opportunities to audit their lectures and seminars.

In the autumn and winter months, when the sun goes down at 4:00 p.m., and there seems little to do outdoors, the collective desire is to bring as many people together as can fit around one table for dinner. On any given night in St. Andrews, there are probably hundreds of dinner parties, organized by students, marked by fun, meeting new acquaintances, eating delicious food, and participating in the most outlandish debates.

At times, I had to look in the mirror to make sure that I was still little Eric Motley, Madison Park's D.U.K. When I look back at all the social and cultural opportunities that were presented to me, a few come to mind that really stand out all these years later. At the top of the list, I was invited to attend a garden party hosted by the Queen of England, placing me in the company of regal finery, millinery, and morning coats—all eye-opening, though not unfamiliar since the women of Madison Park were quick, on invitation, to dress in their finest, especially the queenly Aunt Prince Ella, who'd always worn round-brimmed hats, white gloves, and dresses below her knees.

On another occasion, a birthday celebration in honor of a European friend, I received a handwritten invitation, the lower right hand corner of which read: "Dress: White-tie; Medals, Ribbons, Family Decorations Optional." I remember thinking, thank God they're optional, or I'd have to wear curtain tassels. Other students with ordinary names like

Motley were invited, but many had names accompanied by a storied history, such as Hapsburg, Ogilvy (cousins to the queen), and Tolstoy.

One friend had taken up writing, continuing the legacy of his grandfather, Ian Fleming. Another friend's father was the Lord Chamberlain to Her Majesty the Queen. And then there was the friend whose father brought all eight wives to our graduation, each dressed in native costume and following him about on the Lower College greens, drinking champagne from fluted glasses. I learned later that the friend's father was a dictator from a country I decline to name.

What these experiences reaffirmed was the lesson, taught to me long ago, that each of us, if we are true to ourselves, bring a richness and expansiveness to our relationships with others. Whenever I look back, I can appreciate that what sustained me, amidst all the swift transitions of my life, was the ever-present attitude that everything in life is a gift of grace and that no one, no matter how capable he or she is or what their lineage might be, is more important than another.

The vibrancy and variety of the St. Andrews community ensured that I never had a shortage of friends. And even though we came from radically different backgrounds, my St. Andrews' friends came to mean as much to me as those back home. Scott Kerr, one of the three other Rotary Scholars, arrived at the same time I did. He had an exceptional intellect and a similar curiosity to mine; and he wasn't ashamed to attend church every Sunday. We'd often take long walks and share our spiritual uncertainties and challenges of faith.

Scott and I and the two other Rotarian Scholars, Blain and Juliette, along with our American sidekick Margaret, were inseparable. We studied together, hung out together on weekends, and in a very real sense became as family to one another. Years later, I would participate in the wedding of Scott and Juliette.

The American Rotary International Ambassadorial Scholars,
in Dean's Court, at the University of St. Andrews. Left to right:
Bill Cuthill (St. Andrews Rotary Club President), Scott Kerr,
Juliette Kerr (née Rose), Blaine Kytle (née Roberts)
Photo by Peter Adamson

Ryan Webster arrived about the same time that Scott completed his one-year Rotary fellowship and returned home. Ryan was from Oregon but didn't fit the granola-eating, lumberjack stereotype of the Pacific Northwest. We had many things in common, including a fascination with British humor and traditions. Ryan was even more particular and orderly than I was. He had a keen mind and a big heart, which immediately attracted me to him. But he was also a highly competitive collector of books.

I had established myself among friends and St. Andrews' booksellers as a serious collector of rare and antiquarian books. Behind the register of any local bookstore was a shelf labeled "Eric Motley's Books." I'd developed such an intimate relationship with booksellers that if I couldn't afford a particular volume, they would hold it for me, sometimes for months. I was primarily in the business of acquiring poetry, English literature, and fine decorative bindings. What little money I had to use for collecting came from a small portion of my scholarship's monthly stipend, earmarked for buying academic textbooks, which I allowed for buying "other" books.

Then Ryan unexpectedly arrived with, seemingly, a pocket full of gold (or perhaps it was his life's savings). Before too long he had his own shelf in every secondhand and rare bookshop in town. Mrs. Anderson of Bouquiniste Books would warmly greet me and say, "We just got a good load of fine books last night from an ancient estate in Aberdeen, but Ryan has already been in this morning and picked through the lot." I often would just stand in amazement, very consciously attempting to restrain from any outward expression of my exasperation with this "book thief." I decided that two friends couldn't win at this game. We needed to compare notes and better define our collecting interests so we wouldn't always be competing for the same few treasures. I do not recollect our strategy as such, but I do recollect us having a very long discussion about working together, which meant a lot of compromising.

On weekends, Ryan and I took to the Scottish roads, wherever they led us. And once a week we met over tea to talk about the books we had found and the girls we planned to ask out. In good times, we cheered each other on, and in my low moments, I could count on Ryan to find a literary verse or passage from the Bible to remind me to be of good cheer. He became like a brother to me. I was sad to see him go upon his graduation.

William Cates "Turner" Herbert arrived in St. Andrews from North Carolina in 1998, at the start of my third year. He lived in one of the nicest suites in Deans Court. His mahogany-paneled room with a fireplace and view onto the courtyard was perfect for our cigar conversations, where he smoked and I sat next to the window to breathe. Turner had an intriguing air with his brown curly hair and narrow face; he dressed in fashionable bowties on Sundays and tailored elbow-patched tweeds. He was a man of impeccable taste whose wit and sarcasm equaled those of any Brit.

We became instant friends. We would attend lectures and go out to dinner or parties together. We would have long, heated, intellectual debates about ideas that had influenced our scholarship. Once we took a five-hour hike through the Lowlands north of Crail, a fishing village. "Hey, I am sinking," I cried, as I was nearly sucked in by the marshy earth.

"No, you've sunk!" he called out.

I could tune him out when I felt the need to ignore his admonitions, but he also had an artful but obvious way of tuning me out when I decided to take an intellectual sidetrack that would go on too long. "Hey, hey," he'd say, "I'm lost! Get me back to the point you think you're trying to make."

Turner was always a calm, courteous Southern scholar, no matter the debate. His eclectic knowledge of the world included a love of Motown music. One day, he called me to his room and said, "Eric, sit down and let me first of all explain who Marvin Gaye is," another assumption that Turner had made about my limited knowledge of all things modern. (He was right.) "I've made you a cassette of some of his best music. If you happen to get a girl back to your room one night, do *not* play that classical stuff that you always have on. Reach over and put this cassette on and let Marvin Gaye create the mood." In light of the demands of my academics and my incessant and single-minded desire to complete my Ph.D., there were admittedly few opportunities to put Turner's advice to use.

My closest friend at St. Andrews was Bahbak Miremadi. We met at a dinner party hosted by the locally famous and beautiful Emma Mills. With her four stunning roommates, Emma's flat had the parties everyone wanted to be invited to. That night at dinner, I was sitting so close to Emma I could hardly think. I was too shy to talk to her, much less confess my deepest feelings, which would seem preposterous since I'd met her only twice. Bahbak was sitting on my other side. During dinner, he leaned over and whispered, "She'll only know if you tell her."

Neither of us knew that Emma already had a boyfriend until later in the evening when one of the guests walked by and kissed her.

"Don't despair, dear Eric, there are others to be found, and I'll help you," Bahbak said. For the rest of the night we talked and laughed and became instant friends.

Tall and angular with fine features, Bahbak was comical, amiable, and engaging. His father was born in Iran and his mother in Ireland, and he grew up with both Islam and Christianity. He was educated in one of the best Anglican preparatory schools in England, so culturally he was as English as Prince Charles. By nature, we were both remarkably shy, despite outward appearances, which may be what initially drew us together.

When we met, I was at a critical point in my academic career. I'd just begun my Ph.D. studies with little understanding of what they would entail or any idea of what I wanted to do afterward. The expectations that my mentors, teachers, friends, and I had set weighed heavily on me.

Bahbak too was at a critical point, deciding whether he wanted to continue pursuing medicine or if he could still reverse course. We were both trying to make sense of who we were, what we believed, and what we wanted from life.

For the next three years we remained best friends. He knew me as well as I knew myself. He was sensitive to my opinions, while challenging me to see alternative points of view. When we argued, the conflict was never mindless and only deepened our friendship.

Intellectually we both possessed broad, catholic interests in literature, nature, and art. Spiritually, we both valued silence, reflection, and a constant reexamination of our beliefs. Bahbak often reminded me, "Eric, you shouldn't be judgmental. I see where you're coming from, and I know you're not judging, but you need to come across more sympathetic and understanding." He was always correct in his reproach. We both wanted to live good and worthy lives, and we kept each other on course. We frequently discussed relationships and the type of woman we hoped to marry; neither of us wanted to pursue a good and worthy life alone. I had traveled halfway around the world to meet myself in the embodiment of Bahbak, who was so much like me but at the same time so different. Two decades later, after so much life has passed, we still marvel at the invaluable friendship formed at Emma's dinner table.

CHAPTER 26

"STOPPING BY WOODS ON A SNOWY EVENING"

Hundreds of letters tell the story and remind me of my years away from home. Although long-distance calls were expensive, Mama and I would speak on the phone once a week and exchange letters at least two times a month. Neighbors and friends from Madison Park would send me cards, church bulletins, and newspaper clippings to update me on life back home and to remind me of their love, affection, and admiration. Once a year, the church would send me a "love offering" of fifty dollars. So far away from home and yet so close, Madison Park was with me even on the other side of the pond.

Twice a year, due to the generosity of Pete Hanna, I flew home to spend a brief holiday with my grandparents. I designated two weeks at Christmas and two in June to check on Mama and Daddy. My homecoming, with its accompanying prayers, preparation, baking, and cleaning, had become a loving ritual in our lives. Mama would iron lavender into my bed linen, put fresh flowers in my bedroom, and fill bowls in the dining room and living room with fresh fruit. Aunt Prince Ella would bake three dozen of her famous teacakes.

I could anticipate a flurry of phone calls and visits to 34 Motley Drive from longtime friends. Mrs. Winston, my former Sunday school teacher, expected me to teach her class, and Reverend Washington, the pastor of Union Chapel Church, called on me during morning worship to give the congregation an update on my life. Then the church would pray for me. I would leave feeling that my original foundation was still intact. I never returned home feeling like I could not be myself, but at the same time, I was very much aware that many things I had experienced over the course of my journey were beyond the comprehension of many of my childhood friends and neighbors. Daddy had taught me an important lesson; talk less about yourself and what you're experiencing, and make a deliberate effort to ask people about themselves, their family, and what life is teaching them.

My visit in December 1997 didn't seem particularly different from the others, and yet the moments I spent with Daddy left me concerned. Although his green-hazel, cataract-ridden eyes still sparkled, age was showing—his bad heart had slowed him, and he was less mobile. The last weekend he allowed me to drive him around Madison Park as we used to when I was a boy and he was the driver, except this time we left Mama at home. She wanted to come, but I sensed that we needed to be alone. We toured Motley Drive, Fuller's Road, Jack Drive, Salery Court, Todd Road, and even crossed the bridge and ventured down the hill to Daggerhole. As we silently observed the place that we call home, we didn't need language to communicate our feelings. He asked me to give him a shave that Sunday morning, and even though he was not intending to go to church, he asked if I would shine his shoes, his Sunday shoes. In that moment I was reminded of Wordsworth's idea that "the Child is father of the Man." These were two constant and personal acts that Daddy would perform every Saturday afternoon; in asking me to perform them for him, we closed the circle of life, if you will, and I was now in a position to care for him as he had always done for me.

That afternoon, quiet as usual, he was also more intimate, holding my hand as we sat in our rockers on the back porch, willing time to stand still. I told him about my life, realizing with some guilt that nothing had changed in his. I made sure to say, "I'm doing all the things I'm doing because of the sacrifices you and Mama made for me."

The Motley Trio: My last Christmas with Daddy. Little did I know it would be the last photo the three of us would ever take—four months later, Daddy climbed up the old sycamore tree (December 1996).
The collection of Eric L. Motley

Three weeks after I left, Daddy fell in the bathtub and was hospitalized with a broken hip. He had never broken a bone in his body before. Now frail and weak at the age of eighty-two, his recovery proved all the more difficult. With daily reports, I was under the impression that he was healing slowly, and perhaps, deep down inside, I was more optimistic than realistic. Later that April, I made a surprise visit home to see him in the hospital. I had been told that his recovery was not only slow, but required more attention than Mama could provide alone, so the hospital made allowances for a more extended stay. The reality of the precariousness of the situation was only now beginning to dawn on me.

I had two primary tasks: to visit and love him and to make preparations for his long-term care beyond the hospital. I also intended to take care of a couple of other matters that I kept to myself. I met with the doctors to develop a plan in case Daddy died in the hospital, wanting the assurance that protocol could be bent and that I could be contacted first, instead of Mama. I didn't want her to be by herself when she received the news. Next I visited Ross-Clayton Funeral Home, the African American funeral directors who had buried almost everyone in Madison Park for the last hundred years. If something should happen, I wanted to devote myself to Mama's emotional care and not to last-minute preparations. I chose a cemetery lot next to Daddy's mother, Mrs. Minnie Motley. In going through these motions, I realized that in some respects, I had been preparing for this moment for most of my life. While having to make arrangement for Daddy's final rites was by no means easy, the desire to not burden Mama with such considerations steeled my nerves.

The morning before I left for Scotland I visited Daddy in the hospital one more time. I entered his suite in the intensive critical care unit, where there were four other patients, to spend my allocated fifteen minutes with him in conversation and prayer. Because of the tubes in his mouth, I did all the talking. His eyes filled with joy, and he grasped my index finger. Holding back tears, I whispered, "I love you."

"Stopping by Woods on a Snowy Evening"

All my life I'd recited verses and prayers, at church, alone in the woods, at Aunt Shine's command, while riding my bike along the roads of Madison Park, or at Daddy's request before a meal. Yet no moment of recitation compared to standing in that hospital room reciting to Daddy, not knowing if he would ever hear my voice again—or I, his. I recited his favorite poem, Robert Frost's "Stopping by Woods on a Snowy Evening," the Lord's Prayer, and the Apostles' Creed.

All eyes were on me in that room; no one could speak, eventually not even me. With a heart full, I joined our dear family friend Uncle William in the waiting room. As we sat together, I told him about the arrangements I had made, asking for his assistance should Daddy die. As before, when I was leaving for graduate school, he hugged me and reassured me that he and his wife, Myrtis, would take care of Mama should anything happen.

It was a long plane ride back to Scotland, and as I began to process things, I realized that everything would turn out as I had foreseen. Less than two weeks later, while I was preparing to go to a black-tie student dinner, I received a call from the attending doctor telling me that Daddy had quietly passed away in his sleep. Daddy was eighty-two. He and Mama had lived in the white house at 34 Motley Drive for nearly all of their fifty-two years of marriage. Overwhelmed with disbelief, the stoicism of Daddy kicked in and kept me composed enough to review with the doctor my plans and the immediate steps that needed to be taken. According to hospital protocol, the nearest of kin had to be notified by the hospital first, but they made special accommodation for me, as I had shared with the doctor during my visit; I was concerned about Mama receiving such information by herself, alone at home. I asked him if he could wait an hour before notifying Mama; that would allow me enough time to contact Myrtis and William Winston, asking them to drive to our house in Madison Park to be with her. They in turn also asked Aunt Prince Ella to join them at the house. Myrtis and William phoned me, after they arrived at the house, so that I could speak to Mama. In the end, all of this was done over the course of forty-five minutes. I then phoned Dr. Corts, at Samford University, who I knew would give me emotional and spiritual strength, followed by a call to Mr. Pete Hanna, who would provide me with the assistance of air travel home. But in my mind, all I could hear was Mama's sadness and her request for me to "come home and take care of your Daddy." I immediately phoned the funeral home and asked them to retrieve his body from the Tuskegee Veterans Hospital; he died in the very city where I had been born, some twenty-five years earlier—Tuskegee, Alabama.

After a few calls home to family and friends, and having checked off all the boxes on my well-prepared to-do list, I stepped out on the balcony outside my room, surprised by what a lovely evening it was in Scotland. The sun had colored the sky with a bright orange, and with all the noise around me, a quiet calm settled over me. It was a calmness that was instilled in me by Daddy, who had taught me to always seek an inward strength and peace. I felt an emptiness that I had never known before, but the knowledge of his presence gave me an assuredness that all would be well. Now all I needed to think of was Mama.

Although I was far away from Madison Park, I'd never felt closer as I prepared to return home to bury Daddy. Some of my dearest friends gathered around me with care. Later Simon, Chris, and Noel, my three undergraduate mentees, and I went for a walk along the shore. Resting momentarily on a large boulder, lying on our backs looking up at the stars, Simon whispered in a quiet voice, "Look, I think I see your grandfather shining with all the other stars."

My St. Andrews Posse: Celebrating friendship with classmates from the University of St. Andrews. Left to right: Simon Robertson and Noel Shelley
The collection of Eric L. Motley

As I caught the train the next morning, I felt as if all St. Andrews had gathered to wish me well, as so many friends were standing on the platform as the train approached. For a moment it reminded me of all the people in Madison Park who had gathered, that August morning, to see me off to Samford.

The symbolism was not lost on me that Daddy's funeral would take place in the same church he had built all those years ago. As the organist played "There Will Be Peace in the Valley Someday," I am quite sure that Mama's memory took her back to the Sunday that Daddy was asked to sing the same song, the day before he left for war. The church was full with the people of Madison Park and a few of my closest friends. Mrs. Corts traveled from Birmingham to Montgomery to console me. Everybody knew and respected Mr. George Motley. His coffin, draped in an American flag, also reminded everyone in our town that he was one of the last veterans of World War II, one of the last members of the Greatest Generation. As I sat next to Mama on the front pew, holding her hand and holding back my emotions, I became all the more aware of my increased responsibility to take care of her, and with that came both enormous anxiety and unimagined gratitude. The journey down into Daggerhole seemed longer than all previous trips before. All the years of going down to that sacred place, to bury our dead, had never been as moving as this time. This time I was a mourner and was all too aware that, probably not too far in the distant future, I would be returning for a second time.

Returning to Madison Park to bury my grandfather in 1997.
Left to right: Mamie Motley Arms (Daddy's sister), Chiney
Motley (aka Dot, Daddy's younger brother), Victoria Faison
(Uncle Dot's wife), and Mamie Motley (my grandmother)
The collection of Eric L. Motley

For a little over two weeks, I remained in Madison Park, helping Mama to transition to her new way of life. Our family home was filled with so many artifacts that stood testament to the richness of the life my grandparents shared. One afternoon, before I returned to Scotland, as I was cleaning out Daddy's bedside dressing table, I discovered my letter of acceptance to Samford. He had saved it as a cherished memento— affirmation that the Motley family investment in me had paid off.

CHAPTER 27

"IF YOU'RE NOT READY NOW"

The greatest political lesson Daddy taught me was "never put yourself in a box that you can't get out of." I describe myself as conservative enough not to be a Democrat and progressive enough not to be a Republican. But over the course of high school, college, and graduate school, I had developed a political perspective that aligned mostly with the Republican Party's emphasis on self-reliance, fiscal responsibility, and the role that the community, rather than government, can play in addressing societal issues. At the same time, I'd become increasingly disillusioned at how people in Madison Park often thought one way and voted another. Those who'd most influenced me while I was growing up subscribed to socially and fiscally conservative values in their personal lives but voted for Democrats whose promises seem to contradict those very values. Based on George Wallace's record as governor, I was skeptical that the Democratic Party, at least in Alabama, was interested in the upward mobility of minorities.

In the fall of 2000 as my graduate school days wound down, Vice President Al Gore, Texas Governor George W. Bush, and Green Party candidate Ralph Nader were waging aggressive campaigns for U.S. president. Though far away, I'd stayed attuned to American domestic politics and foreign policy. The more I studied Bush, the more I liked the Republican nominee's straightforward, pragmatic approach. He struck me as a thoughtful person who surrounded himself with highly capable men and women as his personal advisors.

On November 7, 2000, a group of friends from school and I were guests of a classmate for a weekend at his family's seventh-century castle in the Scottish Highlands, attempting to fulfill the "reading week" study tradition observed at St. Andrews each fall, just before final exams. It couldn't have been more different from weekend excursions back at Samford. On our first evening together, after a day of fishing, shooting, and hiking (none of which I did well—I was just along for the ride), the domestic staff prepared a traditional Highlands meal. We dined on salmon, venison, and native greens (but not the type of greens I grew up on in Alabama), accompanied by a lot of wine from the cellars. Afterward we retired to the ballroom for a disco—all Motown music with a little ABBA—and more and more wine. I didn't drink anything harder than ginger ale, and as the night wore on, I was the only sober one.

It was election night in America—of paramount importance to me. But I'd resigned myself to a near information blackout. The castle lacked a TV, and the only radio was in my classmate Charlie's room. He'd brought it along so he could listen to music.

Around 4:00 a.m. I asked Charlie to check on the election news. He retreated to his room and came back downstairs shouting, "Gentlemen and Ladies, can I have your attention please—George Bush has won the U.S. election!"

We all cheered, even those who'd supported Gore or Nader, suggesting that they were too inebriated to tell the difference. I was elated.

An hour or so later, Charlie went back to his room to use the toilet. This time he descended the stairs and announced, "Gentlemen and

Ladies, can I have your attention, please. George Bush has *not* won the U.S. election."

That's when I retrieved the radio so I could get the results for myself. The night only grew stranger, as the networks tried to declare a winner in Florida. We didn't know that it would take weeks to arrive at an answer.

I left St. Andrews in early December having decided, before exams, that it would be easier to complete the last chapter of my dissertation and final editing at Samford, where Dr. Corts had offered me an office in the library and there would be fewer distractions.

I'd enjoyed almost two weeks of farewells. Friends had organized parties, dinners, and afternoon teas. On my last night in town, I took one final walk on the beach with my closest buddies. It was an unusually warm evening, and the stars were bright. We walked on the shore in silence, accompanied by the rhythm of the waves. It was the same beach I'd walked the night that Daddy had died two years earlier, a spot I often returned to. Each of us was mindful that it could be our last time together. Chris, in his proper English accent, said, "Wherever we are, however far apart, I hope we'll always shine brightly, so that when we look up at the stars we'll think of each other."

No statement could top that, so we walked back to town silently and sat at the fountain in the town square until morning, recalling our antics through the years and laughing aloud.

The next day there was one last party. When it ended, tearfully, a friend drove me to Edinburgh to spend the night before I caught an early morning flight. As I passed through the town of Kincaple and ascended the high road of Strathkinness, I looked back to see the same image of St. Andrews that I'd fixed in my mind four years earlier. The view reminded me of a morning the previous spring when I'd woken up, opened my bedroom window, and stepped out onto my balcony. Standing there, all seemed new and beautiful. The blue sky, the smell of the salty sea, and the tree flush with cherry blossoms—my senses had seemed alert, as if for the first time.

It had been a moment of epiphany. I realized that during my time in St. Andrews, I'd become a citizen of the world. The botanizing walks and hikes in the hills; concerts featuring Mendelssohn, Brahms, Bach, and Beethoven; listening to recitations of Wordsworth, Shelley, Emerson, Gwendolyn Brooks, and Langston Hughes; star gazing and learning the constellations; committing quotations by Niebuhr, Aristotle, and Plato to memory—had opened up and unsettled something within me. I'd been transformed by ideas, voices, and experiences.

In the months since then, as I'd prepared to leave, I often turned to a passage that I'd recorded in my teenage journal on one of my visits to the Montgomery County Public Library, from Tennyson's poem "Ulysses":

> I am a part of all that I have met;
> Yet all experience is an arch wherethro'
> Gleams that untravell'd world whose margin fades
> For ever and forever when I move.
> How dull it is to pause, to make an end,
> To rust unburnish'd, not to shine in use!
> As tho' to breathe were life!

I had traveled a great distance from the people of Madison Park—people responsible for my being here—and their ways, hopes and prayers, dreams and encouragement, the folded money secretly slipped into my hands after church by people who had little but cared so much. Standing there, looking out onto the world that morning, I felt I had all Madison

Park at my side. I could see the open fields, the rows plowed neatly and broadly; the faces of family, friends, and neighbors. I could hear their voices in the air, and the words of Aunt Shine came to mind, more resolute than they did when she had spoken them to me all those years earlier, "We believe in you, Motley; now believe in yourself and get an education. But remember you have an obligation to help others."

In all life's ups and downs, twists and turns, education and faith had remained the two great pillars anchoring me. I had been fortunate to study at universities where reason and faith existed together and reinforced one another, so I had never lost hope. But now, I was soon to graduate and head into a world where optimists are too often told to keep their ideals to themselves. I recalled a saying I once heard: "No matter how wise we may become, no one of us knows enough to be pessimistic." And I knew it was my responsibility as an educated person and ambassador of Madison Park to remain optimistic no matter what.

I'd been reminded over and again that "as educated people we have a responsibility to reject prejudices and help close the gaps of justice and opportunity that still divide our nation and our world." To me this wasn't abstract reading; it was personal. I felt called upon to advance human progress. As I descended the hill beyond Strathkinness, St. Andrews vanished from sight. The vastness of the great blue sky and open sea stretched before me like a clean canvas—a new beginning, a brave new world.

In mid-December, by the time the Supreme Court decided that George Bush was to be the next president, I was back at Samford. I spent ten to twelve hours a day editing and revising my dissertation and at least two hours researching job opportunities. I hadn't abandoned the idea that my Ph.D. would serve me well in higher education, because deep down inside, I had always wanted to be part of a learning community. I don't remember at what point I decided I might want to work for the new administration or what purpose I intended to accomplish by pursuing that path, but once I made up my mind, I reached out to several people who could help me make the necessary contacts.

One afternoon I called on a longtime friend, Harold Abroms. We'd met for lunch each Christmas when I was home from Scotland, and I would borrow one of his cars during my stay. Now I revealed my political aspirations to him. A strong but pragmatic Democrat, he first wanted to know why I supported Bush.

I responded by saying that I thought Bush was a capable politician, having proved himself successful as a governor and a businessman and could bring that to bear during his presidency. He advised me to reach out to Margaret Tutwiler, who'd been James Baker's deputy at the State Department, the first female spokesperson there, and an advisor to President George H. W. Bush. She hadn't crossed my mind, though I'd brought her to Samford as part of the speakers' series several years earlier. As a first step Mr. Abroms insisted that I meet Temple Tutwiler, Margaret's brother, who lived in Birmingham. Temple later told me that after our meeting, he'd immediately phoned his sister. "You have got to help this young man," he said. "He is *something*."

Legendary in Republican circles, Tutwiler was working in the West Wing as a special counselor to President Bush after his inauguration. She remembered me, reviewed my résumé, and walked it upstairs. Handing it to Clay Johnson, the director of presidential personnel and deputy chief of staff, and the man who'd overseen the White House transition, Margaret told him, "This is the only résumé I'll ever bring you. Call this kid. My brother thinks he's the real thing, and if my brother says it, then it's so."

Four days later, I received a call from the White House office of Ron Bellamy, deputy director of presidential personnel and former senior advisor to President Bush during his tenure as the governor of Texas. "Margaret Tutwiler suggested that we call you," he said. "Are you interested in a job? When can you come up for an interview?"

After I hung up, I sat quietly, remembering Daddy, and filled with emotion at not being able to share this experience with him. After collecting myself, I left the research office, ran down the library steps and across the quad to the university chapel, a place I'd spent many quiet hours during college, and took a seat in the first pew. Closing my eyes, I repeated one of Mama's prayers: "Thank you, Lord. Let your will be done and prepare me for it."

My next stop was Dr. Corts's office to share the good news.

The following week I flew to Washington courtesy of Dr. Corts. The night before my interview with Mr. Bellamy, I stayed with Brad Heifner, my close friend from Samford. We stayed up so late telling stories that I eventually protested. "I've got to go to sleep," I exclaimed.

"Listen jackass," he said, "you've been preparing for this here interview all your life. If you're not ready now, then you'll never be."

The next morning Brad accompanied me to the metro. As he walked away, he yelled back loudly in his distinct Southern accent, "Motley! You'll walk through the gates a black man and come back through them a White House man."

I met Mr. Bellamy in his flag-draped office. He told me that he'd been collecting flags for two decades but never thought he'd hang them from an office in the White House. That's when the enormity of what I was doing sank in. I remembered how beautiful the flags had looked draped from the wide porches of Madison Park on Veterans' Day. Mr. Bellamy, a gray-haired man with a sincere face, wanted to hear my story, and I told him—every bit of it. When I finished, he said, "Only in America."

After asking me why I wanted to serve in the administration, he flipped through my five-page résumé. I was so naive, I'd listed every talk I'd given at St. Andrews on Plato and Aristotle. "Wow, you sure know a lot about the Greeks," he said, without ridicule.

Next I met Rebecca Contreras, who oversaw boards and commissions in the office of presidential personnel. She had spent most of her professional life working in President Bush's gubernatorial office in Austin. When she told me about herself, I realized that we had similar stories.

After Mr. Bellamy and Rebecca spoke briefly, he invited me back to his office. "We'd like to offer you a job," he said.

"I'm so grateful," I said, "but could you be a bit more specific as to what agency or area I'll be assigned to?"

"Agency?" he asked, confused. "I'm offering you a job here in our office!"

"You mean here at the White House?" I thought I'd be sent over to the Department of State to track passports or the Department of Education to review regional accreditation standards, but the White House?

"Yes, here in the White House, or do you have an interest in working somewhere else?"

My mouth was dry, and my heart was hammering in my chest. I was speechless.

Mr. Bellamy cleared his voice and said, "Eric, you look surprised." I didn't know what to say. I replied "Sir, I am honored."

He explained to me that someone would be contacting me in the next few days to start the paperwork, but that he was willing to answer any questions I had.

A friend back home, who I'd always considered "well-informed," had advised me to clarify a few critical points before taking a government job. "Will there be dental and eye coverage?" I asked.

He and Rebecca must have thought Madison Park was on Mars. He stuttered and said, "I assume so, but you are the first person to ever ask me that question. I will get you an answer, but I am almost certain that all is covered."

And that is how I got to the White House.

Mark Twain was reputed to have once said that history doesn't repeat itself, but it rhymes. I'd made my first trip to Washington, D.C., in 1991, as a delegate to Boys Nation. Ten years later, in February 2001, I arrived in the District of Columbia behind the wheel of my "new" eleven-year-old Honda Accord, following a U-Haul van driven by my good friend Brooks Souders.

The journey was more than a metaphor for just how far I had traveled to get to this point. But I had a feeling that everything was going to be okay. I'd secured an apartment and did my best to make it feel like home.

The night before my first day at the White House I was filled with anticipation. After dinner with Brad, I came home and pressed my new suit, courtesy of Dr. Rod Davis, my former university dean, starched a white shirt, chose my tie—the red-and-blue-striped one that Daddy had worn to my high school graduation—and tried to relax in a hand-me-down Queen Anne chair from Pete Hanna. Between

255

calls from friends and family, I flipped through a few pages of Peter Ackroyd's biography of Thomas More. It was only by chance that I'd pulled it from the shelf several nights earlier. But it poignantly reminded that one could be "a man for all seasons," steadfast and true to one's principles, even in the political realm.

At 10:30 p.m., as I was about to turn off the lights, the phone rang and the caller I.D. showed a Montgomery number. Weary, I picked up anyway, never wanting to hurt those who had helped me most. It was Mrs. Bertha Winston, my elocution coach, Sunday school teacher, and longtime cheerleader.

"Eric," she said, "I hope I didn't wake you. I couldn't sleep. I guess it's because I've had you on my mind all day. So I decided to turn on the light and call. I just wanted to let you know how very proud we are of you. I always had confidence in you to get things done, so tomorrow, you go in there and get to work! When you go into that White House tomorrow, remember you're taking Madison Park with you."

As I hung up, I tried to tamp down my anxiety, reminding myself that I'd come too far to mess up now. Earlier that day, over coffee at a sandwich shop, I'd scribbled the names of people to whom I owed thanks. I've always kept a "gratitude list," registering names of people important in my life, and now I took out that notepad, got down on my knees, and called out each name. "Dear God, thank you for these people and those whose names I've forgotten. I'm here because of them. Bless them each and every one."

Those are the same words I pray today.

On the morning of March 19, 2001, I stood in front of the White House peering once again through the gates. I was carrying the old briefcase that Mrs. Pat Wilson, a former teacher, had "lent" me in seventh grade.

When you work at the White House, you get used to the idea that you don't get to see the president every day, particularly working in the Eisenhower Executive Office Building—a building next to the West Wing. Many people who serve the president never see him at all. So only a few weeks after I'd started, I was stunned to find myself in the Oval Office. Clay Johnson and Ron Bellamy had invited me to accompany them to a meeting with President Bush.

A presidential briefing in the Oval Office with my boss and mentor, Clay Johnson. Left to right: Vice President Cheney, President Bush, Clay Johnson, and Lisa Oliphant (c. May 2001)
Official White House photograph, courtesy of the George W. Bush Presidential Library

I'd never seen such a luminous, sun-filled room. President Bush had decided that he wanted the Oval Office to be decorated in bright hues of cream and soft yellow to reflect light and hope, a reminder of possibility and the brightness before and around us. And surrounded by that symbolism, it did seem to me that it would be difficult for anyone who entered the room to feel disbelief or doubt. My eyes fastened on a painting by W. H. D. Koerner titled *A Charge to Keep*, which hung to the right of the president's desk. The painting depicts a determined horseman blazing a path along a rough mountain trail with others following behind. Moving my gaze across the room, I settled my focus on a painting of Abraham Lincoln, hanging to the right of Rembrandt Peale's famous rendering of George Washington.

I remember Daddy having been similarly inspired by another picture of Abraham Lincoln that hung in his grandfather's house when he was a small boy. Although that humble abode, built by a former slave who had been freed by the Great Emancipator himself, couldn't have been farther from the grandeur of the White House, the principles of liberty and equality beamed just as brightly in both homes.

The spell was broken when the president entered the room from a side door, followed by Vice President Dick Cheney and the chief of staff, Andy Card. Spectacles on the tip of his nose, briefing book in hand, President Bush said, "Okay, Clay, let's get this meeting started," and with that he and the vice president took their seats in front of the fireplace. There were six of us, and protocol dictates that no one be seated before the president. That's when it struck me: "Where am I to sit?"

Ron, who caught my awkward expression, patted the empty place on the sofa next to him.

Clearing his voice, Clay said, "Mr. President, before we begin our meeting, I wanted to introduce you to the newest member of our team, Eric Motley, who started a few weeks ago."

"He's already in *here*?" cracked the president.

"Let me tell you a bit about Eric," Clay said. "He just graduated with a Ph.D. from the University of St. Andrews over in Scotland.

"Scotland?" the president asked. "How'd you get over there? Better yet, how did you get back from over there?"

"He was raised in a small town near Montgomery, Alabama, adopted by his grandparents," Clay answered.

"Scotland's a long way from Montgomery."

"Yes sir," I said, "it is." I couldn't believe I'd spoken.

"Margaret knows Eric and highly recommended him," Clay added.

"How do you know Margaret?" President Bush asked. "Oh, yeah, the Alabama connection!"

"Yes, sir," I said, nodding. "I met her when I was a student at Samford University."

"You mean Samford down in Birmingham? Good school, and you got a good friend in Margaret."

"She's a remarkable woman, and I appreciate her confidence."

That's when President Bush captured what the moment was really about. "Confidence! We all have confidence in you! That's why you're here. I'd already heard about you. Word travels fast, especially in this place. So, welcome. We're glad to have you, and remember, do the right thing. It's an honor to be here, for all of us to be here. We all have a responsibility and must do our best . . . I know your grandparents taught you that, so I don't have to worry."

With that, I was in the White House, and Madison Park was with me.

CHAPTER 28

FROM THE WHITE HOUSE TO FOGGY BOTTOM

I've always kept a journal, but the demands of moving to a new city, starting a career, and working long and full hours at the White House meant that entries were shortened to bullet points. Fear that my observations could be subpoenaed also made me cautious, although I now realize how unlikely that would have been given my cog-in-the-wheel position. My scribblings record events that were important to me at the time, such as on May 6, 2001, when I noted that Pope John Paul II, while visiting Syria, had become the first pope to enter a mosque, or a couple of weeks later, on May 25, when the first blind person reached the summit of Mount Everest. As an Alabamian, I recorded when my home state's Supreme Court chief justice, Roy Moore, installed a Ten Commandments monument in the state judiciary building, leading to a lawsuit to have the monument removed and his own eventual removal from office.

The attacks of September 11, 2001, occurred six months into my tenure. Until then my days in the White House had not fully impressed upon me the seriousness of the job and the sacrifices I might be called on to make. As we anxiously watched the televised coverage after the twin towers fell in New York, we noticed a crawl at the bottom of the screen announcing the evacuation of the White House. Almost at that exact moment, Secret Service agents swarmed our office. "Stay calm, but evacuate immediately," they shouted.

One woman removed her high heels in preparation for the mad dash out of the building. I grabbed my blazer and briefcase and was ready to go before suddenly remembering that the only copy of my dissertation was sitting in my desk drawer on twelve floppy discs. I threw them into my briefcase while a panicked colleague shouted, "What are you doing?"

"I've got to get something really important!" I called.

"You've got to get something really important out of here—yourself."

Finally, I was ready to go, but where? "Just get out of the building," a Secret Service agent answered tersely, in response to my question. "Get as far away from the building as possible."

Despite the overload of calls, Mama got through on the phone, and I assured her that I was okay. We prayed together, her pleading with God to keep me and everyone else safe.

Even in less stressful times than 9-11, loved ones from Madison Park continued to play meaningful roles in my life. In the last years of Aunt Shine's life, I visited her to thank her for all that she had done for me, but she was more intent on influencing my future than in dwelling on the past. As I attempted to offer my gratitude, she firmly reminded me of what Madison Park still expected of me. "You are now a man, an educated man," she began. "You have your Ph.D. You work in the White House. Yet you are no better than anyone else, remember that. Now you have an obligation to use your education to help others. Your education is a valuable thing, an important gift you gave to yourself with the help of many others. Don't let us down, Little Motley. Don't let yourself down."

I looked away for a brief moment, finding it difficult to look her in the eye. As so often when I visited the grand old saints of Madison Park, I was struck by the awareness that one of these seemingly routine visits would ultimately become historic by being my last. As I collected my thoughts, masking my emotion under a serious, controlled face, she mistook my concentration for nonchalance at what she was saying.

She quickly seized my hand, demanding in her strong voice that I look at her while she was speaking. Obediently fastening my eyes on her, jolted from the sentiment of the moment by her voice, she resumed saying what I had heard her say to me over the years as I had progressed through life, "We started the Madison Park tutorial program because of you, Motley, because you were having trouble reading. You were failing and needed an anchor. Young man, never forget that all of this was done for you. Others benefited, thank God, but it was started because of you."

Sometime later, two months before she died, when I was in Montgomery for a few days during my summer vacation, I spent an hour at Aunt Shine's bedside. Mama had prepared me, saying that Aunt Shine was in her last days and, in all likelihood, would not remember me or be able to respond. That was unimaginable, and as I made my way to her house, I felt certain that my face or maybe a verse or two of song—something would surely stimulate her memory. After all I was her "Little Motley." As I sat at her side, she gave not a single indication that she knew who I was or what I was saying. All those years of investment in "Little Motley," those grand texts she had forced me to recite, they were of no effect. I was just another stranger, unknown, speaking unintelligibly.

Over and again I referenced our best memories from the past, her tutorials, all that she said to me during our long walks. I recited the words of "Lift Every Voice and Sing," confident that God's trombone would light a spark, if anything could. It was almost as if her body was already lying in state. She did not remember. But I can never forget.

Working in the Office of Presidential Personnel, I supported the effort to identify, recruit, evaluate, and recommend board members, to the president, for appointment to commissions in the education, defense, and foreign affairs policy spheres. On a daily basis, I interviewed no fewer than ten people or spoke with no less than twenty, from every rank of life. Given the highly politicized context in which I operated, I became acutely aware of how sensitive the work I was doing was, all the more so given how every action taken by our office would reflect on the president. This imbued me with a strong sense of mission and purpose, as I realized that if I were to recommend the wrong person for a high-level government position and push that individual through the process without ample deliberation with appropriate colleagues, there would have been serious repercussions. I constantly asked myself: "Could this be a really bad front-page story in the *New York Times* tomorrow?" Although this was never my only litmus test, it reminded me to be thorough, do my homework, and make decisions that I could defend.

The president, being the "inquisitor-in-chief" that he was, would pepper me with questions related to my recommendations. I recall him having a keen ability to see through bluff and to masterfully ask the right questions. My Ph.D. examination committee could not rival President Bush in this regard. With time, I began to develop a sense for how his mind worked and became better able to anticipate what his concerns might be so that I could address them proactively. Spending more than 150 hours in the Oval Office briefing the president, I developed a wonderful rapport with him, characterized by humor, intellectual banter, and a sense of familiarity that was only made possible by his enormous humility and generosity of spirit. All these years later, our reunions, though fewer and farther between, still bear the hallmark of the close bond we formed then.

The emotional highlight of my tenure at the White House came in May 2003, when I was sworn in to become special assistant to the president (S.A.P.) for presidential personnel. This made me a commissioned officer of the White House, the civilian equivalent of a two-star general. At any given time, there were about thirty-five S.A.P.s. Andrew Card, the White House Chief of Staff, officially swore me in along with fourteen other appointees, in a solemn ceremony held in the Theodore Roosevelt Room of the West Wing, just outside the Oval Office. As I waited to repeat the oath, I remembered Daddy explaining to me the feelings he had when he took the U.S. Army's oath of enlistment. He said he'd been filled with enormous pride accompanied by a heavy feeling of responsibility, which suddenly overtook him—an awareness that he was giving himself completely to the cause of America. I felt the same way.

At that moment my professional life couldn't have been better. In charge of the largest division of presidential personnel, overseeing all boards and commissions appointments, I was seeing years of hard work and sacrifice come to fruition. I was determined not to squander a minute of my time as an S.A.P. Yet my personal life had taken a dive in months previous and left me feeling rudderless. I had lost the love of my life.

After I returned to Alabama in 2000 I'd met a remarkably brilliant and beautiful woman—I'll call her Katherine—who embodied everything I'd dreamed of: she was intelligent, creative, and passionate about life.

We shared many of the same interests and enjoyed attending concerts, lectures, plays, museum exhibits, cultural festivals, and dinner parties.

Katherine and I had grown up differently—she had gone to private schools from K-12, had been afforded luxuries such as piano lessons, equestrian sports, and art instruction, and grew up with the assurance that attending college was a given, with the resources to pay for it secure. But as two Southerners who had so much in common—shared musical taste, deep interest in the arts, a love of nature, an enormous intellectual curiosity about all things, and an abiding faith and belief in the same God—I saw us as kindred spirits. In my mind, I had everything a father could want his daughter to have in a man—character, faith, principles, a good education, a bright future, and the capacity to provide for her and a family. But Katherine's father viewed our relationship differently. I was the wrong color, and he forbade Katherine from seeing me.

I was confounded by his prejudice. In retrospect I was naive. I had secure hopes and expectations that in the year 2000, much had changed in our society. I had come to enjoy so many diverse opportunities and to be accepted by so many different types of people across the world. Up until this point, I'd cleared all of the barriers that had been put before my grandparents, but here it seems I'd reached a wall I was incapable of surmounting. Owing to how deeply I felt about Katherine, I believed, if given a chance, I could prove myself worthy, but how does one prove one's equality? The question began to chip away at my self-worth.

Going against her father's explicit warning, Katherine and I began to date in the fall of 2001. Her mother, a lovely, independent-minded woman, eventually overcame her misgivings, asking only that I respect Katherine and be good to her—the same things that all parents hope for in their children's romantic partners. But Katherine's relationship with her father became increasingly strained.

Despite the anxiety and distance, we grew more deeply attached. In the summer of 2002, Katherine moved to Washington to work as a research fellow. While it was hard to balance the demands of the White House with a relationship, she was a welcome refuge for me from the rigors of the job. We didn't live together, but when I wasn't at work, we spent all of our time together. I couldn't believe how fortunate I was to be with such an exceptional person. I felt that I had found a complement in her. But after a year in Washington, Katherine moved back to the South to pursue a graduate degree. Our relationship continued, though fraught with the usual problems that distance creates, and then, without much warning, it came to an end. Another graduate student pursued her and eventually she relented.

In hindsight, I probably should have understood that the situation with her father would ultimately put a wedge between us. But I can't say that we ended entirely because of her dad's pressure. She was my first real girlfriend. We were wonderfully romantic and idealistic, so the reality that the personal faults we saw in each other might not change unsettled us and came to color our relationship in unanticipated ways. We both learned a lot about love and how it can often take you to unforeseen places or leave you feeling that all has been lost.

From the moment I arrived in Washington, I was aware of how ephemeral political appointments are. During annual staff briefings, Andy Card would always share one truism about the job of a White House staffer: he or she works "at the pleasure of the president, and for the time being." So, in the natural course of things, I knew that eventually even my time at the White House would come to an end. I had the choice of leaving on my own, when the time was right, to pursue other professional opportunities and interests, or I could wait it out until the president's term ended. I remember thinking, "It's only four years!"

I also knew that being at the White House was a once-in-a-lifetime experience and still professionally fulfilling. After exploring other opportunities, I decided to stay until President Bush's first term was up. But the question of what to do next—personally and professionally—resurfaced with the start of his reelection campaign. The expected, and fitting, thing was to serve him through the transition from first to second term if he won. I let my boss, Dina Powell, then director of presidential personnel, who'd succeeded the legendary Clay Johnson, know that I would stay until October 2005.

My choice was to leave government service entirely or to find a new opportunity within the federal government. A good friend who worked on Capitol Hill as a Senate staffer took it upon himself to counsel me: "Whatever you do, don't leave the White House. If you leave, you will no longer be Eric Motley from the White House!"

Wow. Had my good friend become convinced that my identity was solely tied to my job? More alarming, was it true? Wasn't being Eric Motley from Madison Park good enough? Was working at the White House the magnet?

I suddenly remembered something that Clay Johnson had halfheartedly said to an assembly of White House staffers during the early days. "I recommend that all of you prepare yourselves for a personal and professional transition because, one day, you'll have to leave the White House and pass through the gates to the other side from whence you've come. The best way to prepare is to get a dog. Yes, get a dog. And get one *now*. Name him, love him, play with him. Because there is a strong probability that once you leave the White House, you will suffer momentary depression. No one will call you, the invitations will dwindle, and the breakneck speed of getting your calls returned—well, let's just hope your calls will be returned. *But* your dog won't care that you no longer work at the White House. This is real unconditional love."

I didn't get a dog, but I did take Clay's witty counsel to heart, making every effort to expand my circle of friends to include people with little interest in where I worked.

A few months after the start of the second term, Dina invited me to lunch to share her plans. Condoleezza Rice, who had just been confirmed as secretary of state, had asked her to lead the State Department's Office of Public Diplomacy with Karen Hughes—a long-time aide to President Bush, who had previously served as a senior counselor to the president. What sweet music to my ears, as the one program I had been most interested in government was the Fulbright office under the auspices of the Bureau of Educational and Cultural Affairs. Dina said, "Well, Dr. Motley, why don't you come join our team at the State Department, and if you're really interested in Fulbright, then go do your research and come back to me and tell me what division of Fulbright you want to oversee and why."

It took no time for me to follow up with her to make my case for Fulbright. During the course of my research, I learned that the Fulbright-Hays Act, officially known as the Mutual Educational and Cultural Exchange Act of 1961, was created "to enable the Government of the United States to increase mutual understanding between the people of the United States and the people of other countries by means of educational and cultural exchange . . ." What an incredible mission!

So, in October 2005, I gathered my belongings and said my good-byes as I moved down the road from 1600 Pennsylvania Avenue to Foggy Bottom, the home of the Department of State. I was appointed Director of the Office of International Visitors, a division of the State

Department that provides grants for short-term visits to the United States for foreign nationals who are current or emerging leaders in their respective fields. Despite the ominous prognostications of my Hill friend, I'd survived with my identity intact.

All of my life I've found the greatest value in my relationships with people, and it was the relationships developed at the White House that I would miss most. I had come to enjoy a warm friendship with the president and Mrs. Bush, inasmuch as a White House staffer could become friends with POTUS and FLOTUS, and that was largely due to the friendship that had grown between Anne and Clay Johnson and me. Anne and Clay had somehow become my surrogate parents in Washington. Anne was in many ways my Bertha Winston of Madison Park. Once, as I was mending after the difficult breakup with Katherine, Anne took me to lunch and said, as only a mother could, "Honey, you had pretty, and it ended up being ugly, so I suggest that you put looks aside and focus on what matters most. The inside is where real beauty lies."

It is customary that employees in the White House get a photo with the president at the end of their White House service. Three weeks before my departure, I was asked to give the name of the guest I planned to bring with me for that event. The more I thought about who to invite, the more I realized how important this memory would become. I really had no "guest." Most people would bring their spouse or a parent, but at eighty-five, Mama's traveling days were behind her. "Tell President Bush, I'm more than happy to take a photo with him if he ever wants to come to Montgomery, but I'm not coming to Washington, D.C.," she said— one of Mama's many messages I chose not to deliver to President Bush.

Motley's Mentors: Since I moved away from Madison Park, these individuals have
had the most profound influence on my life. Left to right: Dr. Thomas E. Corts,
Pete Hanna, Professor Struther Arnott, and Clay Johnson (c. Autumn 2005)
Official White House photograph, courtesy of the George W. Bush Presidential Library

On reflection I found myself more interested in making this memory
something more than just mine. I decided to make an unusual request
of Clay. I asked to bring the three mentors who made it possible for me
to purse my higher educational aspirations, Dr. Corts, Professor Arnott,
and Pete Hanna. Clay personally arranged to have these three men
with me as I had my photo taken with President Bush. He and Anne
went further by hosting a dinner reception in their home to honor these
"Eric Motley educational benefactors." They invited more than fifty
guests who'd become part of my Washington life: cabinet secretaries,
Supreme Court justices, ambassadors, White House colleagues, local
museum directors, and church and social friends.

Here's what I recorded in my journal:

September 23, 2005

11:00 am: Scheduled photo shoot with POTUS in the Oval Office. Clay Johnson would join the photo. The president warmly welcomed my mentors. Surprisingly, FLOTUS entered the room, "Good morning everyone. I am Laura and I wanted to meet Eric's mentors too, but where are your wives? George, can they come in?" Greta, Marla, and Barbara are brought into the Oval Office. Mrs. Bush never joins departure photos! The Oval Office now is full, ten of us: POTUS, FLOTUS, Clay, Thomas and Marla, Greta and Struther, Pete and Barbara, and Me. The president takes more than the allotted time to walk everyone around the Oval Office explaining symbolism, paintings, desk, and his color choices. My emotions are high. POTUS takes a photo with me and my mentors.

POTUS: "I want to thank you for traveling here today to be a part of this special day for Eric, but what this really underscores is what can happen in America and anywhere in the world when everyone steps up and does their part in helping out. Eric is here today because of a lot of people, but especially because of you, so on behalf of us all, thank you."

As renowned theologian and Civil Rights leader Howard Thurman said, "What I needed to hold me to my path was the sure knowledge that I was committed to a single journey with . . . a single goal—a way toward life . . . and from this flowed an inescapable necessity: to be totally involved."

When I was a small boy wandering through the woods behind my house, I imagined the world as an even more expansive place than the nature I could see, replete with infinite possibilities for self-fulfillment. No one in Madison Park told me otherwise; in fact, my teachers and mentors affirmed my intuition *often*—and in the most unlikely places.

One day while I was picking blackberries, Mama's friend Ms. Daisy Howard appeared, seemingly out of nowhere, like a benevolent genie in a fairy tale. When I tried to start a conversation, she lowered her parasol and gave me advice as profound as Howard Thurman's—and more down to earth. "You mustn't pay attention to me or to anyone when you're working the work that is before you," she said kindly but sternly. "You have to be totally involved in what you're doing and totally consumed with what's before you."

The Zen-like counsel dispensed by a village matron in a blackberry patch reminds me that my life has consisted of many rites of passage that connect in almost circular fashion to my beginnings in Madison Park. From Mama, Daddy, and Aunt Shine to President Corts and then President Bush. From a settlement founded by former slaves in the Deep South to Scotland and the White House. My journey away from my native soil has, paradoxically, constantly brought me back to the values and principles of the loving, nurturing folks who, luckily for me, plucked an African American child from what could have been an abyss and equipped me with strength for the journey I have taken.

CHAPTER 29

"BARBARA ANN"

When I moved to Washington, Mama and I talked almost every morning about what was happening in Madison Park. Who had been born and who had died. Who was getting married or divorced. Who had moved in or out. A frequent topic was Dr. John Winston, my childhood hero and the husband of my elocution coach, Mrs. Bertha Winston. When Daddy was still living but already ill in health, Dr. Winston offered him little jobs, such as changing door knobs, building bookcases, or drawing up blueprints, to keep him active. Now Dr. Winston wheeled his pickup truck into our driveway once a week to check on Mama, medical bag on the front seat.

Picking up the receiver on her end, knowing it was me, Mama would often sing the first verse of the hymn, "I come to the garden alone while the dew is still on the roses . . ." I listened in silence, sometimes joining her at the chorus line—". . . and He walks with me, and talks with me, and He tells me I am his own . . ." The music we made remains even more beautiful in my heart.

When Mama and I were apart, I often thought about her hands, which she saw as guided by God's will. Those hands cleaned other people's houses with the same attention to detail that she devoted to her own house. They helped to plant the seeds of fruits and vegetables that would provide food at the dining table. Most important, her hands reached out to embrace the child of a dying neighbor and friend, and later that child's son, both of whom she and her husband nurtured into adulthood. On one of my visits home, I cupped her small, wrinkled hands in mine. As I patted them, I thought: "If these hands could talk they would tell me all that she has done . . . for our family . . . for me . . . for countless others."

In the spring of 2011, I paid a surprise visit home, and for a few hours on the back porch Mama and I sat, singing, remembering, and updating each other. I didn't realize how little time was left, but it was a precious time for me to remember and to express my gratitude toward one in whose presence I never stopped feeling like the small child whom she had rescued. But heaviest on my heart then, as now, is the awareness of the "debt of love I owe."

June 30 began like any other morning. She rose before the sun, at 4:45 a.m., made breakfast, did laundry, hung it out to dry on the clothesline in the backyard, and checked on the elderly and sick by telephone. She had spent the previous day visiting with friends and neighbors. Despite suffering from chronic congestive heart failure, she had not been noticeably ill. Her only medical procedure that day involved a simple blood pressure check administered by a home health nurse. When offered further assistance, Mama politely but firmly replied, "Ma'am, I've been living in this house for over seventy years, fourteen of them by myself, and I've never needed any assistance. I cook for myself, clean for myself, and take care of myself quite well without any assistance, and I do not need anyone coming in to check on me. I thank you for your kindness, but I do not need your aid." This took place at 10:00 a.m., and after removing her clothes from the line, she tended to more chores before sitting in her chair at the window. A few hours later, while napping, she passed away at the age of ninety.

Whenever a person of Mama's age dies, one concern for those who plan the funeral is "Will anybody come? Has my loved one outlived all of his or her contemporaries, and will there be anyone left who remembers them when they were active in the community?" In Mama's case I need not have worried, for she had touched so many lives as Sunday school teacher, choir member, missionary, volunteer, and overall mainstay for more than seventy years that more than three hundred people packed Union Chapel Church for her funeral. For more than five generations that little parish, site of so much family history, has been the sanctuary and altar around which many in Madison Park gather in times good and bad. Mama herself had been baptized, wed, and worshiped there for more than sixty-five years, and her funeral took place around the same altar that her husband had built.

Friends from around the world had sent flowers, which she loved when she was alive, and their aroma filled the air. The organ prelude was "Amazing Grace," and the choir sang "Blessed Assurance" and "What a Friend We Have in Jesus," favorite hymns that she had sung every Sunday and at her friends' funerals. All of the ministers who had served the church since my childhood took part, and the current pastor, Reverend Szymanski Fields, in his eulogy compared her to a box of M&M candy: deceptively hard on the outside, but soft on the inside, especially once you got to know her. Among those who turned out for the funeral were a white couple in their eighties, Mr. and Mrs. Lowry, whose house Mama had cleaned for almost a half-century. They loved her like a member of the family, and we continue to stay in touch. Also present were important figures from my past and present, including my seventh-grade speech teacher, Susan Mayes; the widow of Samford's president, Mrs. Marla Corts, who had also come for Daddy's funeral; my college mentors, Dean Rod Davis and Professors Mark Baggett and Steven Epley; Birmingham friend Temple Tutwiler and his wife Lucy, who drove to Madison Park to visit Mama monthly; and Clay Johnson, my boss at the White House, who traveled from Austin, Texas, for the service and stayed several days to help me pack up the house and take Mama's friends out to dinner. Childhood friends and college classmates also showed their loving support.

Broken Circle: Surrounded by some of my closest friends as I laid Mama to rest. Left to right: Bonnie Mayes Phillips and Meredith Mayes (Mrs. Susan Mayes's daughters), Mrs. Marla Corts, Andrew Clark (Samford classmate), Sandy O'Brien (Dr. Corts' Samford Chief of Staff), Clay Johnson, Lucy and Temple Tutwiler, Mrs. Susan Mayes, Russ Hovater (Samford classmate), Amy Chandler Simpson (Samford classmate), and Marquis Brown (close friend from D.C.)
The collection of Eric L. Motley

I needed it all, because the last remaining constant support in my life had been removed. The one person who daily preoccupied herself with me and with my concerns was no more. So it was important during my eulogy that I express my gratitude to this loving couple that had become the parents of Barbara Ann and Eric, giving us their precious name, Motley. I also tried to show my thankfulness for the Madison Park community that helped take care of Mama in my absence, allowing me to pursue my aspirations. In my eulogy I said, "People say there is no longer any sense of community in this country, that we're all just concerned with ourselves. But Madison Park is proof that this isn't so. I knew that I could go far away and live out my dreams because the people here in this church would help me bear the responsibility of caring for my grandmother. You said, 'Go, do what you have to do. You're not leaving her alone here.'"

Nor did I leave her alone when I left Madison Park that evening, for she was laid to rest next to Daddy in the Madison Park Cemetery, which I would visit as a child to clean and sweep away the South Alabama pine straw, lay fresh flowers, and cut away wild vines and ivy. It was reassuring to inter her in that same place where so many other loved ones rest—Aunt Shine, Mrs. Frankie Lee Winston, Rev. and Mrs. Seay, and Mrs. Bertha Winston.

During the service, I sat next to Barbara Ann and my half-sister Kesia. We had become one family again about six years earlier, and now we were expressing our love for the woman who had given her life to raising us.

To explain how all of this happened, I need to revisit the story of Barbara Ann's life to that point. I spent my infancy with her in the Motley household, but when I was a little over a year old, she married. "I never loved him," she later told me. "I just had to get out of Montgomery." Why did Barbara Ann need desperately to get away from Madison Park while I've always felt drawn inexorably back to it? I think the answer lies in the difference between our upbringings in those crucial first ten years of our respective lives. Until that point, Barbara Ann had been raised, as I indicated earlier, in a large, unruly household with thirteen siblings and little parental supervision. Suddenly, when my grandparents adopted her, she found herself thrust into a highly disciplined way of life for which her experience had not prepared her. Whereas she had been accustomed to few rules and virtually no responsibilities, suddenly she was living with parents for whom it was "rise and shine" at five in the morning, attend Sunday school and church every Sunday, dress appropriately for every meal, and always do your chores. While this was unsettling to her, I never knew any other life but the one modeled for me by Mama and Daddy. It never seemed unduly restrictive or unreasonable because it was my norm, and similar, if not quite so strict, regimens governed the lives of my friends, so I had no reason to complain or desire to flee. Her husband offered an escape route to the bright lights of Atlanta, and she couldn't resist the temptation to run.

She continued to visit us after their move. But her visits became increasingly rare. At the time, neither my grandparents nor I truly comprehended the emotional and psychological trauma that she was experiencing. In spiritual terms, she now acknowledges that she was lost. More, she lost her sense of direction, identity, and connection with her parents and child. Divorcing him in 1977, when I was almost five, she soon became involved with another man who became the father of my half-sister, Kesia. For several years Barbara Ann drove Kesia down to spend the summers with us, but in my mid-teens Barbara Ann's life seemed to come almost completely undone. Likely embarrassed, she retreated from friends and family. Calls became fewer and visits and correspondence, which at first diminished, eventually stopped. When friends would ask my grandparents, "How's Barbara Ann?" they would answer with white lies. This must have taken an enormous emotional toll on them, but they never spoke negatively about her. "She's figuring out her life," they'd tell me. "Just give her some time. She'll find her way back home."

They lived in the hope that she would return to the family fold, but I became increasingly despondent. While not exactly angry, I was certainly frustrated and disappointed with her. These feelings grew more acute when Daddy suffered a heart attack when I was in junior high. This and other health challenges made me take on responsibilities beyond my years, such as meeting with doctors and making decisions about a pacemaker. As a teenager I'd had to become an adult, playing an ever-larger role in their still largely independent lives, while Barbara Ann, their daughter, did nothing. She became more and more irrelevant to me.

When I went to college, life became more complex and demanding, as it tends to be. Instead of the nurturing, understanding African American community in which I'd been raised, I was now living as a member of various minority groups—African American, rural, and relatively disadvantaged—in a bastion of white, upper-middle-class suburban privilege. That I reacted to my change of surroundings more positively than Barbara Ann has less to do with any inner strength of character than with the fact that I was older than she had been when she underwent this transition, and my grandparents had prepared me for the challenges. They always told me that I would encounter prejudiced people after I left Madison Park but not to let their bias affect the way I viewed myself.

Barbara Ann grew more distant from my concerns when I moved to Scotland. On the long trek from Scotland to Madison Park after Daddy's death, a profound spiritual struggle took place within my soul. On one hand, I knew that I lacked the psychological strength or emotional energy to deal with Barbara Ann, someone whom I no longer knew. But I carried with me on the flight a copy of Victor Frankl's book *Man's Search for Meaning*—why, I'm not sure. In it, however, I read of Frankl's anxiety during World War II over whether or not his wife was still alive in the same Nazi concentration camp. One day it occurred to him that it no longer mattered ultimately whether she was physically alive; he instead found solace in the love that transcends physical presence and even life itself. Quoting the Bible's *Song of Solomon*, he writes, "Set me as a seal upon thine heart, as a seal upon thine arm: for love is strong as death."

Frankl's epiphany prompted me to try to find Barbara Ann's telephone number, but I was too emotionally overwhelmed to put in much effort. I couldn't help but feel that if she'd played a greater role in our lives she would have been there. Finally, torn as I was over what to do, I decided that I could not reach out, even though Mama repeatedly asked, "Don't you want to get in touch with Barbara Ann?"

"I can't now," I said. "If she couldn't be with Daddy when he was in failing health and needed her, I can't deal with her being here when her presence doesn't help anybody."

I refused partly out of a conviction that I had to protect Mama by showing her that I was in control of the situation. And, in truth, neither Mama nor I could take on Barbara Ann's emotional despair—or another burden of any kind. Mama was distressed and emotionally overwhelmed at the passing of her husband, whose death, despite his failing health, had come as a shock—one is never fully prepared for such a separation, especially after fifty-two years of marriage—and I had to make plans for her to stay in the house.

On the day after Daddy's burial, I finally tracked down Barbara

Ann's telephone number. A male voice answered and put her on the line. "Who are you to make such a decision as not to tell me sooner?" she exploded when I told her the news. "I created you, and for you to deny me the right of being at my father's funeral, of burying my own father . . ." Her voice trailed off.

"I did what I believed to be right, for me and Mama," I said. "Where have you been? Your love means nothing to a dead man."

I went on: "I can't talk to you right now. I just hope that you will not allow this regret to happen again with Mama when she dies."

Barbara Ann was crying. "I love you," I said, "but I have to go. I have to take care of Mama."

I had become so emotionally distant from Barbara Ann that I felt no pity for her, even at this time of her loss. Perhaps Daddy's stoicism, which I had internalized over the years, came into play. I felt that I had to separate my emotions from the decisions I had to make, and I didn't want to impose Barbara Ann's lifestyle and shaky finances on Mama. Yet I couldn't forget Frankl's transcendent love for his wife. Hadn't the quotation from Song of Solomon said that love is stronger than death?

For the next eight years I had no communication with Barbara Ann. Then one day a friend of hers asked her, "I know of you, your partner, and your daughter, but I never hear you talk of your mama and daddy. Tell me your life story."

Barbara Ann told her of her life as an adopted child in what she could now see was a loving family and community. She accepted her friend's invitation to begin regularly attending church, leading to her conversion on February 14, 2005, a date that she can still fondly recall. That night, she phoned Mama for the first time in many years.

"It's Barbara Ann. I know it's been a long time, but I've finally found myself, and I want to come home," she began. Then she told her story in a nutshell: "I don't need to tell you all of what life has been like for me, but I feel that God has been calling me for a long time, and I'm ready to see what He wants with me."

Mother and daughter stayed on the phone for more than two hours. Barbara Ann told Mama that she had decided to join the church and get rebaptized in a sign of her renewed commitment to all that she had lost: her faith in herself, in God, in everything. Mama immediately phoned me in Washington. "You'll never believe who phoned tonight," she announced.

Far from being overcome with joy, I felt only confusion and a desire that Mama not be hurt or disappointed again. Yet I couldn't say anything unaffirming, because she said, "I don't know what you're feeling, but this is a moment that I've been praying for for a long time. Don't take it away from me. Don't say anything."

I began to feel joy that this was the beginning of a happy end to Mama's life, and I wanted to do everything I possibly could to make it happen.

Hours later, around 11:00 p.m., Barbara Ann phoned me, to say, "I know that Mama has probably phoned you, and I'm so sorry for whatever pain I've caused you. But I need the past to be the past. I need you to help me move forward."

In my stoic way I encouraged her, "This is great, wonderful. Tell me about your transformation." I approached the situation analytically, seeking intellectual understanding of how she had come to the moment of reconciliation. I didn't cry. I had grown accustomed to suppressing my emotions in dealing with my grandparents' health challenges. Mostly, I wanted to give them the security that they had always given me. Nonetheless, the news from Barbara Ann stirred emotional chords deep within me. For one of the very few times in my life, I was unable to sleep that night.

The next morning, I called Mama. I told her that Barbara Ann and I had spoken and that I was so happy. "I can now die in peace," Mama said. "Everything that I have prayed for has been realized. You are now a young man. You've received an education and you're self-sufficient, and my daughter has come home. What more could I ask for?"

That summer, Barbara Ann found her spiritual way home via her baptism in the Atlanta church that she had been attending. The next day—Independence Day—she made her physical way back home to Madison Park, which she had fled as a prodigal daughter years before, to celebrate her own newfound independence at 34 Motley Drive. Like the elder son in the parable, I was there, alongside Mama, to greet my returning sibling, having been cleansed of the resentment and anger experienced by the biblical elder son at the prodigal's return. All of us had been redeemed and set free from whatever shackles had bound us in the past.

Three years later Barbara Ann married the man with whom she had a long-term relationship. On what has to be one of the happiest days of my life, I had the privilege of walking her down the aisle. In the presence of Mama and Kesia, who stood at Barbara Ann's side as maid of honor, I experienced unadulterated joy.

To further our reconciliation, Barbara Ann and I agreed to talk once a month and to visit Madison Park together twice a year. I bought Barbara Ann an endless supply of Greyhound tickets to visit Mama any time she wanted, and she made solo trips every few months. In the last year of Mama's life, as her health became more fragile, I would phone Barbara Ann, and she would go to spend time with her.

The Winding Road Home: Barbara Ann and I make the journey back to
Madison Park to spend Christmas with our Mama (December 2005).
The collection of Eric L. Motley

Before Mama's funeral, Barbara Ann and I drove together to the
family viewing time at the funeral home. We asked the funeral director
to leave us alone. For about forty-five minutes, we stayed in the room
with Mama's coffin, not saying a word, until Barbara Ann walked to
the coffin and said, "Mama, if I never told you, I hope you knew how
grateful I was that you and Daddy took Eric from me and raised him
and allowed him to become the young man that he is. Thank you."
It was the first time that I ever heard her say anything about having
given me over to their care.

CHAPTER 30

PAID IN FULL

Time has a way of straightening out some of the crookedness of life by smoothing things over. In the end, we sometimes find a new beginning. I've honored Barbara Ann's request to let the past be the past, and it has served us both well. There's more power in moving forward than looking back, as important as the past is; at some point you have to embrace the future. We talk once a week, and at least once a year we meet in Montgomery to lay flowers on our parents' graves, walk the streets of Madison Park, and visit with those who remain in the place that both of us still call home.

Kesia and I speak every few months and also see each other once a year. As much as we have in common, much separates us. Our different upbringings—mine in rural Madison Park and hers in urban Atlanta—have given us different tastes and preferences, so much so that one might think we were adopted rather than natural siblings. Nonetheless, both of us are allergic to shellfish, disdain ostentation, and prefer simple lifestyles. Entrepreneurial by nature, she owns her own successful hair salon and has started her own family of four children.

Now, at my more mature age, I know that every family has its story—a mother, a father, a son, a daughter who has left home, actually or figuratively, in order to find home. As Reverend Brinkley would often say, "Sometimes it is not about us; sometimes it is about the pilgrimage that one feels he must take—the journey of self-discovery." And only now do I have a fuller understanding of the unrelenting love that will never let us go, the love of the Heavenly Father, who celebrated the return of His child.

Whatever our circumstances, no matter what path we take, it is almost impossible to forget home. That is cause for celebration. But we cannot always remain in the home in which we grew up, no matter how beloved it is. Such was the case with 34 Motley Drive.

Immediately after Mama's burial, I began to process all the swift transitions of life and my responsibility to carry out her wishes. Selling the house was one of the hardest jobs I've had to do. Daddy built the house on land that belonged to my great-great-grandfather. Both Barbara Ann and I had been reared in it, and my great-grandmother, uncle, and grandmother had died in it. But maintaining it had become so financially draining that I no longer wanted to pour resources into it if no family members were staying there. So I put the house on the market in the hope that it would bring as much joy to another family as the Motley family had experienced there for more than a century.

This decision touched off a bidding war because every remaining house in Madison Park is owned by descendants of the original owners. The occasion marked the first time in a century that a house had been put up for sale on Motley Drive; moreover, no home in the entire area had been sold within the last twenty years. The prospect of being able to buy a well-maintained property on almost two acres with fruit trees and well-kept flora prompted people to telephone me to say, "I would love to buy the house so that my grandchildren could grow up in the house where Eric Motley was so loved."

While sweeping the wide cedar-plank floor of the almost emptied-out family room, I remembered the tall Christmas tree whose shining silver-foiled star seemed to touch the ceiling. I recalled the smell of fresh pine filling the air, bringing to mind the texture of old ornaments well-worn with time. As I sized up the dimensions of the room, I could almost make myself believe that Daddy built it solely to provide a home for his family's Christmas tree. Who would have then dreamed that a Christmas tree would stand majestically in the family room during each Christmas season for the next seventy years? But without fir tree, ornaments, and silver star, my family home for nearly a hundred years now sat empty and joyless as it awaited a new family's arrival.

I found myself soon thereafter sitting in an empty room surrounded by dozens of boxes as I packed up several lifetimes of dreams, aspirations, memories, and gifts—frames that hold photo memories, clocks, a watch, a Bible, chairs, and all the other important items used every day in the routine of life.

I held a well-worn banker's purse whose zipper had rusted with time, but which eloquently told the story of my grandparents' lives—a marriage certificate, discharge papers from the Army, adoption papers, birth certificate, deed to inherited land, Red Cross donor card, topped off by a collection of old bills with a scrap of paper atop it on which was scribbled "Paid in Full."

When I was a small child, I imagined that everything I needed was in Madison Park—that no place in the world could make me happier; yet seasons change. Heraclitus once said, "No man ever steps in the same river twice, for it's not the same river and he's not the same man." While there are many roads to take and they go by many names, I will always reckon my point of origin as Madison Park. More than twenty years have passed since I left for college, yet the people and the places have remained in my heart and mind almost daily.

To quote Benjamin Button, "It's a funny thing about comin' home. Looks the same, smells the same, feels the same. You'll realize what's changed is you."

Eli Madison would barely recognize the settlement that he and his children and grandchildren established and perpetuated. Today the secure four-lane bridge that carries U.S. Highway 231 across the creek into Madison Park is the best vantage point to see the white steeple of the old Union Chapel Church projecting upward through the tall oak trees. My hometown church sits about a hundred feet from the old railroad tracks, now barely visible through the thick woods, and on a slight hill above a marsh filled with Spanish-moss-covered oak trees.

The racial makeup remains virtually unchanged, but for the families in the immediate vicinity of Madison Park, farming has become nearly extinct. The cotton fields have disappeared, the long, uninterrupted stretches of land giving way to a variety of types of dwellings, including inexpensive manufactured homes and somewhat grander two- and three-bedroom ranch-style houses. The Madison Park School, once a pioneer in the education of rural African Americans, lies mostly empty except for occasional use as a meeting place.

In many ways, Madison Park is still the same place where I grew up. To be sure, it has fared better economically than most other rural communities in part because of its proximity to Montgomery, where most residents continue to work. Some are professionals, especially teachers, but the majority continue to hold blue-collar jobs in manufacturing and construction. Most people probably would not leave even if they had the option, because they draw strength from the fact that their land has remained in their families since the arrival of the freed slaves who founded Madison Park in the 1880s. Some of the worst curses of modern residential sprawl, such as fast-food restaurants and strip malls, have so far been avoided.

The main street on This Side of town, Lower Wetumpka Highway, is less vibrant today than in my childhood because of one simple but profoundly important fact: loss. Everyone used to gather at the Washerteria to see who was coming and going, on foot or by vehicle, to and from Madison Park. At about the time I left for college, in the early 1990s, it closed, and slowly, over time, as in many other rural areas, people stopped gathering as frequently and intentionally as had been the case for generations. Of course they found other places to come together, such as the virtual world of the internet, but face-to-face encounters have diminished.

Madison Park has suffered other kinds of decline experienced by rural America. For example, less care is spent on the environment than when I was growing up. One or two homes have fallen into disrepair, which would have been unthinkable to the folks who built them. Fewer trees line the long, narrow streets, and empty, weed-choked lots have replaced the large frame houses that once stood along Fuller's Road. The old recreational park where the church's annual picnics took place no longer belongs to the people of Madison Park because of a family feud. Speculators bought the land, leaving mounds of dirt where construction projects were started but quickly abandoned.

Nonetheless, despite the changes, the spirit of solidarity remains vibrant in Madison Park, as inspired by its founder, Eli Madison. The original church, Union Chapel AME Zion, still thrives, as do the other churches that have existed almost as long: Old Elam Baptist Church and Madison Park Church of Christ. Community life still centers on the activities at these churches. Over the last few years, I have waded into the debate on whether to rebuild and modernize our Methodist church, the very site where our community began. Like many other people who emigrate away from a community, I want things to remain more or less the same each time I return, so that I can treasure certain markers of memory from my earliest days. Of course those who remain have competing needs for expansion and modernization.

I am reminded that I want to conserve a place where now I am only a visitor, albeit a highly interested and involved one, and that the needs of the new generation must also be accommodated. That will require changes that inevitably disturb my nostalgic longing for an unchanged, fondly recalled landscape. Even so, the communal values of knowing your neighbor's name, lending a helping hand, supporting each other in the ups and downs of life, remain the bedrock beliefs of the place I call home. In the strangeness of this ever-changing world, I experience a deep sense of well-being as I remember the names, faces, places, and memories of Madison Park.

CHAPTER 31

WHEREVER I GO

This is the Madison Park I know. In my rental car, I turn heads as I drive down familiar streets, stopping all along the way to take it in, to visit family friends, to inspect new additions on old houses. I pause in some places long enough to get some tea, to take in some laundry from someone's clothesline, to chat awhile and listen to neighborhood resident Old Peg (I never knew his proper name) tell me about the carburetor he is putting into the old Chevrolet. Old Peg chatters away until suddenly it dawns on him, "Bugs, you don't have the slightest idea what I am talking about, do you?"

I laugh and say, "Old Peg, it sure sounds good to me."

Then he smiles and inquires, cigarette hanging from the side of his mouth, "You still up there in Washington? Boy, you ever going to come back here to Madison Park? You betta never forget home and what your grandparents did for you here!"

I return to be greeted by my childhood friends on Motley Drive because few have left and those who have live right around the corner. Former playmate Bimp, working under the hood of a car, stops and calls me by the only name he knows for me: "Bugs." He has followed in the footsteps of his father, Little Joe, by becoming a barber, and he also owns a lawn service business. His brother Boo-Boo, who is also involved in the business, joins us in the backyard under the old pear trees that Miz Cheney planted a hundred years ago, and we pass time away talking about friends and memories. We exchange updates, and as much as they are interested to hear about the city and the "girls" in D.C., I am more eager to find out what I have missed by being away from home. Their father, Little Joe, comes out and demands I get a haircut on the back porch, the very place I had my hair trimmed as a child. As he cuts, Little Joe provides the vital statistics of the town, who died and who had babies and sometimes who has been born-again. He always talks of my grandparents and what they meant to him. "They were neighbors. They knew what it meant to be neighbors."

These trips back to Alabama keep me from forgetting home and remind me that as much as I know Madison Park, with each return, I know the place for the first time.

I walk through the Madison Park cemetery, visiting the graves of my grandparents and the people of my youth who showed me the way. For hours, I move across the graves, as I used to do with Aunt Shine and Mrs. Winston when I was a child, clearing brush from the stones and whispering their names. As empty spaces are filled, I am reminded that many of the people I once knew are no more, while their children and offspring have never left. All these years later I still know most of the people of Madison Park by name.

The Madison Park cemetery will soon close its gates. Our people's resting place has almost reached capacity, so it has been decided that the community needs to determine how many lots are left and to whom they will be assigned. Last year a trust was formed for that purpose, and the trustees assigned the lots to the fifteen surviving descendants of founder Eli Madison, with a special designation for three additional citizens.

I was moved when I received the letter informing me that the people of Madison Park wanted me to be buried next to my grandparents under the old pine trees on the hill above the creek. I have no immediate plans of filling that lot, nor any certainty of where I will be buried, but my people have reserved a place for me, so I can always be at home.

FINAL REFLECTIONS

A Washington, D.C., friend recently found himself at a conference in the company of a very successful white attorney from Montgomery. My friend immediately attempted to play the name and place game. "Do you know Eric Motley? He's from Madison Park?" The attorney politely replied, "No, I do not know him, and where is Madison Park?" My friend was taken aback because he assumed, after hearing me talk about Madison Park so much over the last decade, everyone in Alabama, let alone Montgomery, knew of Madison Park. Telling me the story, he incredulously added, "The guy looked at me as if Madison Park did not exist, as if it were invisible."

In many ways, I guess Madison Park does not exist on the radar of many navigational systems or printed maps. Except for those who work in the municipal government and public schools of Montgomery, or who know of people or know the story of our community, Madison Park no doubt is invisible. An invisible Madison Park is an incredible idea for me, because to those who hail from the place, Madison Park is as much an idea as it is a living, breathing organism. To those who have never heard of our little community, it may not exist, but to the founders who bought the land, cleared the brush, and laid the cornerstones, and to their descendants who still care for it—whether they live there or not—it is as large as *America*.

The seeds of America were planted and nurtured in the hearts and minds of Madison Park's citizens over 135 years ago, and the people there have been trying ever since to make America work for them, the same as people do in the less obscure places where lights shine bright and all the roads are paved. Eli Madison's vision of a self-reliant and sustaining community where people could come and work to improve their state of life remains the vision of its inhabitants today. Over the last decade, as I have publicly shared the story of Madison Park at Washington dinner parties, Rotary meetings, church, work, and with friends, others have affirmed that they too once lived in a similar place, so in many ways Madison Park has become a metaphor of places that can seem invisible or nonexistent. These places still exist, but are their days numbered? Are they at risk of becoming extinct in the face of increasing atomization? I can only hope not.

Despite the changing landscape and encroaching city, the same strong pride and commitment to community remains among the people of Madison Park. It is planted deep in the earth, carefully and powerfully cultivated by my great-great-grandfather and the freed slaves who began the community and gave it its name. The history of Madison Park is tied inextricably to my sense of who I am. It is a spiritual *locus* that continues to offer inner refuge, solace, instruction, and most importantly, meaning in the ever changing flux of daily existence. Wherever I go, Madison Park goes with me.

When I reflect on the roadblocks that I faced, I'm so grateful for the Madison Park community. They set me on a different path than the external features in my life—my race, relative poverty, rural Southern roots, and the absence of biological parents—would seem to predict.

Final Reflections

The people of Madison Park bestowed their gift of grace, which I can never repay. Life is like that. Blessings come at us so relentlessly; we are forever in a deficit position. We never get all of the thank-yous or goodbyes properly said, which leaves us, each one, living with a burden of gratitude.

For as long as I can remember, my indebtedness to others has been a prism through which my life experience was filtered. That awareness has served to keep my vanity at bay and impel my concern for others. From my first days I was taught by example to count my blessings. Though their total now runs so high I can no longer name them one-by-one, the composite sense of having been blessed is my most cherished possession. The abundance I've found in life—thanks to everyday mentors, fortuitous circumstances, and Providence—far outweighs what I might have earned or what I deserve.

ACKNOWLEDGMENTS

I must confess that writing a memoir is a fitful process, and it demands courage and a commitment to the vulnerability required of honest self-examination. One must earnestly endeavor to not only tell their story, but to fully tell it, opening boxes, literally and figuratively, that have long been packed away. In the end, no one can truly tell your story except you.

There is not enough space to list all the names of those, who in some way, have encouraged my sharing of this story. The first inspiration came from my mentor and former university president Dr. Thomas Corts, who sat down with me a very long time ago to create an outline of what this narrative could look like, and who in turn spent countless hours helping me to find my voice and the courage to put words to paper. He spent way too many hours working with me on this manuscript not to have lived to see it in print, but in many ways, he has shaped the evolution of my life story through his unique and indelible influence.

After an initial spurt of writing, I decided to put my manuscript in a drawer and return to the business of life. Then in 2007, *Washington Post* writer Wil Haygood featured me in an award-winning series, *Being a Black Man: At the Corner of Progress and Peril.* The interest generated by Wil's thoughtfully written front-page Sunday morning story was more than I ever could have anticipated and inspired me to rededicate myself to a more complete telling of my story. It was then that I realized that the story to be told was not just about me, but really about a place and a people whose lives meaningfully intersected mine.

Sometime later, I decided to return to my manuscript, and to my good fortune, Dr. Steven Epley, my former freshman English professor, decided to help me reawaken the spirit and put even more on paper. Having decided to write without a publisher's editorial parameters, I ended up producing a tome just a few pages shy of *War and Peace.* It was then that my good friend Steve Sheppard encouraged me to seek professional help if I ever wanted this book to see the light of day. In the ensuing years, I retained the services of several editors who helped me to trim the excesses and develop an appreciation for the power of memoir—Victoria Rowan, Katharine Cluverius, and the most patient of all, Linda Kulman, who saw me through to the end.

Mel Udeh, a very dear friend and former intern, knew of my own odyssey of grace and gratitude and one day boldly encouraged me to dispense with all the distractions that I had given myself over to, and just get it done. He volunteered to assist me in this effort and has spent the last two years serving as my reader extraordinaire, reminding me of wonderful stories, thoughts forgotten, and the joy of storytelling.

Nearing the end, I realized that I needed a literary agent, so I called my old friend Don Logan, the former chairman of Time Warner, who said he had the very person that I should meet. And the rest is history. Larry Kirshbaum, former head of Time Warner Books, not only took me on, but took my story on and has wonderfully surprised me at times by knowing my story almost as well as I do by heart. He has pushed me and encouraged me and forced me to realize not only the importance but the urgency of this memoir.

As most of my life reveals, relationships have always opened doors, so I am grateful to Dr. Timothy George for introducing me to Stan Gundry, who subsequently brought me to David Morris, Vice President and Publisher of Zondervan, at HarperCollins. It is here that I have found kindred spirits such as my editor John Sloan, and his colleagues Tom Dean, Robin Barnett, and Bob Hudson. All of these individuals have helped to advance this literary project and have become good friends in the process.

Most of what I share in these pages have been stories told to me by the people of Madison Park. I am grateful that three individuals in particular had already provided a historical template for me. Dr. Hagalyn Seay Wilson, when helping to complete her father's memoir, *I Was There by the Grace of God* (written by Rev. S.S. Seay), would talk to me for hours as I helped her tend to her orchids. Dr. Gwen Patton, who published a thorough history of the Madison family, served as an essential reference and provided context that would otherwise have been lost to me. William Winston, the self-appointed Madison family archivist, always told me what he thought I should know and reminded me of what I wanted to forget.

It has been my good fortune that, for the last ten years, my boss, Walter Isaacson, has become a mentor. His example as one of our nation's foremost storytellers has not only captivated my imagination but has also helped me realize my own capacity for storytelling. He remains a constant encouragement.

And then there are all of my friends and colleagues, far too many to name here, who have encouraged my growth and awareness, and have played a significant role in helping me to refine my narrative. Over the years, they have patiently indulged my many retellings of some of the stories that I share here. By patiently lending me their ear, they enabled me to more clearly sketch my life's arc.

In my diaries, I have recorded the names of all the people of Madison Park who I once knew that are no more. In so doing, I have come to the transcendent realization that I owe my greatest debt to a good number of people "whose rest is won"—my grandparents, neighbors, tutors, Sunday school teachers, and many others—who planted and nurtured these seeds a long time ago. To them I offer my sincerest gratitude.